The Website Manager's Handbook

by Shane Diffily

"Very clear and well written...a lot of practical depth...I'm sure that someone managing – particularly a large website – would find [this] genuinely useful to help them think through the key issues in website management."

Gerry McGovern. Author of *Killer Web Content.*

Contents at a Glance

Chapter 1. Website Management Model

A framework for organising site operations, including Maintenance, Development, Governance and Infrastructure.

Chapter 2. Website Maintenance

An overview of the tasks required to keep a website running smoothly on a day-to-day basis.

Chapter 3. Website Development

A roadmap of the activities needed to plan, create, release and review a website (or add a section to an existing site).

Chapter 4. Website Governance

The role of leadership and standards on a successful site.

Chapter 5. Website Infrastructure

How to select and build an internal website hosting infrastructure.

Web Tools Quick Reference

This 'Quick Reference' lists many of the tools used to support the activities of Website Management.

Of course, the extent to which you deploy such systems is strongly influenced by the scale of your website and the availability of finance. It should be remembered that many sites operate very well with far less equipment than shown here. In this sense, skilled staff remain the most important resource for successful Website Management.

The Tools of Website Maintenance

- Website Content Management system (pages 35 & 365).
- Software for website quality assurance (pages 48).
- Software for administering website feedback (page 53).
- Software for website analytics (page 65).
- Software for monitoring the performance of website infrastructure (pages 76, 243 & 371).
- A 'Publishing Pack' for each member of a Publishing Team (page 40).

The Tools of Website Development

- A software package to assist project management (page 96).
- Software for design and image editing (page 43).
- Software for content development (page 118).
- A WYSIWYG editor for writing site code (page 212).
- A MarkUp Editor or Integrated Development Environment (IDE) for writing advanced code (page 212).
- A website testing suite (pages 222, 224 & 227).

- Tools for managing website publicity (page 267).

The Tools of Website Infrastructure

- The hardware and software of website hosting (pages 259 & 342).

- Search engine software (page 359).

- eCommerce (shopping cart) software (page 361).

- The software of website security (pages 232 & 351).

The Website Manager's Handbook

International Book Serial Number (10 digit): 1-4116-8529-6

International Book Serial Number (13 digit): 978-1-4116-8529-1

First Published August 2006

Copyright © 2006

Disclaimer

Every effort has been made to make this book as complete and as accurate as possible, but no warranty of fitness is implied. The information is provided on an as-is basis. The author shall neither have liability nor responsibility with respect to any loss or damages arising from the information contained in this book.

A variety of products are referred to in this book. In no instance should this be interpreted as an endorsement or recommendation. Furthermore, the lack of reference to a particular product must not be construed as an opinion. Readers are advised to exercise due diligence when purchasing services and technology.

For acknowledgements please turn to the back-inside cover.

With thanks to my colleagues Tommy Hopper and Tom Geraghty.

Table of Contents

Foreword

A curious omission from the reams of literature that has been written about the web in recent years is that related to the structures and procedures of site management. While volumes have been produced about disciplines like design and coding, very little has been suggested about how these activities should be organised.

For example, what techniques should designers and developers use to co-ordinate their activity? What resources do they need? What rules govern their tasks? These are the questions that have been left hanging. Yet, it is precisely these issues that take up so much time for website managers.

Indeed, it was my own difficulty in finding advice on such items that prompted me to write this book. My idea was to suggest a model of Website Management that could encompass all the practices needed to successfully administer a site. These practices have been derived from research, from conversations with other managers, as well as from ideas I myself have developed.

Having said that, I do not pretend that this is 'the' definitive guide to website management. Although I have tried to make this book as comprehensive as possible, it encompasses topics that are (by nature) in constant flux. Furthermore, I may have overlooked some issues, simply because they have not been within my realm of experience. For that I apologise.

Nevertheless, I do believe that many managers will find the ideas outlined here useful as a means for validating or directing their own operations.

Shane Diffily. August 2006.

Introduction

This book presents a model for the management and maintenance of your website. Such a site can be of any size and in any industry — from an intranet of a few dozen pages to a huge online music store. The fundamentals are the same.

Through this book you will learn about all the activities you need to manage a website successfully. You will also learn about the people, processes, technology and other resources required to sustain it. In effect, this book tells you exactly **what** you need to do, **when** you need to do it, **who** needs to be involved and (most crucially) **how** things should be done.

Roles and Responsibilities

Of course, the extent to which you can apply these principles depends to a large degree on the scale of your operation. For example, a small business may find that a single individual with the right skills is sufficient for many of the activities outlined. If so, this book may be useful simply as a means for defining that person's responsibilities.

In contrast, a larger organisation may have several departments involved in the activities of site management, e.g. IT, Marketing, etc. In this case, the text should assist with the allocation of roles. It might also be valuable as a template for structuring relationships and assigning responsibility.

Increasingly, technology is automating many of the activities of Website Management. Developments in this area include everything from simple programs that check for broken-links, through to enterprise-scale Content Management Systems. Where appropriate, options in this area are explained in the text.

How to read this book

This book is intended as a 'manual' for site operations. As such, rather than reading from cover to cover, you may find it useful to dip in and out, in order to get advice on issues as they arise.

Having said that, the overall narrative does follow a definite course from beginning to end. That is, initial sections deal with short-term operational issues of site maintenance. Later parts consider more strategic aspects like development and governance. By reading in a linear manner you may gain a more complete understanding about how these elements link together.

What this book is not

This is a book for website managers—not designers or developers. That is, it explains how tasks like design and coding should be administered—not how to do them.

That said, a basic introduction to the principles encompassed by these topics (as well as some others) is provided. The purpose is to equip managers with the knowledge they need to make informed decisions about development.

Intranets, Extranets and Portals

Finally, it should be noted that while this book refers to 'websites' throughout, the same principles can be applied to intranets, extranets and portals. Where a different approach is required, this is highlighted in the text. As such, for the purposes of this book, the following definitions are used:

- A **website** is a collection of documents or files that are published on the World Wide Web and intended for use by the general public.

- An **intranet** is a collection of documents or files enclosed within a private network, that are viewed using web technology and which cannot be accessed by unauthorised persons.

- An **extranet** is a restricted area of a website in which information intended for customers, partners or suppliers is published. Access to an extranet is normally only possible using a password or other means of controlled access.

- An **(intranet) portal** is a web-based application that provides a single view of all information required by employees, including email, intranet, calendar, search, etc. Portals are commonly created using software from vendors such as SAP, Oracle and Microsoft.

x

Chapter 1
Website Management Model

Remember the early days of the web, when the internet was all about alien abductions and freedom of expression? Wasn't it great! There were no rules, everyone was a geek and anything could happen.

And then it did.

Somebody, somewhere offered goods for sale online and nothing was ever the same again. As a result, the Developers who had dominated the web since its genesis began to collaborate with Designers to build better interfaces. Journalists and copywriters also got involved as the need for professionally written content was realised. Marketing and general managers were next onboard as angel-investor fuelled 'dot.coms' outgrew their garages and moved into business parks. And finally — horror of horrors — lawyers were drawn in as the legal challenges of the web began to emerge. The metamorphosis was complete.

Or was it?

In fact, many of the website management techniques in use today continue to betray their untidy origins in the chaos of the early internet.

Indeed, it is still relatively easy to find websites where disorder and loose controls persist. For example, many sites have no clear goals and no dedicated development team to support them.

Needless to say, it is now past time that such mayhem was done away with. The internet has changed beyond recognition in the past ten years and there is no longer any excuse for muddle and disorder. It is time for a well-founded and practical standard for website management to emerge.

That is precisely what is proposed by the Website Management Model.

The Website Management Model

The Website Management Model is a framework for organising all the activities of site administration. That is, it identifies the people, processes, technology and other resources you need to support a web venture of almost any kind.

This model is useful for those who already operate a site, as well as those who are just starting out. For example, if you currently supervise a website, you may be confused about how some tasks are carried out or how they relate to one another. If so, you should find the Website Management Model useful as a means for evaluating current systems and filling in any gaps.

On the other hand, if you have been tasked with overseeing a freshly released site, you could use this model as a framework for creating a new system of control. In this way, you can feel confident that all of the activities needed for sound management are in place.

The Elements of Website Management

The Website Management Model is composed of four elements, each of which encompasses a set of management activities. These are:

- Website Maintenance.
- Website Development.
- Website Governance.
- Website Infrastructure.

To introduce the model we will begin with a brief overview of the elements from which it is composed. These will then be explored in detail (in the following chapters) in order to reveal the people, processes, technology and other resources upon which they rely.

Figure 1. The Website Management Model.

Website Maintenance

Website Maintenance comprises all the activities needed to ensure the operational integrity of a site. In other words, it is about making sure a website runs smoothly and according to plan. In **Chapter Two**, we will learn exactly what this means in terms of administration and workload.

Website Development

Website Development encompasses the broad set of activities needed to create and review a website (or add a new section to an existing site). The activities from which Website Development is composed are:

- Planning
- Content
- Design
- Construction
- Testing
- Hosting
- Publicity
- Review

These activities are themselves bounded by the objectives of the business and the needs of users, which in turn help determine the overall character of a site.

The options you have for Website Development are explained in **Chapter Three**.

Website Governance

Presiding over the elements of Maintenance and Development is Website Governance. While frequently upstaged by more visible aspects of management, this represents the true centre of gravity on a site.

The objective of Website Governance is to ensure a controlled approach to site management—from planning and design through to maintenance and infrastructure. Without Governance there is no-one to say what is or is not allowed. Ultimately, this means no control and no direction. Website Governance is investigated in full in **Chapter Four**.

Website Infrastructure

Finally, providing a secure foundation for technical operations is Website Infrastructure. Website Infrastructure embraces all of the activities and resources needed to select and build an internal hosting solution, including hardware, software and staff skills.

These are explored in detail in **Chapter Five**. (External hosting is examined separately within Chapter Four)

That summarises the elements of the Website Management Model. As you have seen, a wide range of activities are covered. No doubt, this may have set some alarm bells ringing.

"Oh my God, I am going to need a dozen people to manage this thing!"

Needless to say, you won't.

Many websites operate very effectively with small teams—often just two or three people. Activities that cannot be covered internally are contracted to external consultants on an as-needed basis. All that matters is that the website is being properly managed for the benefit of your customers.

And it is with customers that we will begin our review. After all, they are the people who really matter, right? Yet, how can you be sure customers are satisfied by their online experience or that your website is performing well on a day-to-day basis?

The only way to find out is to advance towards the coal-face and evaluate how well the activities of **Website Maintenance** are carried out.

Chapter 2
Website Maintenance

Visit any large European city and you will probably notice that it is surrounded by suburbs full of concrete tower-blocks. The majority of these were built in the 1950s and 1960s when pre-fabrication was seen as a solution to the post-war housing shortage. Such structures were cheap to make, easy to assemble and provided much needed shelter.

However, as the construction of these new neighbourhoods came to an end, little money was left over for ongoing repairs. Inevitably, the telltale signs of neglect soon became obvious — paint started to peel, the plumbing clogged-up and elevators stopped working. In the end, these buildings simply disintegrated through lack of care.

Guess what? The same thing can happen to your website.

After some heady initial enthusiasm and conspicuous spending, experience shows that many sites are in danger of being abandoned. Indeed, websites that have suffered this fate are easy to recognise. For example, do any of these problems sound familiar?

- Broken links

- Unanswered feedback

- Badly spelled text

- Missing page titles

One of the greatest challenges of Website Maintenance is to ensure appropriate systems are in place to avoid such an outcome. By necessity, this demands a team of skilled personnel who can rely on the support of good technology and sound procedures. If any of these are missing, the results can be embarrassingly visible.

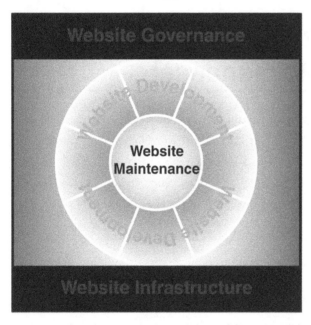

Figure 2. Website Maintenance as an element of the Website Management Model.

For this reason, it is necessary to understand the activities from which Website Maintenance is composed. As we will discover, these are:

- **Website Publishing**: Keeping content up-to-date.

- **Website Quality Assurance**: Spotting errors on a site.

- **Website Feedback Monitoring**: Managing communication with website visitors.

- **Website Performance Monitoring**: Measuring site success.

- **Website Infrastructure Monitoring**: Supervising website hosting.

- **Change Control**: Managing technical and other changes in a co-ordinated way.

However, before exploring each of these in detail, it is useful to find out more about the people who are actually responsible for them.

Website Maintenance Team

If one thing is true about the internet, it is that no two companies ever use the same set of descriptions for their web staff. For example, job titles like 'Webmaster', 'Internet Administrator' and a plethora of other labels are all in common use. Though often funny (or just plain confusing) the selection of naming conventions is not terribly important. The culture of an organisation usually sets the mark in this regard. However, given the importance of the tasks carried out by these people, a discussion about team structures is definitely worthwhile.

The 'News Room' Model

This debate continues to develop as several web commentators advocate that the structure of a Maintenance Team should mirror that of a news room[1]. Their argument is that websites are mainly about publishing — just like newspapers and magazines — so the same model ought to be applied.

There is an undeniable logic to this and the model has many adherents. This is due in part to the gradual migration of website control from IT departments to Communications/Marketing. However, as was seen in the list of activities above, maintenance incorporates many more tasks

---

[1] Content Critical by Gerry McGovern. ISBN 0 273 65604 x. www.gerrymcgovern.com

than publishing alone. As such, the news room model may not be suitable in all circumstances.

In fact, (as illustrated below) the variety of skills required on a Maintenance Team is quite broad.

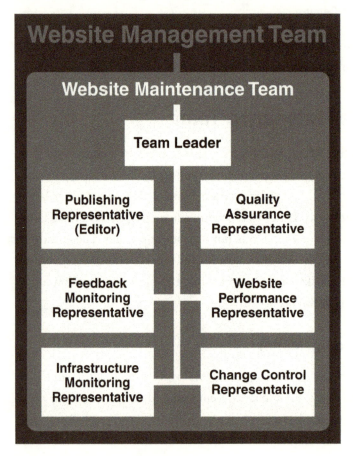

Figure 3. The Website Maintenance Team.

As can be seen, a minimum of seven roles are represented — one for each activity and a Team Leader to supervise them.

The **Team Leader** is the individual accountable for the overall operational integrity of a site. That is, he must ensure each activity is expedited in a timely and high quality manner. To do so, a regular

Maintenance Review Meeting may be convened at which operational issues are discussed. (The responsibilities of other team members are explored later in this section.)

For some busy sites this meeting may need to occur on a daily basis, though a weekly or fortnightly session should be adequate for most. Typical agenda items include:

- A report by each team member on their area of responsibility

- A discussion of operational issues

- Agreement on a plan for forthcoming changes

However, because websites come in such a wide variety of shapes and sizes, it is rare to find a team that reflects the recommended structure exactly. For example, many smaller sites function very well with less than seven people—simply by combining several roles into one. Yet, even such a small team must still have all necessary skills represented. This is because each one is vital for maintaining a good quality web presence.

Staffing a Website Maintenance Team

Deciding on the right levels of staffing for a Maintenance Team can be tricky. The sad truth is that many organisations badly underestimate the amount of work required to keep their sites operating smoothly. They somehow imagine that once a website is put live, it magically looks after itself. As a result, only the barest bones of a proper team are ever put in place.

Fortunately, the problem of defining the number of people required for maintenance is not insurmountable. A useful device for arriving at an answer is the concept of Website Scale.

The Concept of Website Scale

Website Scale is a means of classifying a site in terms of three parameters:

- Size

- Complexity

- Levels of activity

Almost any site can be represented in this way—from a small website of plain text to a massive corporate intranet with dozens of applications. As a matter of fact, the concept of Website Scale is so important that we will encounter it again and again as we progress through the four elements of Website Management. This is because it is so useful for estimating the number of people required on a web team.

For example, the website of the British Broadcasting Corporation (www.bbc.co.uk) in London can be described as much greater in scale than that of the Icelandic channel, Ríkisútvarpið RUV (www.ruv.is). That is, the BBC site is bigger in size, uses a wider variety of more complex technology and receives substantially more traffic than its Icelandic equivalent. It can therefore be concluded that a greater number of people are required to support it. The actual quantity may be gauged by examining each of the elements from which Website Scale is composed.

Website Size

In simple terms, the bigger a website is, the more personnel are needed to maintain it. Yet, how can the size of a site be measured? Is it simply a total of all the megabytes of data it contains? Or, perhaps a count of the number of pages online?

In fact, neither of these is satisfactory.

For example, a website could contain hundreds of megabytes in just a few video files. Another could be host to thousands of pages, though each may only contain a few words.

The best means that has been found for calculating website size is to estimate the total man-hours required to produce and maintain all of its content. This can then be used to approximate the number of people required for support—particularly for the activities of Website Publishing and Quality Assurance.

How to estimate staffing from the size of a website

For example, it may take 3 hours to produce, edit and publish a 500 word feature on a corporate intranet, e.g. information about medical benefits. This could then be scheduled for review every six months (to ensure it remains accurate), at a cost of 30 minutes each time. As a result, an intranet of this type requires 3.5 man-hours to produce and maintain a 500-word article.

If 100 similar features are planned, 300 man-hours (seven and a half weeks) are needed for production and 50 man-hours (just over one week) for review.

As the average hours available per person per year is about 1,750, we can now see how staffing is calculated. For example, the content described above could be maintained over the course of a year by a single person with plenty of time to spare: 1,750–350 = 1,400.

Although the math itself is fairly straightforward, recommending precise levels of employment is somewhat more complicated. This is because of the ways in which websites differ from one another. For example, video needs much more time for production than text. As such, a Team Leader must know exactly what type of content his site contains in order to calculate the resources needed for maintenance. (Go to Chapter Three, page 118 for more about content formats.)

What will normally be found is that a site that contains a lot of frequently updated features will need more staff than one that is home to only a few, static pages.

The following table illustrates some indicative staffing levels for the three most common grades of website size[2].

Small Website	Content Man Hours per Annum : 1,500–4,000
	Staffing Levels for Content Publishing and Quality Assurance: About 1-2 people.
Medium Website	Content Man Hours per Annum : 4,000–10,000
	Staffing Levels for Content Publishing and Quality Assurance: About 2-3 people.
Large Website	Content Man Hours per Annum : 10,000+
	Staffing Levels for Content Publishing and Quality Assurance: From 2-3 people upwards.

Figure 4. The three levels of Website Size.

The well known web content consultant, Gerry McGovern has completed some excellent analysis on the subject of staffing in his book "Content Critical"[3]. Gerry shows not only how long it takes to produce content, but also what it costs, i.e. skilled writers can produce content more quickly, but they are paid more.

---

[2] Health Warning: As mentioned, these numbers are indicative only! Actual employment levels may differ based on the circumstances of your business.
[3] Content Critical by Gerry McGovern. ISBN 0 273 65604 x. www.gerrymcgovern.com

Website Complexity

Differences in manpower can also arise as a result of the technology used to develop a site. This is because highly intricate websites usually require larger numbers of personnel to look after them — in particular for the technical activities of Infrastructure Monitoring and Change Control. (These are explained in detail on pages 73 and 80)

In this way, there are said to be three levels of site complexity:

Basic Website

Often referred to as 'brochureware', this is the most straightforward type of website. Such sites merely contain information in plain text with perhaps a few supporting images and downloads, e.g. PDFs. No interactivity is included. As such, most Basic sites are used for rudimentary information purposes only. Their uncomplicated nature also means they are relatively easy to maintain. For example, a single person with low-level skills may be all that is required.

(Learn more about the technology that underlies a Basic website in Chapter Five–Website Infrastructure, page 335).

Dynamic Website

On a Dynamic website, content is stored in a database and published according to the requirements of site visitors. Such sites are frequently used by businesses that publish large volumes of information in a standard way. A good example is the news website www.wired.com which contains thousands of stories in a similar format. Some Dynamic Sites also offer basic interactive services, e.g. Discussion Forums.

Although the user experience of a Dynamic website is similar to that of a Basic Site, the technology that underlies it is much more involved. As such, a team of one or two people with good technical skills may be needed for a medium-sized site of this type.

(Learn more about the technology of Dynamic websites in Chapter Five, page 339).

Transactional Website

A Transactional website is one that uses the internet for facilitating business operations or generating revenue. Some of the world's best known sites, e.g. Amazon.com, exploit this as a model for their operations. Sites of this type rely on databases and other advanced technology for collecting and processing orders. As this activity often involves financial dealings, it has come to be known as eCommerce.

eCommerce is defined as the purchase of goods and services over the World Wide Web by means of a secure connection. The practice of eCommerce is divided into different segments, based on the type of consumer being targeted. The most prominent of these are:

- **B2C** (Business to Consumer). For example, Amazon.com sells consumer goods directly to individuals.

- **B2B** (Business to Business). For example, Forrester.com sells intelligence reports to businesses over the internet.

- **B2G** (Business to Government). Many of the same firms that engage in B2B also engage in B2G. For example, both categories are reflected on the Dell® website, www.dell.com.

However, not all Transactional sites are monetary in nature. For example, many corporate intranets can be considered Transactional because of the features they contain, e.g. timesheets, expenses submission, etc.

(Learn more about the technology that underlies Transactional websites and eCommerce in Chapter Five, page 339).

As with a Dynamic website, a Transactional site requires highly skilled staff. For example, a medium sized site could employ two or more people to perform all the duties of technical maintenance. The largest and busiest such sites frequently hire many more.

Given these differences in complexity, some indicative figures for the staffing of a Technical Team are indicated in the following table:

Basic Website	**Content**: Plain content (HTML/XHTML). **Staffing Level for Infrastructure Monitoring and Change Control**: 1 person (for a small to medium sized site).
Dynamic Website	**Content**: Dynamically generated from a database. **Staffing Level for Infrastructure Monitoring and Change Control**: 1 or 2 people (or more on a very large or busy site).
Transactional Website	**Content**: Fully transactional content, e.g. eCommerce. **Staffing Level for Infrastructure Monitoring and Change Control**: From 1 or 2 people upwards (many more on a large or busy site).

Figure 5. The three levels of Website Complexity.

Website Activity

Website activity is the last and possibly most important factor when planning the manpower requirements of a Maintenance Team. This is because a busy website inevitably has to deal with mountains of queries, problems and general issues of upkeep. In this way, it has a very strong influence on staffing.

A commonly accepted means for measuring website activity is a 'Page Impression'. As explained in more detail later, Page Impressions are a count of the number of pages accessed by website visitors. As a general rule, a site must receive a minimum of 1,000,000 Page Impressions per month to be considered 'Busy' (though some receive far more than this).

Such heavy activity means a website is unlikely to function properly without a full complement of maintenance personnel. Indeed, a **Busy** site that is also **Large** in size and **Transactional** in nature may need dozens of staff to keep it going.

Quiet Website	Page Impressions: 0–100,000 a month
	Total Team Staffing: Between 1 and 3 people.
Intermediate Website	Page Impressions: 100,000–1,000,000 a month.
	Total Team Staffing: About 2-3 people.
Busy Website	Page Impressions: 1,000,000+ a month.
	Total Team Staffing: From 3 people upwards (many more on a very busy Transactional site).

Figure 6. The three levels of Website Activity.

Staffing Problems

Unfortunately, there is little support on many sites for such high levels of employment. While this is sometimes due to real financial constraints, it can also be explained by a lack of understanding about the need for Website Maintenance itself. If truth be told, some managers simply don't 'get' why a site requires close attention. Their opinion is that 'the website will look after itself' and are unwilling to invest much time or effort in it. Overcoming this attitude is among the greatest challenges to be faced by a Maintenance Team.

As such, to understand why maintenance is so essential, we need to explore it in more detail. If we can demonstrate how these tasks lead directly to a higher quality site, it could be used to sell the idea of maintenance to senior managers.

And what better place to start than with the most visible of all such activities, **Website Publishing**.

Activity 1
Website Publishing

From the first words placed on the web by Tim-Berners Lee over 15 years ago[4] to the wealth of online newspapers available today — publishing remains at the heart of site maintenance.

Yet, an extraordinary thing about the World Wide Web is how often standard publishing practices are ignored. For example, while an Editor is usually appointed for even the most basic of printed newsletters, such a role is missing on many sites. As a result, the web is littered with misspelled text, poor quality images and other carelessly produced content. This shoddiness is a hangover from the turmoil of the early internet and has no place in modern management.

For that reason, it is important to learn about the systems and procedures by which content may be supervised effectively. After all, there is no point in having great information online, if there is no mechanism for looking after it. As we will now see, any good system of this type must

---

[4] A copy of the very first web page can still be seen at
http://www.w3.org/History/19921103-hypertext/hypertext/WWW/TheProject.html

be built on the twin pillars of a **well resourced team** and an **orderly process.**

Website Publishing Team

As mentioned in the introduction to this chapter, a popular way for organising a Maintenance Team is to mimic the structure of a news room. Although we discovered that this model may not always be appropriate (due to some missing roles), it can be very effective for Publishing Teams.

A **Publishing Team** is the group of people responsible for managing the lifecycle of online content. Such a team is typically composed of an Editor and representatives from each major area of activity, including:

Content Contributor

This person creates and maintains site content. Several types of Contributor may be represented depending on the content to be developed, e.g. a writer, a video editor, an illustrator, etc.

Designer

The role of Designer is to build the visual templates required for effective communication. As explained below, more than one type of Designer may be involved in publishing.

Developer

The Developer's job is to merge content and design into a physical web page by the use of various coding languages.

Moderator

This person is required to supervise the behaviour of site visitors where facilities like Online Chat or Bulletin Boards are used.

Legal Reviewer

The Legal Reviewer is responsible for ensuring all content adheres to the law, industry regulations and company policies.

Figure 7. The Website Publishing Team.

The degree to which an organisation is able to mimic the set-up of this archetypal Publishing Team is determined by the volumes of content it maintains and the availability of resources. For example, a busy website like bbc.co.uk demands a full complement of publishing staff. Indeed, several people might be needed within each discipline because of the amount of information to be expedited. In contrast, a small Basic site may survive very well with just one or two individuals, who share several roles between them.

Yet, no matter what the size of a team, at the very least the role of Editor should be clearly defined. This is because the Editor is responsible for setting the tone and monitoring the quality of all online activity.

Website Editor

As the person in charge of publishing, a Website Editor is answerable for everything that appears on a site, e.g. the accuracy of information, suitability of images, etc. In fact, the Editorial role is so central that this individual may also be appointed as overall Maintenance Team Leader. This is because of the influence he has for achieving site goals.

Notwithstanding this, the core activities for which an Editor is accountable are those concerned with the lifecycle of content, including:

Reviewing and editing work-in-progress

As the individual responsible for the quality of web content, the Editor must review and edit all items submitted for publication. This includes checking for spelling, presentation and tone.

Maintaining existing content

The Editor must also keep a watchful eye on existing content, for example, by setting a rule that all pages be reviewed at least annually.

Responding to user comments about existing content

Such comments are normally sourced via email from website visitors. Feedback of this type can even be used as content itself. For example, on the BBC News website readers opinions about news coverage are published and discussed[5]. However, where significant volumes of

---

[5] For example, http://news.bbc.co.uk/2/hi/uk_news/magazine/4080206.stm

feedback are received, a dedicated Feedback Co-ordinator may be needed (as explained on page 51).

Planning and commissioning new content

The Editor must expedite updates based on an agreed schedule. This schedule is decided during a Website Publishing Meeting. Production is then allocated among various Content Contributors.

Website Publishing Meeting

The Website Publishing Meeting is a session that gathers together everyone involved in the creation, review and approval of online content. In principle it is exactly the same as the daily editorial meeting that takes place in many newspaper offices. The aim is to monitor Work-in-Progress and decide on a publishing schedule.

Title	Actionee	Summary	Content	Site Section	Golive
New Product Catalogue	Nina Kleiner, Marketing.	The product catalogue for Spring 2007.	Text. Supporting images. PDF of the catalogue.	Products	23rd August
Interview with CEO	John McFadden, Marketing.	CEO plans for 2007.	Video. Supporting text.	Shareholders	30th August

Figure 8. A sample Publishing Schedule.

A **Publishing Schedule** is a calendar that identifies content changes for a site. It also stipulates who is responsible for each item and when they must be completed. The advantage of such a schedule is that it allows an Editor to arrange updates in advance, as well as the allocation of scarce resources.

When agreeing on such a schedule, it is common to find that some sections of a site require changes more frequently than others. For example, 'News' may need to be modified weekly, whereas 'Annual Reports' may only call for a review every 12 months. In circumstances like this, a device known as a Publishing Calendar can be useful for tracking items and highlighting when they need to be expedited.

A **Publishing Calendar** is an extension of the Publishing Schedule that allows recurring content to be identified in advance. Keeping a calendar like this up-to-date is the responsibility of the Editor.

Title	Actionee	Recurrence Date
Christmas Catalogue	Marketing	Mid October
Annual Report	Marketing	May
Graduate Recruitment Campaign	Human Resources	End July

Figure 9. A sample Publishing Calendar.

Content Contributor

Next to the Editor, the most important members of a publishing team are those who actually create and maintain content. Called Content Contributors, these people are commissioned to produce new features or update existing content based on the requirements of a Publishing Schedule.

In ideal circumstances, Contributors should be experienced professionals, e.g. journalists, who have been specially recruited for their skills. Some busy sites have several fulltime people in this role, as well as others who are hired on a contract basis.

In contrast, the Content Contributors on a small website might simply be ordinary members of staff who have been asked to assist the publishing process. This is especially so for intranets. As such, it is usually necessary to provide training to ensure these people can produce high quality information. Thankfully, many educational programmes are now available in this area, e.g. writing for the web[6].

Briefing Document

To support Contributors when creating new content, a written description of what is required is often helpful. Called a Briefing Document, this is a dossier that contains an overview of a given assignment and a list of resources to aid production.

For example, a Briefing Document for a new piece of content about 'Global Warming' (to be published in text format) might appear as follows:

Title	Global Warming for Beginners
Summary of the theme and key points to include	Define Global Warming. Identify the evidence. Identify the causes. Consider the effects. Suggest methods to solve problem.
Resources that may be required for inclusion, e.g. images	Images of glacier retreat. Sources of CO2.
Required length in words	650 words
References and resources	Kyoto protocol agreement
Date for delivery	21st July 2007.

Figure 10. A sample of the elements to include in a briefing document.

---

[6] For example, at BBC Training. www.bbctraining.com/newMedia.asp

In the event that a feature is required in a form other than plain text, e.g. video or audio, the Briefing Document must be modified in response. This is especially useful where work is contracted to an external company.

For example, in the case of video, a Brief may stipulate the length of the required footage in minutes and seconds, as well as the preferred screen-size and file format. The document may also include guidelines regarding a company's editing preferences, e.g. images of competitor products or logos may not be allowed.

(For an overview of many different content formats, go to Chapter Three–Website Development, page 118.)

Moderator

Bulletin boards, Chat-rooms and Wikis[7] are online features that allow visitors to a website to communicate with each other or create content, often in real time. Facilities like this are popular for knowledge sharing and fostering community. They also offer a low cost means of customer support.

However, the open nature of such features means they are very prone to abuse. This can range from the trivial (e.g. unwanted advertising) to the sinister. Press reports continue to show how chat rooms are used by fraudsters and sex offenders to target victims[8]. It is essential therefore that steps be taken to protect the privacy and security of legitimate visitors, as well as the integrity of your own organisation. The first step towards this is to appoint a Moderator.

---

[7] Wikis are explained in more detail on page 125.
[8] BBC News Online "Can we really police online chat?"
   http://news.bbc.co.uk/2/hi/uk_news/3791603.stm Accessed October 2005.

A **Moderator** is the person responsible for the regulation of an online communications tool. When carrying out her duties, a Moderator may create a set of groundrules that stipulate the type of behaviour that is acceptable on a site. These are sometimes referred to as 'Netiquette' (i.e. 'etiquette for the internet') and include principles like:

- Respect other users

- Do not launch personal attack

- Do not stray from the topic being discussed

- Do not post advertisements

- Report suspicious or anti-social behaviour

Websites with vulnerable audiences may need even more detailed guidelines. For example, both MSN and MySpace.com provide extensive information on safeguarding young people from internet hazards, such as how children can recognise suspicious behaviour[9].

It may even be helpful to give a Moderator a limited editorial role. This could prevent unknown persons joining a chat room unless they come recommended by an existing member. Similarly, a Moderator may decide that no updates can be made to a noticeboard until they are reviewed for acceptability. In this way, she can be proactive in ensuring online safety.

The Limits of Moderation

While such measures can go a long way towards protecting visitors, the 'live' nature of many features means anti-social behaviour can never be completely eliminated. Consider the example of the LA Times which, in 2005, published a content item known as a 'Wikitorial'. The purpose of

---

[9] MSN Safety Resource Centre. http://www.msn.co.za/security/family/default.asp
MySpace.com http://collect.myspace.com/misc/safetytips.html?z=1

the Wikitorial was to create "a constantly evolving collaboration among readers in a communal search for truth" by inviting visitors to contribute to a daily online editorial[10]. However, this noble effort was quickly undermined by a few pernicious users who defaced the site with adult material. In the end, the experiment had to be discontinued.

While the experience of the LA Times is extreme, it shows what can happen. In this case, the Moderator acted correctly by removing the feature as soon as it began to be destabilised. While this may seem drastic, the unfortunate reality is that the disciplinary options available to a Publishing Team are quite limited. The only real power they have (besides completely removing all content) is to exclude certain users, perhaps by revoking logon privileges.

However, even this can be ineffective because of the manner in which the internet is constructed (as a loosely regulated network of networks). For example, an abusive user could simply reapply for access using a different name.

Legal Reviewer

The assessment of content for legal issues before 'going to press' is familiar in several industries, especially printed media. In contrast, this activity has been overlooked on the web for many years. For example, it used to be common for Publishing Teams to ignore copyright by 'cutting and pasting' images at will from other sources without permission. Some even went so far as to reproduce entire designs for their own purposes[11]! Fortunately, this is now changing and the practice of Legal Review is becoming more common.

---

[10] LA Times. Wikitorial. http://www.latimes.com/news/opinion/editorials/la-wiki-splash,0,1349109.story Accessed January 2006.
[11] Many examples of this can be viewed at http://www.pirated-sites.com

The purpose of such a review is to ensure that content intended for publication on the web is in compliance with the law (and any other regulations or policies). This commonly includes:

- **Data protection and the privacy of customers.** Is anything that may compromise customers' integrity being published?

- **Freedom of Expression.** Is any content unlawful, e.g. inciting racial or religious hatred?

- **Criminal Damage.** Is anything that has the potential to harm a visitor's computer being published, e.g. a virus that is hosted unknowingly?

- **Libel.** Are any unsubstantiated rumours being published, that may be libellous to a person's character?

- **Copyright Protection.** Is any content being reproduced without the consent of the owner?

- **Consumer Protection.** Are adequate measures in place to protect consumers' rights?

In a small organisation where no legal department exists, a website Editor may adopt this review function. However, a large site with its own lawyers could benefit from having a person dedicated to this role.

(A more detailed examination of the legal issues impacting Website Management is provided in Chapter Four–Website Governance, page 301.)

Designer

The role of a Designer is to find the optimum solution for the visual and interactive presentation of content on the web. To this end, Designers work closely with Content Contributors, Developers and Editors to create an agreed outcome. Indeed, several different design disciplines may be incorporated into the production process. Among these are:

- **Information Architecture**. This involves the structuring of information.

- **Interaction Design**. This is concerned with the creation of elements such as online forms.

- **Visual Design**. This is the most commonly understood notion of design. Visual Design applies colour and imagery to a website.

(The individual disciplines of design are explored in greater detail in the Chapter Three–Website Development, page 144.)

As with other aspects of Website Management, the extent to which these disciplines are employed depends on the financial resources available. For example, a busy website that relies on the ease with which customers can complete transactions may have to employ many such staff, e.g. an online bank. However, a smaller website could operate effectively with just a single highly skilled Designer who is responsible for all work.

Developer

A Developer is the person tasked with converting content and design into a web-readable format and publishing it on the internet. When doing so, Developers work closely with Designers and the Editor to ensure planned layouts can be reproduced satisfactorily. On a small website the Designer and Developer may even be the same person, i.e. someone who can both design and code a site.

The traditional approach for making a web page is to build a HTML file in which to display text, images and other media. However, depending on the scale of a site, Developers may also use other languages, e.g. ASP, PHP or JSP. These are referred to as 'Server-Side Scripting' languages and are used to power the interactivity seen on Dynamic and Transactional sites. For example, Dell.com uses Server-Side Scripting to facilitate eCommerce by collecting credit card numbers and processing orders.

(HTML and Server-Side Scripting are explained in more detail in Chapter Three–Website Development, page 173.)

However, in recent years the experience of many organisations has been that—as the need for publishing has grown—Developers have been unable to cope with the volumes of material submitted. This has resulted in bottlenecks that delay activity. As a result, the responsibilities of Developers are being superseded by the introduction of a new technology for managing publishing activity called Website Content Management (WCM).

Website Content Management

The great advantage of WCM is that it allows Content Contributors to publish directly to a website without having to ask a Developer to do anything. For example, a writer can simply type the information they want directly into a WCM program, click 'submit' and it will publish immediately. In fact, many systems allow writers to create articles in word processing applications like Microsoft Word. The WCM software then handles the conversion of the content to HTML and sets up all necessary links.

In this way, a typical WCM package encompasses such functions as:

Content Creation	Content Management
Allows many authors of content.	Allows version control and archiving.
Creates metadata automatically.	Follows a strict workflow.
Publishing	**Presentation**
Allows site design to be altered.	Generates web accessible code.
Supports multiple formats e.g. RSS.	Produces standards compliant HTML.

The ability of WCM to allow devolved publishing can result in great savings of time for Developers. Instead of spending hours at the tedious task of converting text into code, they can be allocated to more valuable activities, e.g. application development. WCM also has many other features (e.g. link checking and reporting) that reduce the time needed for site upkeep. (More of these will be encountered as we progress through the activities of Website Maintenance.)

Website Content Management Vendors

A large number of WCM vendors are currently in operation, though the industry trend is towards consolidation. The market itself can be divided into five tiers based on product cost and functionality. These are:

Enterprise Tier

The Enterprise Tier comprises products that cater for very large organisations for whom stringent document management is an urgent priority, e.g. pharmaceutical or law firms.

Products in this category incorporate functionality that goes well beyond that required for ordinary Website Content Management. Indeed, these products are best described as Enterprise Content Management (ECM), of which WCM forms only a small part. ECM encompasses the creation, delivery, management and archiving of all content across an organisation.

The high specification of such systems is reflected in list prices between $250,000 and $1 million+. Some of the better known ECM vendors include Documentum®, Vignette® and Interwoven®.

Upper Tier

Products in the Upper Tier are aimed at firms for whom the creation of content is a key business activity, but do not face the same regulatory constraints as the Enterprise Tier. This typically includes businesses for whom publishing is a core activity, e.g. newspapers, magazines.

The list price of such systems is between $100,000 and $500,000, and some familiar vendors include OpenText® and Percussion®. Upper Tier products are ideal for large and busy Dynamic or Transactional sites.

Mid Tier

The Mid Tier encompasses systems aimed at companies for whom content creation is not a core activity, but who have a strong interest in knowledge/content management. This includes most mid-sized firms.

While some Mid Tier vendors have an international presence (e.g. Microsoft®, Terminal4®), many serve local markets only. As such, list prices tend to be quite varied — between $10,000 and $150,000. In general, Mid-Tier products are flexible enough to meet the needs of most Medium–Large sites.

Bottom Tier

Bottom Tier products cannot truly be considered WCM. This is because they only provide quite poor functionality and do not support many of the features considered necessary for WCM, e.g. workflow. As such, they are better referred to as 'Publishing Systems'. Many systems like this are created by Developers in design agencies and bundled free with project work. However, one widely used commercial product called Contribute™ is manufactured by Adobe® (from $149). Bottom-tier systems are best suited to small, basic websites.

Open Source

Open Source is software in which the underlying code of a program can be viewed and modified by anyone. The key advantage of Open Source is that it can be downloaded from the internet and put to use for free. On the other hand, it doesn't come with any support services. This means skilled Developers must be hired for maintenance. Nevertheless, OpenSource is still very popular with many large organisations.

With regard to WCM, some popular Open Source programs include Mambo, Magnolia and OpenCMS. These provide a similar level of functionality to licensed Mid Tier or Upper Tier products.

That completes our overview of the major roles of Website Publishing. While many of these positions may be familiar to you, your own organisation could have implemented a structure somewhat different to that described here. For example, you may have more grades of Editor (sub editor, editor-in-chief) or different types of Designer. If that is the case, the difference is simply a matter of scale—the core responsibilities remain the same.

Website Publishing Process

Now that we know what people belong on a Publishing Team, we can start to explore the process by which they actually carry out their tasks.

The objective of a Website Publishing Process is to ensure content is created, reviewed and approved in a controlled manner, before being made available to visitors. A typical system of this type consists of a workflow through which content is expedited from one role to another.

On a site with a small Publishing Team (i.e. where many roles are combined into one), this process may consist of just one or two steps. However, a large or busy site that publishes hundreds of documents each week (e.g. a news website) needs to be much more thorough. In this case, the website Editor must make sure updates are progressed in a supervised way.

There are several benefits to insisting on such an exacting system. These include:

- It prevents unauthorised content being published.

- It allows work to be monitored and scheduled more effectively.

- It allows publishers to anticipate the stages through which work must pass before going live. (This helps shape expectations about how soon items can be expedited.)

- It has the knock on effect of encouraging Content Contributors to produce better quality content (as they know it will be reviewed before being released).

Based on the roles reviewed above, a typical process of this type could reflect the following:

Step	Roles	Description
Step 1	Content Contributor	Content is produced by a Content Contributor in accordance with the stipulations of a Briefing Document.
Step 2	Editor	When received by the Editor, he reviews it and makes whatever changes are necessary.
Step 3	Legal/Regulatory Reviewer	When approved by the Editor, the completed content is sent for Legal/Regulatory Review.
Step 4	Designer & Developer	Following Legal/Regulatory clearance, it is prepared by the Designer and the Developer.
Step 5	Editor	When the content is complete, it is common for the Editor to have a final review. In the case of sensitive items, e.g. homepage, the Website Management Team may wish to clear changes before they golive.
Step 6	Developer	The content is returned to the Developer who places it on the live website.
Step 7	Editor	When the content is live the Editor conducts a final review to ensure it is presented as intended.

Publishing Workflow

As already explained, WCM is now facilitating many aspects of publishing. Indeed, several packages include functionality that allows a publishing process to be controlled electronically. Called 'workflow', this permits content to be expedited in a far more disciplined manner than was previously possible.

For example, an individual who is asked to produce an article for an intranet may do so using WCM. After the content has been written, the Contributor clicks a button labelled 'submit' in order for publishing to occur. This prompts an email to be sent to the Editor advising him to review the new contribution. Only when this has been approved, is it put live. In this way workflow is one of the most useful features of WCM.

Of course, in smaller organisations a Publishing Process may have to rely on much simpler technology. Email is commonly used in such circumstances. For example, content might be emailed from person to person, with changes and edits being added at each step. However, email can become cumbersome when large volumes are worked on. It can also be difficult to know where in the workflow a piece of content is located. This is because there is no automatic means for tracking progress.

As a result, WCM is fast becoming indispensable in many organisations. This is because it provides Content Contributors with the freedom they need to make changes and gives Editors a mechanism for monitoring updates. However, essential though WCM is, it is only one of a range of tools needed by a Publishing Team. As we will see next, a variety of other resources are required to ensure good content can be consistently produced.

Publishing Resources

What self-respecting Editor would be without a good dictionary, or Designer without a library of images? Hopefully none! That is because these are among the most fundamental tools they need to do their jobs.

In fact, each member of a Website Publishing Team needs some form of toolkit to help them produce content. As a consequence, many organisations create special resource packs that contain all the supports required by publishing staff. While the cost of these packs is low, the benefits for content quality can be very high.

We will now look at the tools recommended for inclusion in such a pack for each member of a Publishing Team.

Editor's Publishing Pack

The Editor's Publishing Pack contains all the resources required to ensure rules for language, style and design can be properly adhered to. These include:

Website Standard

The Website Standard is the document that sets out the approach of an organisation to all aspects of site management; including design, content, navigation, coding and maintenance. As such it is the most important document an Editor can have.

(Go to Chapter Four–Website Governance, page 298, for a comprehensive overview of Website Standards.)

Website Style Guide

A Website Style Guide is a document that details how language on a site should be written and structured. Style Guides are an essential feature of printed media production and are increasingly used on the web. For example, a Style Guide may stipulate that only British-English spelling be used, or that sentences should be no longer than 15 words. Such guides are indispensable for creating a common approach to the use of language. Fortunately many examples of Style Guides are available for download from the World Wide Web[12].

Company Policies

The policies of an organisation set limits to the scope of content that can be developed online. For example, a company Security Policy may stipulate that web transactions may only be processed using encryption. Similarly, it could be against an Equal Opportunities Policy to publish anything that implies discrimination.

(Turn to Chapter Four–Website Governance, page 317, to learn how Company Policies affect Website Management.)

Organisational Identity Manual

An Organisational Identity Manual governs the utilisation of a company's logo and any associated imagery, colours and typefaces. Many organisations create such rules so that trademarks can be correctly rendered and protected from misuse. For example, an Identity Manual may state the minimum size of a logo. It may also list exactly what colours need to be employed.

Dictionary

While this might seem obvious, it is surprising how often the requirement for a good dictionary is overlooked. A dictionary is needed both for checking the meaning of words, as well as their spelling.

---

[12] BBC News. http://www.bbctraining.com/styleguide.asp
The Guardian. http://www.guardian.co.uk/styleguide/0,5817,184913,00.HTML

The selection of an appropriate reference work depends mainly on the language in which an organisation is working and the level of detail required. While a 'pocket' book may be sufficient on many sites, a more robust volume is needed by companies that undertake a lot of publishing. This is particularly true for websites that focus on a specialist topic, e.g. medicine or computing.

Of course, a huge variety of such publications are available. Two in particular are:

- Merriam-Webster's Collegiate Dictionary

- Concise Oxford English Dictionary

On the internet, www.dictionary.com is a useful resource, as is Oxford's Online Dictionary, www.askoxford.com/dictionaries/compact_oed/.

Finally, a dictionary to cover aspects of spelling and labelling within an organisation itself may be needed. Such a dictionary would stipulate the correct rendering of department names and products for the purposes of consistency and trademark protection. (Such a dictionary is commonly included as a section in a Website Style Guide.)

Thesaurus

A useful resource for maintaining richness and variety in written content is a thesaurus. It should be noted that Microsoft Word has a built-in thesaurus that can be activated by highlighting a word and pressing 'shift' + 'F7' on the computer keyboard. Some other useful reference works include:

- Roget International Thesaurus

- Merriam-Webster's Collegiate Thesaurus

Grammar Guide

A grammar guide is used by an Editor to check constructions and ensure standard rules for language are adhered to. As with dictionaries and thesauri, the choice of guides to English grammar is very wide. One of the most popular is Oxford Reference Grammar from Oxford University Press.

Content Contributor's Publishing Pack

The Content Contributor's Pack generally contains all of the same elements as the Editor's Pack, though some material may appear in abridged format only, e.g. Identity Manual, Company Policies.

Legal Reviewer's Publishing Pack

This pack consists of extracts from legislation and regulations, as well as a collection of company policies against which content can be compared.

(An overview of legislation that impacts Website Management can be found in Chapter Four–Website Governance, page 301.)

Designer's Publishing Pack

The Designer's Pack contains the same resources as found in the Editor's Pack, with the exception of the dictionary, thesaurus and grammar guide. However, other specialist items are substituted — in particular a Design Library and Design Software.

Design Library

A Design Library comprises a selection of photographs, graphics, typefaces and other audio-visual material that has been licensed for use by an organisation. These can then be used to support the creative process. Such a library helps to maintain a fresh and professional appearance for a site. Libraries of this type come in two forms:

1. Custom Library

2. Stock-Art Library

To create a **Custom Library** a professional photographer is employed to take pictures on themes of interest to a business. This could include images of the Board of Directors or company products[13]. Similarly, an illustrator may be contracted to create specialist graphics or icons.

However, a Custom Library may be unnecessary for all but the largest of firms. This is because design material can easily be purchased from 'Stock Art' suppliers. A huge variety of **Stock Art** is available, covering almost every theme and medium imaginable. These resources can be purchased online for delivery on CD or by download, e.g. www.gettyone.com.

Design Software

The design software used across the web industry is remarkably uniform. In fact, the look-and-feel of most websites is designed on a small number of systems referred to as image-creation or image-editing tools. The most popular of these are:

- Adobe® Photoshop® (from $649)

- Adobe® Illustrator® (from $499)

- Adobe Fireworks™ (from $399)

- Microsoft Expression® Graphic Designer ($n/a)

Of course, other specialist software may be needed if formats other than simple images are required, e.g. video, animation, etc. (These are explored in Chapter Three–Website Development, page 118.)

---

[13] This can also be done on the cheap by investing in a digital camera–especially for an intranet, where image quality need not be as good as for public communications.

Developer's Publishing Pack

The elements of a Developer's Pack are generally the same as those of the Designer, though a different assortment of specialist resources are required. This typically encompasses the software required for creating and editing website code. The most popular tools in this regard are explored in the next chapter (page 212).

As we have now seen, the provision of good quality resources means that content is more likely to be produced to a high standard.

Yet, even if all systems and procedures are strictly adhered to, errors can still arise. For example, a Developer may accidentally delete or move a file. This could result in broken links or other problems. The difficulty is that unless someone is checking for such mistakes, they may go unnoticed — until a customer complains!

That is why the activity of **Quality Assurance** is so important.

Activity 2
Website Quality Assurance

Quality Assurance is the activity that makes sure a website is operationally sound and in conformance with an organisation's standards. Basically, it is about preventative maintenance — so that small issues do not become big business problems!

In some ways Website Quality Assurance can be compared to the system of compulsory Vehicle Testing that exists in many countries. The purpose of these tests is to examine vehicles that appear to be roadworthy (i.e. operationally sound) but that may contain undetected flaws. These can then be fixed before they become dangerous.

The same logic may be applied to a website. While a site might appear to be operating smoothly, there could be small errors that have been overlooked. The purpose of Quality Assurance is to isolate and deal with these.

Website Quality Assurance Activities

The activities of Website Quality Assurance encompass two areas: **Data Collection** and **Data Analysis**.

Data Collection

The aim of this task is to collect the data against which a website can be examined for issues of quality. In practical terms, this requires a site to be validated against a series of checkpoints. These include:

- Checking for broken links

- Checking for missing content, e.g. images

- Checking for missing browser titles

- Checking the spelling and grammar of content

- Checking for missing metadata

- Checking the file sizes of pages to ensure they are not too large

- Checking for browser compatibility

- Checking that applications are functioning correctly, e.g. an online hotel reservation form

- Checking that legal and regulatory guidelines are being adhered to, e.g. data protection and privacy

- Checking that pages conform to your organisation's Web Accessibility standard (if any)

- Checking that the Website Design standard is maintained

Data Analysis

Data Analysis examines all the information that has been collected for a site and from that an Issues Log is compiled. The purpose of this log is to list items that are in violation of a QA checkpoint, e.g. broken links, oversized images, etc. These can then be allocated to Developers for adjustment.

The Technology of Quality Assurance

On many sites the activities of Data Collection and Analysis are performed manually, often by a Junior Developer. That is, he or she is instructed to review all content and validate it against the list of QA Checkpoints. Experience suggests that this task needs to occur on at least a weekly basis for all but the smallest of sites.

However, it should be obvious that this process can be very time-consuming, as well as unbelievably boring! Indeed, some sites are so large that effective Quality Assurance simply cannot be undertaken in this way. Imagine trying to manually check every one of the tens of thousands of links on a Dynamic site like www.bbc.co.uk — every week! Practically impossible.

Fortunately, this has been recognised for some time and an array of automated software is available. The advantage of such products is that they can undertake the legwork of Quality Assurance while leaving staff free to concentrate on more valuable assignments.

Although several Quality Assurance products are low in cost or free to download from the internet[14], they are generally poor in quality. Fortunately, a number of systems from established manufacturers are also available. These are configurable to a high degree and can be set up to conduct a wide variety of checks. Some of the better known include:

---

[14] A comprehensive list of such tools is maintained by Rick Hower at the website
http://www.softwareqatest.com/qatweb1.HTML

Dreamweaver™ from Adobe (www.adobe.com, from $399)

While Dreamweaver is primarily a website authoring tool (as explained in Chapter Three), it also incorporates basic QA capability, including link checking, filesize checking, accessibility monitoring, etc. Dreamweaver is best suited to Basic websites that are small to medium in size.

Expression® Web Designer from Microsoft (www.microsoft.com, $n/a)

The website creation tool from Microsoft includes similar functionality to Dreamweaver, such as code and link checking.

HiSoftware Web Site Monitor™ (www.hisoftware.com, from $495)

Originally focussed on simple hyperlink validation, HiSoftware Web Site Monitor now includes additional tools for reviewing filesize, page titles, accessibility and metadata. This product is suitable for Basic, Dynamic and Transactional sites up to several thousand pages in size.

WebQA™ from Watchfire® (www.watchfire.com, from $1,100)

WebQA is one of the internet's most widely used Quality Assurance tools due to the comprehensive range of options it provides. This includes filesize checking, page titles, accessibility, privacy and metadata. It can safely be used on Basic, Dynamic and Transactional sites up to 10,000 pages in size.

WebXM™ from Watchfire (www.watchfire.com, price dependent on website scale)

As the premium product from Watchfire, WebXM offers a much wider set of features than most tools. This includes privacy, brand and legal checking. It also incorporates a function that allows any content that is linked to, to be monitored for suitability, e.g. to ensure it is not offensive or adult in nature. Because of this, WebXM is best suited for the largest and busiest of websites, as well as those for whom integrity and reliability are key business values.

(The online assessment tool WebXACT™ at www.webxact.com, provides an introduction to the functionality of both WebQA and WebXM.)

Website Content Management

Finally, as described on page 34, WCM is now taking on many of the tasks of site maintenance—including several features of Quality Assurance. For example, a number of WCM products encompass functions like link checking and accessibility validation. However, few systems encompass the full suite of options necessary, which means a dedicated QA tool is generally necessary.

One of the most notable features of Website Quality Assurance is the level of discipline it needs for proper implementation. This is because, in the absence of strict enforcement, wear and tear could soon erode the ability of a site to operate to a high standard. This type of discipline is also mirrored in other maintenance activities, e.g. **Feedback Monitoring** (examined next), where a close attention to detail is required to maintain good customer relations.

Activity 3
Website Feedback Monitoring

Website Feedback Monitoring is a process for regulating and responding to communications from site visitors in a controlled and timely manner. It should be remembered that the only way many customers will ever make contact with you is via the web. As such, it is the one and perhaps only chance you have to convince them their needs are taken seriously.

A problem on many sites is that feedback is never responded to, simply because no process for managing communications has been put in place. This is regrettable because feedback is both extremely valuable as a source of customer information and relatively straightforward to administer. All it requires is someone who can monitor and respond to messages in a professional way.

Website Feedback Procedure

On many sites the task of Feedback Monitoring falls between the cracks because everyone thinks it is someone else's job and no-one wants to 'waste' their time checking email. In circumstances like this a

Maintenance Team Leader may be obliged to appoint a Feedback Co-ordinator to care for communications.

The role of a **Feedback Co-ordinator** is to ensure customer messages are acknowledged and responded to in a timely manner. The volume of communication received by some companies (e.g. an online bank) may be so great that the assistance of a professional Service Centre is required. If so, expert procedures should already be available.

However, for organisations where this task is dealt with internally, other systems are needed. These typically encompass the following activities:

1. **Collect the feedback**: Though this regularly occurs via email, it can also be collected from other channels (as we will see below).

2. **Acknowledge receipt of the query**: This is done as a matter of courtesy, so that customers know their message is being attended to.

3. **Investigate (if appropriate)**: If a query cannot be responded to immediately, further investigation may be required.

4. **Make a full response and manage any follow-up correspondence**: Following any investigation, a complete answer must be provided. This may involve several rounds of communication back and forth with the customer.

5. **Archive**: When complete, customer messages may be recorded in a Feedback Archive.

While these steps are common for all types of feedback, the manner in which they are managed can differ based on the channel through which correspondence is received. This includes:

- Email

- Bulletin Board

- Chat

- Instant Messaging

- Satisfaction Ratings

- Telephone

- Post

Email

The vast bulk of website feedback usually arrives by email. Messages like this are sent either by way of a simple contact address or via an online feedback form.

If a contact address is chosen, it is best that a generic destination be selected, e.g. feedback@website.com[15], rather than that of a named individual. A generic address means that communication can be monitored even if the nominated co-ordinator is away from the office.

Contact Form

Message Type:	⊙ feedback* ○ site fix ○ new ○ business ○ reprints ○ wire *Note: We may publish message: Raves letters to the editor feature published, please let us know in y
Send to:	
	Note: We have too many contribu use the reply link in the story byli

Figure 11. Web form from Wired.com showing how feedback can be sorted by type.

---

[15] The format for such an address is also worth considering. It may be advisable to rewrite it in a way that spamming programs cannot recognise. For example, feedback@website.com could be rendered as 'feedback at website dot com'.

However, web forms do have some advantages over direct mail. For example, they allow customers who do not have email accounts to contact you. (This is because such emails are sent from your website, not from the customer's computer.) Similarly, customers who happen to be away from their usual email location can use it to get in touch. Finally, forms also facilitate the sorting of queries into different categories. This is achieved by asking customers to tick a box indicating the type of feedback they are submitting — as seen in the example from Wired.com.

Where feedback is received by email, receipt of customers' messages should be acknowledged either immediately or within 24 hours. Acknowledgement emails may also be automated if large numbers are received. The text in such an email could indicate what the customer can expect to happen next, as well as a procedure for escalating the inquiry if an answer is not received. In some cases a reference (or 'ticket') number may be supplied. This number allows issues to be tracked and customers to monitor progress.

Feedback Bulletin Board or Discussion Forum

Bulletin boards are sometimes used to gather feedback on sites built around a specialised subject. For example, a website about astronomy may have a bulletin board reserved for 'Feedback' or 'User Suggestions', as well as others for discussing the subject matter itself. Such a bulletin board could be used to encourage visitors to submit questions for the attention of the Editor.

Feedback received in this way may be responded to in a manner similar to email. That is, acknowledgements and subsequent messages are posted on the board for the attention of all users. However, if a visitor indicates they want their query dealt with privately, that should be respected.

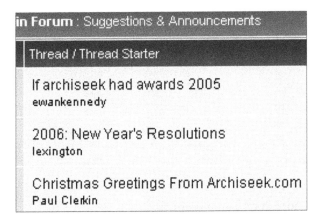

Figure 12. Feedback bulletin board on www.archiseek.com

Online Chat

Some organisations (notably large online service providers) may use Chat as a means of customer contact. Chat allows a customer to engage in real-time communication with a company representative, thereby facilitating instant service. However, chat is resource intensive and is only recommended for websites that have appropriate levels of staffing.

Figure 13. Online chat service from the self-publishing firm, Lulu.

Where communication is authorised by this method, one of the most important requirements is to set the times during which service will be available. For example, it may only be feasible to run chat for a few hours every day. These times (as well as time zone differences) should be clearly indicated on the site. During the noted periods, customers will expect an instant response, so someone must always be available.

Instant Messaging

Instant Messaging follows much the same model as Online Chat. The drawback is that website visitors must have appropriate software available on their computers. However, as this can be downloaded free from the internet[16], it is not a serious impediment.

smile **contains high levels** of customer service

smile's award winning customer service team is available via email or telephone 24/7. Here's how you can get in touch:

 secure message - To talk about your account always use our specially built, private secure messaging system which you'll find in **smile** banking after login

Figure 14. Messaging service on internet bank Smile.co.uk

Satisfaction Ratings

Many websites now include in-page features that allow visitors to rate content and provide comments about it. Such ratings are then sent to authors, who use them as a basis for improving information. When many such ratings are taken together, they provide a good way of estimating overall user contentment.

---

[16] For example at AOL (www.aim.com) and MSN (messenger.msn.com).

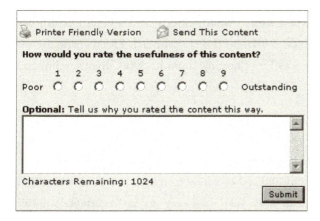

Figure 15. Satisfaction rating form from Microsoft.com

Telephone

In the event that a website is unavailable, one of the few remaining feedback channels is the telephone. Contact in this way may be necessary if, for example, a website is undergoing maintenance and needs to be shut-down temporarily. An interim web page may be published to indicate a phone number that can be used to contact the organisation in the meantime.

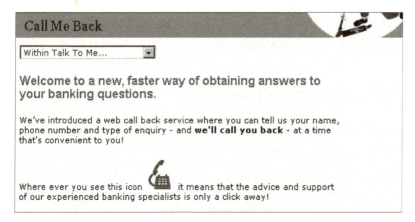

Figure 16. Call back facility on the website of the Australian bank, Adelaide Bank.

Telephone contact can also be used in ordinary circumstances. A common such facility is referred to as **Call Back**. This occurs where a customer logs a query via a web form, together with their phone number and a note indicating a suitable date/time for contact. The website owner then accepts the cost of a call by phoning them back (as illustrated above on the website of Adelaide bank).

Post

Finally, good old 'snail mail' can also be used to submit feedback. That said, it is quite an unusual method of contact. In fact, it is so unusual that any feedback received in this way is likely to be a lawyer's letter demanding that you "cease and desist" from some activity!

> **CORPORATE HEADQUARTERS**
>
> **Corporate Headquarters**
> 56 Top Gallant Road
> Stamford, CT 06904-7700
> U.S.A.
> + 1 203 964 0096
> Driving Directions
>
> **U.S. — West Coast**
> Gartner, Inc.

Figure 17. Postal addresses for the business intelligence firm Gartner on www.gartner.com

Website Feedback Archive

As part of the Feedback Monitoring procedure, the creation of a communications archive can prove useful for chronicling site issues and queries. At a minimum this should contain details about:

- The nature of feedback received

- The channel by which it was received

- The date it was received

- The action taken

- The date the query was resolved

This can then be used to assist service improvement, perhaps by highlighting trends. For example, a web page of 'Frequently Asked Questions' could be created based on commonly occurring themes.

Of course, care should be taken not to retain actual customer messages for longer than necessary. Data Protection legislation in many countries means that correspondence must be disposed of once the reason for the initial communication has been expedited. For example, an email from a website visitor asking for help should be deleted once they have been informed of the answer, i.e. it should not be used as a sales opportunity.

(For more about the law as it applies to the internet, go to Chapter Four-Website Governance, page 301).

Lastly, as with all aspects of site maintenance, an update on Website Feedback should be included as an agenda item in a regular Maintenance Review Meeting. Indeed, as feedback helps throw light on the quality of site operations, it may sometimes be dealt with within the broader activity of **Website Performance Monitoring**, examined next.

Activity 4
Website Performance Monitoring

Website Performance Monitoring is the activity that gathers and analyses data against which the success of a website can be evaluated. Much discussion in this area revolves around the notion of 'hits' and website traffic. This is unfortunate because such statistics are poorly understood. Besides, Performance Monitoring is much broader than simple traffic analysis alone. It encompasses many other methods for evaluating achievement, e.g. revenue earned, user opinions, etc. Consequently, it is important that a Maintenance Team have a clear idea of the Key Performance Indicators (KPIs) against which their site is being evaluated.

Key Performance Indicators

KPIs are the targets that have been selected by Website Management as devices for determining success. While such measures can encompass a wide variety of metrics, the three most commonly represented are:

- Website Activity

- Visitor Feedback (this was explored in the previous section)

- Subscriber/Sponsor Feedback

Each of these is examined in more detail below.

Website Activity

"My website gets 50,000 hits a day!"

Great, but does that mean...

- 50,000 pages are viewed on my website everyday?

- 50,000 people are visiting my website everyday?

- Or, my site is visited 50,000 times everyday?

In fact, it does not mean any of the above. What it means is that 50,000 files of several different types are transferred from your website to the user agents of the people accessing it. A user agent is a device that can browse the World Wide Web and display content. For example, some common user agents include:

- A web browser on a desktop or laptop computer

- A Personal Digital Assistant (PDA)

- A mobile phone with web access

The files sent to a user agent could include anything from plain text to images. For instance, a web page may have five images embedded in it. When that page is accessed, the website transfers six files and so records six 'hits' — one hit for the page itself and five more for each of the separate images. Depending on the design of a site, a figure of 50,000 'hits' may therefore show little or nothing about user activity.

As a consequence, a more robust set of metrics is required. This is particularly important because (as we saw earlier in this chapter) traffic has such a major influence on team staffing. Yet, if 'hits' are next to worthless for tracking activity, how can a concept like 'busy-ness' be measured effectively?

The best means that has been found is by monitoring each of the following:

- Website Visits

- Website Visitors

- Website Page Impressions

Website Visit

A visit is an instance of a unique visitor accessing a website. Most sites aim to maximise both the number of visits they receive and their duration. However, this is not true for everyone. Think of a Transactional website for reserving airline tickets, e.g. Ryanair.com. A visit that exceeds 20 minutes probably indicates that the reservation process is too difficult.

Unfortunately, accurately defining visits can be problematic because they are often interrupted. For example, if an individual browses a website for 15 minutes, takes a break for an hour and then returns—does that constitute one visit or two? In this case, a decision on the length of the allowed interval must be made (though 30 minutes is considered adequate in most circumstances).

Website Visitor

A visitor is the originator of a visit, i.e. the person[17] who browses a website. Every visitor to a site can be identified by the Internet Protocol (IP) address of the device they use to access it. An IP address is the unique identifying number that is allocated to every object connected to the internet. Such numbers are formatted in the following way, e.g. 123.456.789.012. This means that the total number of visitors to a site can

---

[17] Actually, it is more accurate to say the visitor is the 'user agent' used to access the site. However, because most devices are controlled by human beings it is safe to say that visitors are in fact people!

be calculated by counting the number of unique IP addresses it has recorded.

However, it is worth bearing in mind that some large organisations (e.g. colleges and banks), allocate a single IP address to every person on their network. That means that even if 100 different people from inside a bank visit your website, they will only be counted as one visitor.

Similarly, some Internet Service Providers allocate different addresses to a single visitor within a single visit. This means that one visitor can be made to look like many. As you can imagine, this makes it very hard to get a grasp of real activity.

Website Page Impressions

A Page Impression is actually a 'hit'. However, Page Impressions only record 'hits' on pages that contain content. That means that images and other files are automatically filtered out. As such, only true pages are counted.

As already mentioned, a high traffic website is one that receives a minimum of 1,000,000 validated page impressions per month. However, it should be noted that many busy Dynamic and Transactional sites receive millions more. For example, the news website of the BBC attracts over 23 million page impressions **every day!**[18]

Financial Return on Website Activity

While visits, visitors and page impressions can be used to evaluate the popularity of a website, they say very little about the value of such activity. For example, the owners of a Transactional website like Amazon.com are less interested in the number of visitors they receive,

---

[18] BBC News online. "Record Traffic to BBC New Site".
http://news.bbc.co.uk/2/hi/technology/4672869.stm . Accessed August 2005.

than in the percentage who actually purchase something. Indeed, financial KPIs are of far greater importance for many firms. Such measures generally encompass three themes:

- **Acquisition**: The cost and value of attracting visitors.

- **Conversion**: The cost and value of making a sale.

- **Retention**: The cost and value of customer loyalty.

KPI	Calculation
Customer Acquisition Cost	Marketing spend / Number of visitors to a site
Conversion Rate	Number of visitors who purchase something / Number of visitors to a site
Average Revenue per Order	Total Order Value / Number of Orders
Average Revenue per Conversion	Total Order Value / Number of visitors who purchase something

Figure 18. Sample measures of website financial performance.

Unfortunately, a study conducted by DoubleClick™ in 2004 found that as few as 4 or 5 out of every 100 visitors to a Transactional site actually buy something[19]. Although other reports show that this number has the potential to grow[20], aspects of bad design often frustrate customers. The phenomenon of 'Abandoned Carts' presents a stark illustration of this.

An **Abandoned Cart** occurs when a shopper (who has selected a product for purchase) chooses not to complete their transaction. Research has shown that up to 75% of visitors abandon their carts before completing

---

[19] DoubleClick.com. "DoubleClick Q3 2004 E-Commerce Site Trend Report (November 2004)" http://www.doubleclick.com/us/knowledge_central/trend_reports/e-commerce/ Accessed April 2005.

[20] Useit.com "One billion internet users" http://www.useit.com/alertbox/internet_growth.html Jakob Neilsen, December 2005. Accessed December 2005.

the checkout process[21]. This can happen for many reasons. Perhaps they do not understand the instructions for inserting credit card numbers or maybe they cannot find the 'submit' button. In fact, some customers intentionally abandon their carts, simply because they were only using them as a means of price comparison and had no intention to buy.

Validating Website Traffic

As well as serving as metrics for a Website Management Team, KPIs can also be used to promote the success of a site to investors and advertisers. Yet, differing definitions for some of the figures of Website Traffic has called their usefulness into question. In response, agencies such as the Web Analytics Association (www.webanalyticsassociation.org) and the International Federation of Audit Bureaux of Circulations (www.ifabc.org) have become popular as a way of standardising and verifying traffic numbers.

IFABC is "an industry owned, non-profit organisation that works with the media to achieve a better understanding of the data they use". Websites subscribe to such a service so that their figures can be verified by an independent body. This is very similar to the circulation ratings that are created for newspapers and magazines.

The Tools of Website Traffic Analytics

While scrutinising the metrics of Website Traffic is all very well, many managers have no idea where the numbers underlying this information actually come from. Although the answer itself is quite straightforward, the process for extracting and analysing data is somewhat more complex.

---

[21] Clickz "20 Tips to minimise shopping cart abandonment"
http://www.clickz.com/experts/crm/traffic/article.php/2245891 August 2003.
Accessed November 2005.

In simple terms what happens is that every time a visitor comes to a site, the computer upon which it is hosted records their activity in a file. It is this file (called a 'logfile') that is the source of the metrics we have seen. A logfile is basically a long page of text that lists all the characteristics of a visit.

One of the problems with logfiles is that they are well-nigh impossible to read in a normal way. For example, could you make sense of several thousand pages that looked like this:

```
193.120.81.130  -  -  [02/Aug/2005:19:38:01 +0100]  "GET
/articles/index.htm      HTTP/1.0"      200      6810
"http://www.diffily.com/"  "Mozilla/4.0  (compatible;
MSIE 6.0; Windows NT 5.1)"
```

(For those interested, a partial explanation follows)

Logfile	Explanation
`193.120.81.130`	This is the IP address of the visitor.
`"GET /articles/index.htm HTTP/1.0"`	This denotes the exact file that was accessed.
`200`	This is the 'HTTP Status Code' for the file that was transferred.
`6810`	This is the size of the file (in bytes) that was transferred, i.e. 6.8kB.
`"http://www.diffily.com/"`	This is the address from which the visitor originated.
`"Mozilla/4.0 (compatible; MSIE 5.5; Windows NT 5.0; T312461)"`	This is the user agent and Operating System used by the visitor.

In response, a huge market has grown around technology called **Website Traffic Analytics**.

Website Traffic Analytics encompasses tools that extract and analyse data from a logfile. Many products of this type are free and can be downloaded from the internet. However, high quality analysis usually requires investment in a professional system (with a starting price of about $4,000). These come in two forms:

- **Standalone Solution**: Where software is installed directly on the computer that hosts the website.

- **Application Service Provider Solution**: Where measurements are gathered remotely.

Standalone Solution

The Standalone solution comprises software that is installed directly on the computer hosting a site. The benefit of the Standalone model is that it is self managed. The disadvantage is that in-house technical support is required. Some sample vendors in this area include:

- Sane Solutions®

- Visual Sciences

- WebTrends®

Application Service Provider Solution (ASP)

The ASP[22] solution encompasses services operated over the internet by third parties. These systems function using customised 'tags' that are placed into every page of a website. A tag is simply a short line of code that monitors visitor activity. Every time a page is visited, the tag is activated and sends information to the external provider where results are collated.

The main benefit of the ASP model is that very little set-up is needed. The disadvantage is that tags must be inserted into every page, which may number in the tens of thousands on a large site. Furthermore, this

---

[22] Not to be confused with the Server-Side Scripting language, Active Server Pages (ASP).

model may not work for intranet sites (because of security issues) and can sometimes be very expensive due to licensing arrangements.

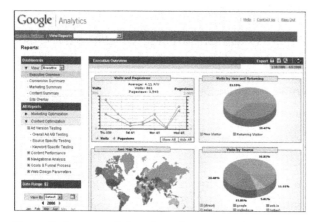

Figure 19. A screengrab from the website of Google Analytics.

In general, the ASP model is most suited to highly resourced sites where detailed analysis is required. Some sample ASP vendors include:

- Omniture

- Coremetrics™

- WebSideStory™

- Google Analytics™ (now available for free)

Visitor Characteristics

As well as monitoring visitor numbers, Website Analytics can also be used to track the characteristics of visitors to a site. While such analysis may not provide any immediate measures of success, it is useful for highlighting trends, e.g. preferred user agents. This can then be fed into a process of site review. Among the types of analysis that may be performed in this way are:

User Agent Type

All analytics tools are able to identify the type of devices that are used by visitors. This can have an important impact on design. For example, if more and more people use PDAs or mobile phones for web browsing, a special version of a site may be needed to cater for them. (An overview of how this is achieved is provided in Chapter Three–Website Development, page 195.)

Time of Visits

Analysis of user behaviour can reveal the most popular times for visits to a website. This could be used to influence the publishing process. For example, if large numbers of visitors access a site every Monday morning, new content should be made available for them at that time.

Sources of Internet Traffic

A useful feature of such tools is that they can record the place on the World Wide Web from which the visitors to a site originated. For example, if visitors use a Search Engine such as Google® or Yahoo!, the logfile records this fact, as well as the search terms that were used.

Geographic Location

Finally, an analytics tool can record the geographic location from which people are accessing a site. While this feature is not 100% accurate, it is a useful indicator of the scope of a business. For example, if many people are logging-on from Germany and Austria, perhaps it implies that an alternative language version should be created?

Subscriber/Sponsor Opinions

As seen in the previous section, the activity of Feedback Monitoring is crucial for any site that wishes to maintain a happy audience. However, the opinions of ordinary site visitors are only part of the story. There are two other classes of user whose comments and suggestions are of even greater significance. These are the 'Subscriber' and the 'Sponsor'.

A **subscriber** is a power-user of a site, e.g. someone who has registered as a member of a discussion forum and who uses it very regularly.

A **sponsor** is someone who is willing to pay for the services provided by a website, e.g. by paying a fee to access an online newspaper.

Many Dynamic and Transactional websites boast large audiences of both subscribers and sponsors. One of the best known is eBay.

Sponsors on eBay.com

eBay has a revenue model that relies on sponsors to pay a small fee for placing ads online. The upshot is that the users of this service are more than just 'visitors' — they are 'customers'. They therefore constitute an important stakeholder group whose opinions must be listened to. In response, eBay has pioneered a system for involving sponsors in decision making, e.g. by actively requesting opinions about site development and services.

A variety of other sites follow a similar model (though often without financial incentive). For example, the success of Flickr.com can be related directly to the quality of the relationship it has fostered with subscribers.

Subscribers on Flickr.com

Flickr started life as an online gaming site but over time developed into a photograph sharing platform. The positive relationship that was cultivated with subscribers helped make this transition possible. This itself has enticed more and more people to get involved and increased business value as a result. (Flickr has now been bought by Yahoo!)

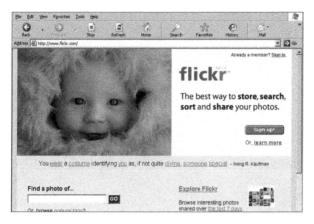

Figure 20. The homepage of Flickr.com

Yet, it must be noted that subscribers and sponsors can make their feelings known in more ways than one. Indeed, criticism is never slow is coming if decisions are taken that adversely affect their interests. For example, on one occasion Flickr redesigned their site by placing navigation on the left-hand side of the screen. The flurry of objections that soon began to arrive prompted a quick retreat back to the original set-up!

One area of site administration that causes more complaints than any other is that of inadequate Website Infrastructure. Unreliable website that cause 'hanging' screens and loss of data are enough to drive visitors mad! That is why the activity of **Infrastructure Performance Monitoring** demands such a lot of attention.

Activity 5
Website Infrastructure
Performance Monitoring

How many website managers have ever seen the physical computer upon which their site is hosted? Indeed, how many regularly talk to their technical personnel in order to understand the issues that affect website performance?

Unfortunately, not that many.

There seems to be an attitude among some managers that technical maintenance is beyond their ability. As a result, many sites seriously underperform in this area because systems are not monitored closely enough.

The aim of Infrastructure Performance Monitoring is to plug this gap by recommending procedures for the supervision of site hosting. As explained in Chapter Three (page 256) hosting refers to the service that allows a website to be stored on and accessed from the internet.

Naturally, the creation of a team with the right expertise is the most important requirement for good infrastructure support—particularly if hosting is undertaken internally[23]. As we saw in the introduction to Website Maintenance, the group in charge of this area is called the Technical Support Team.

Technical Support Team

The size of a Technical Team and the range of skills represented on it depends on the complexity of the infrastructure to be maintained. For example, a single person with rudimentary skills may be able to handle a small Basic site, while a busy Transactional website requires many more.

Basic Website	**Content**: Plain content (HTML/XHTML). **Staffing Level for Infrastructure Monitoring and Change Control**: 1 person.
Dynamic Website	**Content**: Dynamically generated from a database. **Staffing Level for Infrastructure Monitoring and Change Control**: 1 or 2 people (or more on a very large or busy site).
Transactional Website	**Content**: Fully transactional content, e.g. eCommerce. **Staffing Level for Infrastructure Monitoring and Change Control**: From 1 or 2 people upwards (many more on a large or busy site).

Figure 21. Staffing a Technical Team.

Notwithstanding differences in size, the range of skills embraced by this group remains the same. These are:

- **Server Software Management**: This deals with the maintenance of the software used to host a site.

---

[23] The process for deciding whether an internal or external hosting solution is appropriate is explored in Chapters Three and Five.

- **Server Hardware Management**: This deals with the maintenance of hosting hardware.

- **Information Systems Security**: This deals with issues of website security.

- **Data Maintenance**. This deals with issues of data storage.

(More detail on these is provided in Chapter Five, page 367.)

A **Team Leader** should also be appointed. This person's role is to co-ordinate technical administration and ensure ongoing performance. A common means for facilitating this via a Service Level Agreement (SLA).

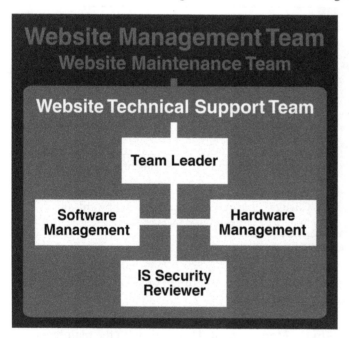

Figure 22. Website Technical Support Team.

Service Level Agreement

An SLA is a document that stipulates metrics by which the technical performance of a site can be assessed. Arrangements like this are most common where hosting occurs externally (as explained in Chapter Three, page 259). However, a similar deal may be instituted if support is provided internally. In this case, it is referred to as an Operational Level Agreement (OLA), as explained in Chapter Five (page 369).

The most common measures represented within an SLA (or an OLA) include:

- **Website Availability.** This is the percentage of time that a website is up and running. Many hosting companies offer targets of between 99.8% and 100% on this.

- **Website Reliability.** This equates to the number of unplanned outages that occur on a website, i.e. many outages = poor reliability. In many SLAs this is set at zero, meaning the hosting company certifies there will be no interruption to service.

- **Website Responsiveness.** This is the speed with which a website responds to traffic. This is often set in milliseconds and is dependent on factors such as the specification of the website hardware and the speed of the link to the internet.

(Issues affecting performance are explored in Chapter Three, page 262 and in Chapter Five, page 369.)

The most basic means of checking site performance is to logon at busy periods and assess how well it is responding. However, monitoring a site in such an ad-hoc way cannot possibly provide the quantitative data needed to evaluate SLA compliance, especially for a Transactional site. The unfortunate result is that (in the absence of other resources) many teams choose to ignore this area and rely instead on indirect methods for finding out when problems arise. For example, in 2004 the business intelligence firm Forrester® found that 74% of alerts regarding site performance came directly from visitors who emailed to complain[24]! Needless to say, this is less than satisfactory.

Performance Monitoring Technology

In response, a range of technology is now available to help monitor site Availability, Reliability and Responsiveness. Among the analysis they can provide is:

- Server response times

- End-User response times

- Server error rates and types

- Processor loads

- Hard disk utilisation

- Bandwidth utilisation

- Traffic patterns

- Queue sizes

- Timeouts

Entry level products (from $4,000 upwards) are generally used for measuring site responsiveness and for creating alerts in the event of a problem. Some well known vendors include:

- BMC Software®

- Mercury®

- Computer Associates®

- HP® Openview™

---

[24] Copyright © 2004, Forrester Research Inc. "Managing Performance from the End User Perspective". November 2004. www.forrester.com

Higher-end products provide a much broader suite of services and demand a correspondingly higher price (dependent on website scale). This includes analysing the devices that are accessing a site and identifying the cause of problems. Some sample vendors in this space are:

- Coradiant®

- Keynote Systems®

- Premitech

- Wily Technology

Nearly all these products also provide some form of real-time monitoring. This means that when an error occurs (e.g. an application fails), an alert can be sent to the Technical Support Team. Such alerts are commonly sent by email or SMS.

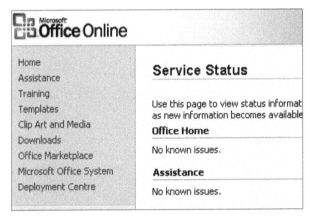

Figure 23. Microsoft publishes a page at http://office.microsoft.com/status/ that allows visitors to check the availability and status of its online services.

Performance Monitoring tools like these are essential for sites that aim to provide a high level of service. This is particularly true for eCommerce firms who use the web as a means for generating revenue. For example, any dip in the performance of a site such as Amazon.com means less money can be collected, which can have an immediate impact on business prospects.

Infrastructure Review Meeting

As a further step towards monitoring SLA compliance, an Infrastructure Review Meeting may be convened at which technical problems are analysed. Such a session can also consider planned technology changes that have the potential to impact site operations. For example, a plan to deliver new services over the web (e.g. eCommerce), could mean a review of the SLA is required. The effect of this can then be assessed and fed back into a regular Maintenance Review meeting for consideration by the entire team.

Indeed, the need for the proper management of site updates leads us into the final activity of Website Maintenance, **Change Control**.

Activity 6
Website Change Control

We have now looked at all aspects of maintaining a website in its current form. Yet, the responsibilities of site maintenance extend beyond issues of immediate operations. They are also concerned with developments that have the potential to affect future integrity. In this sense, a Team Leader must be able to make guarantees about performance, even as changes occur.

To do so, a mechanism is needed by which the impact of amendments can be managed — particularly those that affect site visitors and business operations (as well as the activities of maintenance themselves). The means by which this is achieved is called Change Control.

Change Control is a process for implementing technical and other updates to a website in a timely and non-disruptive manner. Because most sites are composed of a huge assortment of different technologies, this presents a considerable technical and administrative challenge.

For example, a large Transactional website may be host to several complex applications, including a Content Management System, Search Engine, a Performance Monitoring Suite, as well as security software. It is vital that any revisions to this set-up be implemented in a way that minimises the possibility of disruption. In most organisations this activity is supervised by a Technical Support Team.

The Change Control Process

The process by which Change Control is managed comprises four steps. These are:

1. Identify the nature of the change

2. Identify the scale of the change

3. Identify any possible impact

4. Proceed or re-evaluate

1. The Nature of the Change

The most common amendments covered by Change Control are those concerning the infrastructure of site hosting and the technology used to deliver content[25]. These can be grouped into four categories:

1. Changes arising as a result of software maintenance

A large part of all technical changes involve software maintenance of some kind. For example, security problems may be found in the operating system used to run a site, which means emergency patches are required.

---

[25] Amendments that arise from the ordinary activities of Publishing or Quality Assurance are excluded (unless they involve significant new technology).

2. Changes arising as a result of hardware maintenance

To ensure consistently high levels of performance, regular hardware maintenance is required. This can involve the replacement of faulty components, or upgrades to cope with high levels of traffic, e.g. extra memory.

3. Changes arising as a result of the initial release of content using a new technology

New content represents an unknown quantity for a Maintenance Team and demands careful deployment. For example, the first use of video on a website could require significant planning.

4. Changes arising as a result of marketing activity

Aside from technical changes, marketing activity can also produce an impact that requires attention. For instance, a campaign to attract more traffic to a site may lead to additional resources being needed to cope with increased activity, e.g. a faster connection to the internet.

2. The Scale of the Change

The scale of a change measures the amount of an existing infrastructure that is affected by it. It also determines the quantity of resources required to make the change happen. In fact, these usually go hand-in-hand. That is, a big change often needs a lot of resources. For example, the implementation of a Website Content Management System is significant both in terms of its effect on an existing infrastructure and the number of people required to expedite it.

However, the interpretation of scale can differ from site to site. For example, replacing the computer used to host a small Basic website represents a major change relative to its size. Yet, the same activity on a big Transactional site could be considered quite minor.

3. The Impact of the Change

The impact of a change is a measure of its effect on site visitors, business operations or site administration. Managing impact is all about minimising the risk that any of these will be affected.

For example, a change that results in a site going offline for a period of time is high-risk because it prevents customers using the web to engage with a business. In contrast, an amendment that merely requires minor alterations to internal maintenance procedures may have no noticeable effect at all.

It is worth noting that large changes do not always have a big impact. For example, suppose the software used to run a website needs to be upgraded. While this will have a significant effect on site administration, it could be invisible to visitors (if properly managed). On the contrary, small changes frequently have a huge impact—especially when they go wrong. For example, a botched hardware repair could result in a site being unavailable for several hours.

In this regard, there are a number of attributes that should be reviewed before any activity commences. These attributes provide a means of identifying elements that are particularly vulnerable to adjustment, such as:

- **Event Sensitive Applications**: This encompasses technology that—from experience—is known to be very sensitive to amendments of the type planned.

- **Business Critical Content**: This includes elements that—if adversely affected—would have a very negative impact on the business, e.g. the loss of an online shopping application.

- **Frequently Used Content**: This concerns applications that could inconvenience many customers in the event of unavailability, e.g. an intranet phonebook.

The challenge for the Maintenance Team is to avoid or minimise such effects through appropriate control procedures.

4. Proceed or Re-evaluate

Once all the facts have been considered, the decision to proceed with the change (or not) must be taken. This assessment is normally made by the Maintenance Team Leader.

Where the evidence suggests that the risk of a negative impact is within acceptable limits, the project can proceed as planned. However, where the risk is unacceptable, the change itself or the process of implementation must be reconsidered.

The Green Light

In the event that an amendment is given the green light, it is advisable that it be scheduled for a time when any negative effects are minimised, e.g. after business hours. It might also be necessary to notify particular audiences (e.g. site visitors) that disruption is expected.

Figure 24. An 'outage' notice for visitors to www.chrisgavin.net

For example, a message on a website homepage could state that a change is set to occur, indicating when it will take place and its planned duration. Alternative methods for contacting the organisation could be provided as this happens, e.g. a telephone number.

Contingency and Testing

In case things go wrong, a contingency plan should be put in place for every change that occurs. For example, if a software upgrade fails, it must be possible to halt the implementation and revert to a previous state with no loss of data. This is particularly important where the risk of error is high.

Finally, once a change has been made, website testing must ensue to make sure the site continues to function as intended. A full range of assessment methodologies are outlined in this regard on page 217. The affected site should also be closely monitored for several weeks. This is because the full impact of a change may not become obvious for some time afterward.

Change Control Schedule

An essential prerequisite for managing change is to make sure all relevant teams are kept informed. The best means for achieving this is a **Change Control Schedule.**

Date/Time	Action	Outage Period
April 12th 19.00.	Launch of new application to monitor website traffic.	No outage.
April 13th 20.00–20.05	Server software patching.	No outage.
April 14th 20.00–20.30	Replacement of hard disks.	10 minutes.

Figure 25. Example of a Change Control Schedule.

A Change Control Schedule is a calendar that lists every item with the potential to impact website visitors, the business or site operations. The benefit of such a schedule is that it ensures no two changes occur at the same time. For example, it would be disastrous for a new marketing campaign to begin on the same day that a significant hardware upgrade is to take place. A review of the Change Control Schedule provides a mechanism whereby any such conflicts can be ironed out.

That now completes our review of the activities of Website Maintenance. Of course, these tasks only cover the tactical operations of site management. By nature, they do not go into deeper strategic questions regarding site goals, design or direction. These are the issues that belong to the realm of **Website Development**. And it is these which we will explore next.

Chapter 3
Website Development

In a well known episode of The Simpsons[26], Homer is introduced to Hank—the older brother he never knew he had. After an emotional reunion, the two siblings set about getting to know one another. It turns out that Hank is a wealthy car magnate, who in a fit of generosity decides to offer his new brother a vehicle from the company show room.

When Homer rejects every model on display, Hank is undeterred and instead asks for his help to create a new class of automobile—a car for the common man! It seems an inspired idea and in his enthusiasm to get going, Hank allows all the usual rules of motor design to be ignored (forgetting that these are the things that helped him get so rich in the first place!)

After a few weeks of excited toil, the fruit of Homer's labour is unveiled. Unsurprisingly, the new car is a tasteless monstrosity—a bubble-domed eyesore, complete with tail fins, chrome trimming and a horn that plays

---

[26] 'Oh Brother, Where Art Thou'. The Simpsons™ & © Twentieth Century Fox Film Corporation. All rights reserved.

`La Cucaracha'. Unfortunately for Hank, no amount of stylish marketing can conceal this disaster. Almost immediately, he is out of business.

A Website like Homer

There are several parallels between the development process followed by Homer and that of many failed websites. For example, sites like this often originate with an enthusiastic but inexperienced manager who is asked to oversee production. Although skilled staff might be appointed to her team, personal or political preferences are more important than the advice they have to offer. The inevitable result is a clumsy and tacky site that costs a fortune to build, yet satisfies neither any business objectives nor customer needs.

Naturally, creating a website in such an ad-hoc manner is inadvisable. This is because a process that ignores established guidelines will always end up missing some important detail—causing embarrassment for the organisation and dissatisfaction for customers.

In contrast, a site that intends to satisfy business objectives **and** user needs must be based on a far more careful process of development. Although this process needs to be meticulous, it does not have to be long winded. All it requires is a system for ensuring work can happen in a predictable way.

In this chapter we will learn about such a process and explore the resources needed to support it. Our first step is to identify the activities from which it is composed.

Website Development Cycle

Website Development is an eight-step process for co-ordinating the creation of a new website, or implementing changes to one already in use. These steps are:

- Planning

- Content

- Design

- Construction

- Testing

- Hosting

- Publicity

- Review

In simple terms, the development process represents a framework within which all the activities of lifecycle management—from inception to review (and eventual demise, if necessary)—can take place.

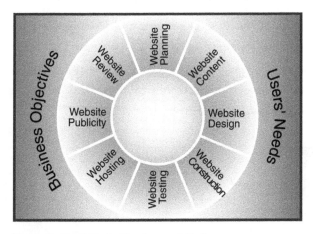

Figure 26. The Website Development Cycle.

For example, a business that wishes to create a new website can use this process as a means for structuring their work. Similarly, a site that has been live for some time can rely on it as a method for making incremental changes or undertaking a redesign.

In this sense, Website Development never really stops, but proceeds as a series of cycles. As soon as one rotation is complete, planning for another can begin. The diagram above shows how these activities may be joined together into a 'Development Cycle'.

Business Objectives and User Needs

Yet, this is not the complete story. That is, website development does not happen just for fun — it must be initiated in some way.

For instance, a business that wants a new website might be compelled to go online by some objective that can be fulfilled by the web, e.g. to sell more goods. Similarly, a site that is already in operation may want to commence another round of development in order to improve some aspect of its online experience, i.e. to satisfy user needs more effectively.

In fact, it is these elements of Business Objectives and User Needs that guide the course of the Development Cycle. Without them a website could not survive simply because it would have no reason to exist! Therefore, a thorough understanding of how they influence production is essential for the creation of a successful site.

Business Objective	The outcome that is to be achieved by a website.
User Needs	The expectations of the intended audience.

Figure 27. Business objectives and user needs.

However, before we explore these elements in more detail, it is useful to learn more about the structures that underpin the development process itself. That is, what project logistics and other resources are required to ensure work can be carried out effectively?

The danger is that — in the absence of such supports — production could become chaotic and arbitrary. Not surprisingly, projects like this are almost certainly doomed to failure. As such, before the planning of a site can even begin, all necessary provisions must be made to ensure activity can occur in a co-ordinated way.

Website Development Project Management

Although Website Development encompasses a set of quite specialist activities, the processes that underlie it are the same as for any other project. That is, it needs a team to carry out the work, a timescale to operate within and a set of resources to sustain it. As such, when initiating a development of this type, a number of basic elements must be in place to ensure a successful outcome. These are:

- Website Development Team
- Project Objective
- Project Budget
- Project Timeframe
- An Analysis of Project Risks
- Systems for Project Management & Communications

Website Development Team

A Website Development Team is the group responsible for the implementation of a new site (or managing additions to one already in existence). The most common roles represented on this team include:

Website Development Team Leader

This individual is responsible for organising group activity and ensuring project deliverables are achieved. Though she need not be an IT expert, a good grounding in the basics of Website Development is useful.

Designer

A Designer is responsible for building the visual templates required for the effective communication of web content. Several types of Designer may be required depending on the scale of the site that is planned, e.g. Information Architect, Interface Designer, etc. We will learn more about these later in this chapter.

Developer

The Developer's job is to merge content and design into web pages through the use of various coding languages.

Technical Support Team

If a site is to be hosted internally, this team ensures adequate infrastructure is in place to support ongoing performance. If the site is hosted externally, it manages the relationship with the chosen hosting company.

Marketing

Upon the release of a website, promotion may be required to attract the attention of the public. This is the responsibility of Marketing.

Website Maintenance Team

As we discovered in Chapter Two, a Maintenance Team is required to ensure a site can continue to perform to a high standard after it has been released. It is important therefore, that this group have some involvement in development in order to be familiar with its design and content.

As may be seen, several roles of Development overlap those of Maintenance, i.e. many of the same people are represented in both teams. In fact, in some cases the Team Leader for each might even be the same person. This is because of the advantages that accrue from having one individual with complete visibility of everything going on within a site (e.g. by recognising how day-to-day operations tie-in with major changes). This is frequently the case on smaller websites.

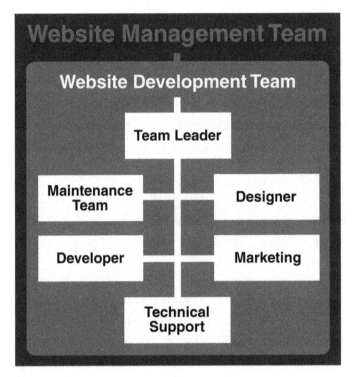

Figure 28. The Website Development Team.

On the other hand, a Development Team may be kept entirely separate from that of Maintenance. In such circumstances, the Development Team is convened with the sole purpose of creating a site, and when that is done it is transferred to Maintenance. Ongoing additions are conducted in the same way—as soon as new elements of content are created, they are handed over.

The Website Management Team

Ultimately, the composition and structure of such a team is the responsibility of site management. As explained in Chapter Four, a Website Management Team (WMT) is the premier authority in charge of a site. As such, they can choose whatever organisational system they like. For example, a WMT could decide that an external agency will carry out development. This might be suitable if in-house skills are unavailable and a site is required quickly. However, projects of this type can result in some loss of control, as well as ongoing maintenance difficulties (especially if continuous referrals are required). For that reason, a site for which constant updates are planned is better off employing its own staff.

Project Objective

A project objective is a description of the outcome of a piece of work. For example, the objective for a website development project is just that—a website!

However, (as we learned in Chapter Two) websites can vary significantly in scale from one to another. Website Scale is a means of classifying a site in terms of its size, complexity and levels of activity (see page 14 for more.)

For example, the type of content on a small Basic website is quite different to that of a large Transactional intranet. Consequently, the objectives for each are also different. As we will soon discover, the first step of the Development Cycle (Website Planning) provides a useful means for clarifying project objectives and deliverables.

Budget

Unsurprisingly, one of the most important constraints on the process of Website Development is finance. In ideal circumstances enough resources would be available to meet all the requirements of a project team. However, such a 'blank cheque' scenario is extremely rare, which means most sites must be cropped to fit the budget at hand. For example, it is all very well to want a Dynamic or Transactional site, but if there is only budget enough for simple Brochureware, it is a waste of time planning for anything else.

A final decision on budgeting normally occurs at the end of Website Planning, when Deliverables have been agreed and the exact scale of a site can be predicted.

Project Timeframe

An unfortunate characteristic of many web projects is the degree of pressure exerted on Development Teams. For example, a common demand from senior management is to get their site live 'yesterday'!

However, forcing such a tight timeframe can be a double-edged sword. While it may be positive in terms of concentrating effort, it can also damage the value of a deliverable. For example, a high quality site requires sufficient time (or staff) for all tasks to be completed. By cutting down on such elements, you are in effect agreeing to a reduction in quality.

Indeed, when time is tight there is often the temptation to bypass a few steps of the Development Cycle in order to go live early. Planning and Testing are the two areas that suffer most in this regard. But this is a risky strategy. For example, a Transactional website that goes live with a faulty application (due to inadequate testing) could lead to severe embarrassment if customers are inconvenienced.

The best approach is to be pragmatic. That is, either allow more time for development to occur or set aside some deliverables. These can then be completed during a follow-up phase.

Project Risks

Almost all projects have some degree of risk associated with them. For that reason it is useful to identify any issues that could prevent a site going live. For example, a common project risk is that a lack of resources (people, money, technology or time) might inhibit site quality. Similarly, management indifference or internal politics could lead to delays.

Identifying issues like these can prove a non-threatening means for communicating concerns to senior management.

Systems for Project Management & Communications

Every Development Team requires a set of tools to help them carry out their work[27]. For example, basic productivity software like Email and Microsoft Office should be made available to all participants and augmented with other specialist resources as necessary. This is particularly important for a Team Leader, given her role is primarily one of co-ordination.

Also useful is the 'check-in/check-out' and 'design notes' functionality included in website authoring tools like Dreamweaver from Adobe. This can be helpful for co-ordinating activity on small developments. In a similar vein, the project management resource 'Basecamp' (www.basecamphq.com, from $24 per month) has shown itself particularly suited to organising web assignments. Finally, enterprise-scale software like Microsoft Project® (from $599) or IBM Rational® ProjectConsole (from $1,370) provide a means for administering very large pieces of work.

As soon as all these supports and logistics are in place, production of the website itself can begin.

---

[27] This excludes the equipment needed for the actual tasks of design, development, testing etc, which are explored later.

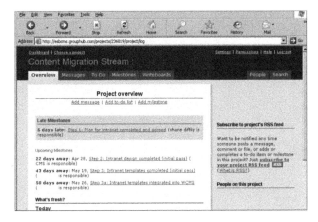

Figure 29. An image from a project screen in Basecamp.

In the surge of enthusiasm to get going, some teams may be tempted to plunge straight away into the details of design, programming and code. This is a mistake. The best way to start a new web project is not to focus on technology, but to explore the reasons why a site is required.

The recommended course of action, therefore, is to return to the concepts of Business Objectives and User Needs, and from them clarify the Goals and Deliverables of the website. These can then be used to drive and direct project activity.

The actual discovery of these elements takes place during the first step of the Development Cycle, **Website Planning**.

Step 1
Website Planning

Website Planning is a process for identifying the Business Objectives and User Needs that drive the Development Cycle. From these, a set of Goals and Deliverables can be devised and used to steer site production. In this sense, planning is the first step for building a successful website.

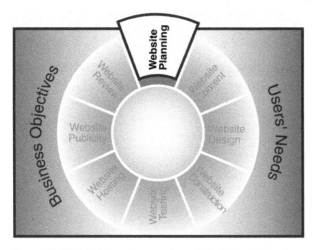

Figure 30. Website Planning as a phase of the Website Development Cycle.

Unfortunately, there is evidence to indicate that this phase of development is skimmed over on many projects. For example, numerous sites display the lack of focus and poor attention to detail that are symptomatic of inadequate planning.

While the embarrassment of low quality content ought to be enough to dissuade anyone from ignoring this activity, there are many factors that recommend it. Chief amongst these is the fact that planning provides a valuable opportunity for exploring some of the most fundamental issues of site development. For example:

- Why are we doing this?
- What value will we get from it?
- Who is our audience?
- What do they want?

Arriving at answers to these questions and, by extension, agreeing a credible set of Goals and Deliverables are among the greatest benefits to be derived from this process.

Business Objectives

Why do you want a website?

"Because it is a great medium for attracting people to our Global Warming campaign."

"Because it is an ideal mechanism for helping our team stay in touch."

"Because it is a perfect channel for selling our music."

"Ehm...because everyone else has one!"

Nobody is forcing you to create a website. You do it because you want to. The hope is that if you do decide to build a site, you have a convincing and compelling motive in mind. However, it is often the case that many website owners cannot clearly articulate this motive. The only business objective they seem to have is 'keeping up with the Jones'.

Yet, it doesn't have to be like this. There are many excellent reasons for developing a web presence. Some of the most common include:

- **To influence people**. Think of the websites for George W. Bush and John Kerry in the US Election 2004.

- **To generate revenue**. A website can sell more by targeting a wider market.

- **To create cost savings**. By putting customer service information online, the number of calls to a service centre can be reduced.

The challenge is to identify objectives that are compelling enough to justify the initial (and future) investment of going online. As we saw in the previous chapter, a website comes with many costs with regard to maintenance and upkeep. To offset these, it must produce some value in return.

One of the most useful ways of identifying this is to convene a workshop of stakeholders who have an interest in the site. These delegates can then agree the reasons why a website represents good value and express them as business objectives. The typical attendees at such a workshop include the Website Management Team, the Development Team and other functional departments.

Website Planning Workshop

The purpose of a Website Planning Workshop is to arrive at a shared vision of the objectives for a site. For example, is it just for show? Or is there real commercial sense behind it?

Setting the Scene

Although workshop delegates may be enthusiastic about going online, they may not have much experience of the factors that drive web production. As such — before commencing such a session — it is worthwhile taking some time to equip them with the knowledge they need to recognise the type of sites that are suitable.

To this end, an explanation of the context within which development takes place can prove helpful — particularly regarding the cost implications of any final decision. It can also put the ambitions of the organisation in perspective and ensure discussions remain realistic.

Among the most useful aspects to include in such a review are:

- Global Internet Factors

- National Internet Factors

- Local Internet Factors

- Website Management Factors

- Development Costs

Global Internet Factors

The purpose here is to understand the factors that drive web development at the highest of levels. This encompasses things like new technology (e.g. broadband, video, etc) and demographics (e.g. numbers of older people going online).

(Many of these issues are explored in more detail Chapter Four–Website Governance, page 301.)

National Internet Factors

This touches on themes similar to the above, but at a national level. Typical areas of review include the law (e.g. legislation affecting the internet), politics (e.g. government support for eCommerce) and social trends (e.g. the numbers of people with web access).

(These are explored in Chapter Four, page 309.)

Local Internet Factors

Local factors encompass business or industry pressures that affect website development. For example, company policies (e.g. security), the impact of competitor sites and insight from literature (e.g. design and usability) are often incorporated here.

Website Management Factors

A review of the obligations of Website Management (that is, Maintenance, Development, Governance and Infrastructure) is useful for ensuring delegates have a clear idea of what they are getting into before going online. A primary reason for the failure of many websites is that no finance is allocated for future upkeep. Therefore, a fundamental constraint must be that the requirements of the proposed site do not exceed the available budget.

Development Costs

Aside from the costs associated with site management, a chief concern for delegates will be the price of initial development. Although identifying an exact figure is not possible until after Goals and Deliverables have been agreed, some estimates are available. These may be arrived at by calculating the average spend required to produce a site of each type within the concept of Website Scale.

Website Scale

As we learned in the previous chapter (page 14), Website Scale is a means of classifying sites in terms of three parameters:

- Size

- Complexity

- Activity

Almost any kind of website can be represented by this model, from a basic intranet to a large eCommerce venture. As a consequence, website scale can also be used to estimate the level of investment required to develop a site. The parameter of 'complexity' is particularly helpful in this regard.

Complexity is a description of the technology used to develop a site. As a result, it has a direct influence on the type of infrastructure used for hosting and the number of staff required for support. Given that these are two of the biggest costs of production, complexity provides a useful means for estimating overall investment.

There are three levels of site complexity:

- Basic site

- Dynamic site

- Transactional site.

Estimated Costs of a Basic Website

A Basic website constitutes plain text with perhaps a few images or downloads. Due to its relatively uncomplicated nature, a medium-to-large site of this type is unlikely to cost more than $15,000 to design/build (perhaps by an external agency) [28]. Hosting could then be provided by a Website Hosting company for as little as $500 a year.

---

[28] The figures noted here are based on standard industry rates for early 2006. They do not take into account the cost of maintenance, which can often be greater than development.

However, a busy site (over 1,000,000 page impressions a month) could cost a lot more.

Estimated Costs of a Dynamic Website

A Dynamic website is one that generates content directly from a database. Such a site represents quite a sophisticated web presence and a large project could cost anything up to $50,000. Hosting charges are also higher, being of the order of $1,000 per annum (or more, depending on traffic). Where hosting is done internally, extra costs are also incurred. (Learn more about internal hosting in Chapter Five-Website Infrastructure.)

Estimated Costs of a Transactional Website

A Transactional website is one that uses the internet as a means of facilitating business operations or generating revenue, e.g. eCommerce. While development costs are similar to those of a Dynamic site, millions of dollars more are frequently spent by companies such as Amazon.com. Transactional sites also require an extremely robust hosting infrastructure to ensure performance can be guaranteed. While large firms may choose to invest in their own customised infrastructure, a site with lower levels of traffic may be satisfied with an external host.

By the end of this process of Scene Setting, workshop delegates should have a reasonably good impression of the type of site they are going to produce—particularly in terms of complexity and cost. For example, the stakeholders of an organisation that is new to the web (or that has a limited budget) may find themselves gravitating towards a Basic website. In contrast, delegates from a business with a lot of online experience (or lots of money) may wish to exploit the internet as a new revenue channel. In this case, a Transactional website could emerge as the best option.

The Cart before the Horse?

Yet, it should be noted that preliminary discussions of this type are sometimes in danger of putting the 'cart before the horse'. This is because the type of website that is appropriate for an organisation must **not** be set at this stage. That can only emerge from an understanding of Goals and Deliverables, which will not be known until the exercise of planning is complete.

As such, care must be exercised when 'Setting the Scene' so as not to bias workshop attendees too much in favour of a preferred outcome. The aim of this introduction is merely to equip them with the knowledge they need to make an informed decision. The purpose of the workshop itself remains to identify business objectives, which (when combined with user needs) can then be used to establish the type of site that is required.

Discussing Business Objectives

Having learned about the context of website development, the Planning Workshop can switch its attention to identifying business objectives. Such a discussion can usefully be initiated by posing the simple question, "Why do we want a website?" This should spark a debate about the organisation's reasons for going online.

Although there should already be several clear and compelling motives for developing a site, a useful starting point is the mission of the organisation itself. It can then be decided how this can be facilitated by the web[29].

For example, a charitable organisation may have as its mission, "to foster and integrate marginalised communities into society". In this case, there

---

[29] If no ideas are forthcoming, perhaps a quick prayer to St.Isidore of Seville may help. In 1999 St.Isidore was named 'Patron Saint of the Internet' by the Vatican.

is a clear and compelling reason for going online — because the internet presents a powerful new tool for pursuing this aim.

As discussions progress, ideas should begin to converge on objectives that are suitable for the web. As we saw earlier, these can frequently be segmented along the lines of:

- Revenue generation

- Cost savings

- Influencing people

For example,

- "We will use our website to sell more tickets for our airline."

- "We will use our extranet to reduce the administrative workload for students at our university."

- "We will use our intranet to improve morale and loyalty in our organisation."

When all ideas have been exhausted, they can be reviewed and checked for suitability. A final list can then be agreed and used as input into the Goals and Deliverables of the site itself.

However, before this takes place another round of information gathering is required. This is because a successful website must do more than simply reflect the objectives of a business — it must also address the needs of users.

User Needs

Having completed the process by which business objectives are identified, we can start to explore that other major determinant of site development: user needs. Not surprisingly, this often requires detailed research—the first step of which is to find out exactly who 'they' are. That is:

- Who is our intended audience?

- How do they use the web?

A website audience is unlikely to be a homogeneous mass. Most organisations find they have at least two or three core audiences (as well as numerous secondary ones) that are attracted to their site. As such, it is necessary to split these groups into smaller segments, so that particular needs can be identified.

Audience Segmentation

Segmenting an audience means arranging it into units based on a shared set of characteristics or preferences. This can be carried out in many ways, including:

- **Segmentation by Demographics.** Many organisations separate customers into groups based on age, education or spending power.

- **Segmentation by Location.** If a website audience is widely dispersed it makes sense to segment it according to place of residence or language, e.g. Europe/US/Asia or German/English/Japanese.

- **Segmentation by Lifestyle.** Also referred to as 'psychographic segmentation', this clusters people with reference to interests, cultural affiliations and other lifestyle attributes.

How to Cope with Huge Audiences

It can sometimes happen that an organisation has a huge number of audience segments. Consider the variety of services and products offered by Unilever and the number of potential visitor types they have. How can such a large number of people be served from a single website?

In circumstances like this, the key is to focus on a manageable number. As already mentioned, most sites have at least two or three audiences that stand out from all others. These may be the groups that are most profitable or most important to the business. As such, these are the segments upon which to concentrate. All other groups should be treated as secondary.

Understandably, this can sometimes be difficult to put into practice because of internal political or other pressures. However, a decision like this is bound to be taken sooner or later, simply because serving too many audiences dilutes return on investment.

Nevertheless, it should be noted that some organisations may actually be prevented from pursuing such a strategy. For example, a government agency may have a legislative imperative to service every audience equally. In this case, there is no alternative but to attempt to satisfy everyone.

Identifying User Needs

Once user segments have been identified, their needs can be extracted. There are many methods for doing this, ranging from the cheap & cheerful to the comprehensive & expensive. However, in all cases the purpose is to find out what the audience would like 'To Do' or 'To View' when visiting the site. This data can then be used to define the required content.

To Do

Ideas that correspond with 'To Do', can be used to identify key tasks or **transactions** that a visitor wants to complete online, for example:

- To submit expenses over an intranet

- To reserve a flight over the internet

- To refresh an order via an extranet

- To chat with friends on the internet

These can be used to gather ideas for online **applications**. If any such content is required, it typically means a Transactional website is needed.

To View

Ideas that correspond with 'To View', may be used to identify needs regarding **informational** content, including:

- To read a bus timetable

- To watch the news

- To explore new movie releases

- To listen to music

These can be used to identify text, video and other informational content that does not (usually) facilitate any form of interactivity or transaction. Content of this type is typically delivered from Basic and Dynamic sites. For example, a transportation company with hundreds of services could decide to use a Dynamic site to list its timetables. In contrast, a small bus operator would be better off with a Basic site.

Weighting Audience Responses

When conducting such research, an audience may also be asked to weight its choices in order or preference, e.g. from 3 to 1. These weightings can then be used to establish development priorities:

- A weighting of 3 means an item is a 'Must Have'

- A weighting of 2 means an item is a 'Nice to Have'

- A weighting of 1 means an item is on a 'Wish List'

Researching User Needs

Without doubt, the best way to establish the needs of a website audience is to get out and talk to them. This ensures the planned site will reflect 'actual' user preferences — not those that have been assumed by the Development Team. However, direct contact is not always possible (or may only happen in a limited way) due to budget or project constraints. As a result, a variety of research techniques may be needed. Some of the most popular of these include:

Surveys and Focus Groups

A survey is a means of collecting market information by directly interviewing a small number of individuals who are representative of a larger group. Surveys can be conducted in a number of ways, e.g. via the web, by telephone or in person (by stopping people on the street).

In contrast, a Focus Group engages an invited audience for the purpose of gathering data. While such discussions can go into greater depth than is possible in a survey, the disadvantage is that a smaller sample of the population is used.

Feedback

For those who manage an existing site, feedback is a valuable method for collecting audience opinions. For example, if a news website gets a lot of comments requesting more video, this could be prioritised for development. Feedback is also good for compiling anecdotal remarks about online experience, e.g. broken links, site responsiveness, etc.

Review of Website Activity

For a website already in place, a review of traffic analytics can also reveal features that are popular with visitors. These can then be given priority during the development cycle. However, interpreting web statistics is something of a black-art (as discovered in Chapter Two, page 61) and also suffers from a lack of real customer contact.

Compare with Common Experience

A review of competitor sites and design literature is handy for revealing elements of web content that are universally popular. For example, a musician who wants to go online should be aware that similar sites almost always include MP3 downloads. It can therefore be assumed that a common user need is to listen to song samples. However, a comparison with common experience is less valuable than a survey or focus group because it is not based on data from the actual audience being targeted.

Personas

Because direct contact with users is not always possible, it is often up to a Development Team to envisage the type of content that customers want. A useful technique for doing so is to create a "Persona".

A Persona is a description of an idealised website visitor that matches the attributes of the audience being targeted. These attributes may be gathered from the evidence of website activity, feedback or common experience. For example, a website that aims to influence young people about Global Warming could create a Persona to match the characteristics of its intended audience, e.g. a young person at college. To give the Persona a greater sense of reality, the design team could also select a name and photograph to attach to the description (as below).

"Sally is 25. She attends college where she is studying engineering. She is interested in the environment but has only a limited understanding of Global Warming. However, if made more aware of the issues, she would like to get involved somehow. Sally feels intimidated by the variety of ecological organisations and is not sure how to contribute."

Figure 31. An example of a website Persona.

Personas have been shown to be of great assistance when gathering information about user needs. This is because they provide a focal point for discussing requirements. A Persona can be talked about as if she were a living, breathing individual and the website was being designed to address her needs.

One significant drawback of this approach is there is no way of knowing if the Persona is correct or not. This is because (as mentioned) there may not have been any direct contact with real audience members. However, this need not always be the case. For example, Personas can sometimes be created as the output from a survey or focus group. In this case, they provide a means for summarising known user attributes.

Website Goals and Deliverables

Now that Business Objectives and User Needs have both been identified, they can be combined into a set of Goals and Deliverables for the website itself. Together these can be used to steer overall development.

Website Goals

A Website Goal is a statement of intent that combines an understanding of business objectives with important characteristics of the site audience.

For example, an organisation that has the objective of 'selling more music online' may have identified people under 30 as its most attractive user segment. Further research may indicate that this group is willing to spend up to $100 a year online. A resulting Goal could be "to sell at least $80 of music per year to visitors aged 30 and under."

Some other examples of well worded Goals include:

- "Our website will generate at least $1,000,000 revenue by 2008 by selling more tickets for our airline to budget travellers."

- "Our extranet will reduce the administrative workload on students at our university by 2 hours per week."

- "Our website will increase awareness of the issue of Global Warming among an extra 25% of young people in Canada, aged 18–26."

- "Our intranet will reduce HR administration costs by 15% for our European office."

When agreeing Goals like this, it is important that only a limited number be selected. If too many are produced, the focus of a project can become blurred. Between one and three is usually adequate.

Smart Goals

Yet, it is not enough simply to produce eloquently worded statements. Goals must also be reasonable within the constraints of the organisation itself. Consequently, any final list must be sanity checked to ensure they are SMART. That is, all Goals must be:

- **Specific**. Goals must focus on a particular area of activity and not be so broad as to be meaningless.

- **Measurable**. It should be possible to gauge when a Goal has been achieved. For example, if a website Goal is to "increase awareness", the key measure will be public knowledge. A survey can help establish if that has happened and how much of it was due to the online campaign.

- **Achievable**. There is no point setting a Goal that cannot be achieved, e.g. would the Goal "to increase revenue by 250%" be achievable?

- **Realistic**. A target must also be realistic. That is, it may be possible to achieve a 250% increase in revenue, but it would require 100 extra staff. How realistic is it that these resources will be available?

- **Timely**. Finally, the Goals must be timely, meaning they should be bound by a timeframe. For example, you may set yourself 12 months within which to achieve your target.

Website Deliverables

A Deliverable is a high level description of the content (i.e. applications or information) to be published on a site. For example, some sample website Deliverables could include:

- "This website will provide a mechanism for visitors to purchase airline tickets in a secure manner."

- "This extranet will provide appropriate course material to students online."

- "This website will include information that introduces visitors to the concept of Global warming."

- "This intranet will provide staff with a means of logging expenses online."

The ideas from which this list is drawn are collected during user research (whether direct or indirect), though some may also originate from staff at a website planning workshop.

In general, as many Deliverables as necessary should be produced in order to indicate the scope of content that is required for a site. However, it is often the case that only a small number of these can be implemented during an initial project cycle—mainly due to resource constraints. As such, a decision by Website Management on which Deliverables are most important is required before work can commence.

The mechanism by which such a judgement is made could be based on the priorities assigned during research. For example, ideas that received the highest number of priority 3 ratings can be expedited immediately (with remaining content scheduled for a later date). The task of actually producing these items occurs during the next phase of the Development Cycle, **Website Content.**

Step 2
Website Content

In the previous section we saw how a preliminary list of website content may be arrived at by a process of user research (perhaps involving surveys or feedback). The output of this investigation is then expressed as a series of high-level Deliverables, each of which describes a particular site feature.

The next step is to refine these Deliverables into a more detailed list, down to the level of individual files. The resulting inventory can then be used to plan and expedite the tasks of content production.

Content Inventory

A Content Inventory is a catalogue of everything to be published on a website. When creating such an inventory, the physical expression of some Deliverables may already be clear from the way they have been worded, e.g. "This website will provide an application form that allows visitors to join our organisation". In this case, the information or application intended for publication can be easily identified. However, other Deliverables may not be so transparent.

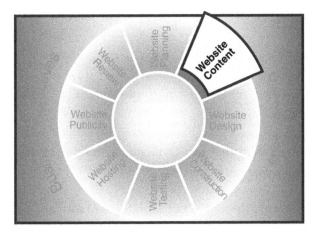

Figure 32. Website Content as a phase of the Website Development Cycle.

For example, the Deliverable "This website will include information that introduces visitors to the concept of Global Warming" is somewhat woolly. As such, it is up to the Development Team to determine what it means in terms of real content. This includes a decision on the required format.

Item	Content	Format(s)
Homepage	Short explanation of the website.	Plain Text.
How to Join	An overview of the joining process.	Plain Text.
Joining Details	How to join online.	Web form.
Joining Details	How to join by post	Plain Text.
What is GW	Overview of Global Warming.	Plain Text.
Introduction	General review of Global Warming	Text & Video.
History	Review of Global Warming through history.	Flash-based timeline.
Action	A calendar of events.	Text.

Figure 33. A sample website content inventory.

Content Formats

As we have learned, web content comes in two varieties. These are:

1. **Information.** This is used for display purposes only and cannot facilitate any interaction.

2. **Applications.** This is content that can facilitate some form of user response, e.g. an online reservation process.

Both of these may be expressed through a range of different formats, the most common of which include:

- Plain text

- Graphics

- Multimedia (video and audio)

- Flash™

- PDF

- Java Applets

- Shockwave™

(Each of these is examined in more detail below)

The task for the Development Team is to identify the formats they believe best reflect the Deliverables agreed during Website Planning.

For example, a team that is developing a website about Global Warming may decide that the Deliverable "information to introduce visitors" can best be provided by means of a simple text description. On the other hand, a video could provide more of an emotional impact. It is up to the Team Leader (with the assistance of a Website Editor) to decide on the format that is most appropriate. Many factors can influence this selection, for example:

- Budget constraints.

- Audience attributes, e.g. age, accessibility requirements, etc.

- Development parameters, e.g. coding languages, broadband availability, etc.

(Many of these are examined in more detail in the next section, Website Construction)

It is useful to remember that the choice of suitable web format is often just a judgement call. For example, two sites with a similar Goal could end up being quite different simply because the preferences of each Development Team are different. An example of this can be seen in the application 'Search for a Cruise' on the website of Princess Cruises[30]. While this form has been built using Adobe Flash (explained below), a similar application on Travelocity.com is based on plain HTML[31]. Although both sites fulfil the same function, they use a different format to do so.

The Uses of Content

As a matter of fact, it is surprising how alike content is across many websites. While formats can vary, the purposes for which they are used are often the same. In this way, content can typically be classed into one of three types:

1. Content that 'Persuades'

This is content that attracts people to a website by providing a basic introduction to what it is about and what visitors can do there. Almost any format can be used in this regard, e.g. text, video, Flash, audio, etc. The aim is to familiarise people with a topic in a trustworthy and non-

---

[30] http://www.princess.com/find/index.jsp
[31] http://www.travelocity.com/Cruises/0,,TRAVELOCITY,00.html

threatening way. For example, a website about Global Warming could include:

- Campaign news.

- An online poll, e.g. "Do you recycle? Yes/No".

- Interviews with existing members.

- Online chat with an ecology expert.

- A moderated discussion forum about Global Warming.

- Downloadable screen savers, desktop images and other marketing material.

2. Content that 'Sells'

'Sell' content focuses on the core objective of a website. Sites that use such content well frequently have a clear and explicit call-to-action that entices visitors to do something. For example, a retail site might display a compelling description of a newly released movie beside a prominent link that says "Buy This DVD Now". In contrast, the 'Sell' content on a site about Global Warming could comprise an emotional message that prompts visitors to complete an online membership form.

3. Content that 'Reassures'

This content is used to encourage people to maintain an active interest in a website. It also seeks to 'comfort' visitors by making them feel they have done the right thing by trusting you. Good after-sales services like this contribute to a sense of being 'cared for' and 'involved' somehow. This itself can be used to entice other people to get aboard via 'word of mouth' (or 'word of web') recommendations[32]. Examples of such features commonly include:

- A members' area that contains extra content such as private discussion forums, multimedia, etc.

- A help and support area.

- A members' newsletter.

When sorting through reams of options like this, it easy to get carried away and overload a site with unnecessary features. In most cases this simply leads to problems down the road, because budgets are not big enough to keep everything up to date. For that reason, a balance must be preserved between the scale of the intended site and the resources at hand. In this regard, a Website Publishing Team should be appointed (if one is not already in place) to help plan and expedite the tasks of content production.

Website Publishing Team

In Chapter Two–Website Maintenance, we explored the structure and functions of a Publishing Team. We learned that the main roles from which it is composed (aside from Designers and Developers) are:

- Editor

- Content Contributors, e.g. a writer, a video producer, etc.

- Legal Reviewer

---

[32] This type of content is referred to as 'inukshuk' by the usability consultants at UIE. "Reassuring users with inukshuk content" http://www.uie.com/events/roadshow/articles/inukshuk_content/ December 2005. Accessed December 2005.

We also discovered that this team relies heavily on a series of procedures and tools in order to produce content to an appropriate standard. What we now find is that many of the same systems can be used when creating a new site.

For example—just as in Website Maintenance—a **publishing schedule** is useful for ensuring content can be developed in an orderly way. Agreement on such a schedule can generally be reached during an initial Publishing Meeting.

Website Publishing Meeting

The purpose of this meeting is to allow an Editor to review a site's Content Inventory and devise a plan for production (which also needs to align with overall project timescales). Tasks can then be allocated among Content Contributors based on their own areas of expertise. Some organisations employ trained professionals in order to produce content, including journalists for textual information and illustrators for animation. (Learn more about these in Chapter Two–Website Maintenance, page 27).

Conversely, a great many firms simply rely on ordinary staff to populate their sites—especially intranets. Indeed, this is usually adequate for things like plain text. Yet, in circumstances where more complex features are required, external contractors may be needed. This is particularly true for elements that call for considerable technical skills or hardware investment, e.g. video, audio, Flash.

This diversity of content means it is useful for an Editor and Development Team Leader to understand (at least in rough terms) the methodologies by which such features are produced. This allows them to plan the allocation and scheduling of work in the most sensible way.

Consequently, we will now investigate some of the most popular formats for the presentation of content on the web.

Plain Text

Plain text is the most straightforward of all content to be published on the web. This is because it can be authored in any word processor (e.g. Microsoft Word) and shared easily via email.

However, it would be a mistake to think that good writing is effortless. In the previous chapter we learned that it requires the support of many resources, including a style guide, dictionary, thesaurus — as well as adequate time.

Nevertheless, the benefits of a well written site are clear. Content of this type allows visitors to become engaged more easily and also builds trust. Indeed, trust is key for engendering a positive relationship between a site and its audience. For example, an online retailer who writes well structured, clear descriptions is much more likely to make a sale than one who does not. This is because the confidence of visitors is strongly influenced by the manner in which information is presented. In this regard, there are said to be four stages for building trust online.

1. **Consistent**: A website demonstrates an ability to maintain a consistent level of quality, i.e. in content, site performance, etc.

2. **Credible**: A website demonstrates that its promises are credible, e.g. by providing testimonials from legitimate sources.

3. **Reliable**: A website demonstrates its actions are reliable, e.g. by responding to email queries in a timely manner.

4. **Trustworthy**: A website earns the distinction of being trustworthy, e.g. the customer feels at ease when sharing financial details.

The Rules of Good Web Writing[33]

In order to write effective content, it is necessary to be clear for whom it is being produced. When a writer does not know their audience well, they can easily fall into the trap of creating information that makes sense to themselves, but is meaningless to customers. In the previous section, we saw how Personas can be used to assist the design process. This technique may also be used to guide the task of writing, by providing a concrete image of the audience for whom it is being prepared.

Similarly, writing must also be well structured. Research has shown that visitors do not read text online – they scan it, looking for trigger words associated with their need[34]. For example, someone who wishes to reserve a hotel room may have trigger words like "Reservations", "Bookings" or "Beds". If they find these phrases, they will engage with the site – if not, they will move on. As such, if you have something to say, it is best to keep sentences short and snappy.

The Supremacy of Text

Adherence to such rules is vitally important given the way in which text dominates most successful sites. Some of the reasons for this supremacy include:

- Text is the default format of the web

- It is very fast to download

- It can be accessed from any user agent

- It is simple to maintain

---

[33] More excellent writing guidelines are available from Gerry McGovern, a leading authority on web content (www.gerrymcgovern.com).
[34] Useit.com 'Why Web Users Scan Instead of Read'.
http://www.useit.com/alertbox/9710a.html

Yet, the real reason why text is so highly favoured is because of its flexibility. As we have already seen, there are three functions for website content:

- To persuade

- To sell

- To reassure

Unlike graphics or video, a line of writing can be easily used for any of these. As a matter of fact, new uses and treatments for text are still emerging. Two in particular that have gained substantial attention in recent times are 'Wikis' and 'Blogs'.

Wiki

A Wiki is an application that allows visitors to a website to add or edit information. The phrase 'Wiki' refers to the software used to run this system. Such software is often free and can be downloaded from the internet. Alternatively, it can be purchased as a component within a Website Content Management (WCM) System (for more about WCM, turn to page 34).

The interesting thing about a Wiki is that—unlike a Discussion Forum or similar collaborative environment—there is usually no process of review before contributions go live. The theory is that by allowing free and open access, knowledge can be shared more easily.

However, in Chapter Two we learned about the experience of the LA Times and how this freedom can be abused. Similar issues are also emerging on other sites. For example, following a high profile incident in December 2005, the online encyclopaedia Wikipedia® has been forced to implement a registration procedure in order to keep track of changes more effectively[35]. This type of control is likely to become the norm.

Figure 34. The homepage of www.wikipedia.org

Blog

A blog is an abbreviation of the term 'web-log' and is used to describe any diary-like journal that is published on the web. Although blogs have been in existence since the mid-1990s, they first started to gain public attention in 2004. This was due to the large numbers created in the run up to the US presidential election.

The idea behind a blog is to stimulate public interest by producing a frequently updated chronicle of thoughts and comments. Most blogs simply comprise plain text with perhaps a few supporting images or downloads. To avoid the maintenance issues associated with the numerous changes they involve, several automatic blogging services are available. The most popular of these is Blogger.com, while some WCM tools include similar functionality.

---

[35] Wikipedia. "Author of Wikipedia character assassination takes responsibility" http://en.wikinews.org/wiki/Author_of_Wikipedia_character_assassination_takes_resp onsibility Accessed December 2005.

In the corporate arena, a variety of firms have started to exploit blogging for business purposes. For example, the research company Gartner maintains a series of journals on its public website[36]. These are written by in-house experts and are used to keep customers up to date with industry developments. Many other companies encourage employees to create blogs on their intranets — the objective of which is to encourage internal knowledge sharing.

Figure 35. A blog on the website of Gartner.

Graphics

While graphics may seem like a fundamental part of the World Wide Web, the first online image was not published until 1992 — three years after the web's invention[37]! This late start was due to most initial focus being on text and hyperlinks, as well as to a lack of graphics-enabled software. However, with the release of the first 'real' browser (NCSA Mosaic) in April 1993, all this changed and the web as a visual medium was born.

---

[36] Visit http://blog.gartner.com/blog/index.php?catid=25&blogid=8
[37] This image can still be viewed at
   http://en.wikipedia.org/wiki/First_image_on_the_Web

What is interesting is that the format of images in use since then has hardly changed. The overwhelming bulk of online graphics continue to be in one of just two formats, JPEG or GIF.

JPEG

JPEG (Joint Photographic Experts Group) is an image format most suited to the production of graphics that contain many gradients or tones, e.g. photographs. The main benefit of JPEG is that images can be saved to a very small filesize. This means that downloads over a slow internet connection can happen much more quickly than would otherwise be the case.

For example, an image in the standard Microsoft Bitmap format (BMP) can be reduced in size by a factor of 10 through conversion to JPEG — with almost no visible decay in quality. This is achieved though the use of 'lossy compression'. Lossy compression is means of image optimisation that trades filesize against reproduction accuracy. The drawback is that visual degradation can occur if high compression is chosen. However, this can be avoided by testing an image at different levels of quality until a desired outcome is found.

JPEGs can be created in a variety of image editing and graphics programs, the most popular of which include:

- Adobe Photoshop (from $649)
- Adobe Illustrator (from $499)
- Adobe Fireworks (from $399)
- Microsoft Expression® Graphic Designer ($n/a)

GIF

GIF (Graphics Interchange Format) is the other graphical mainstay of the web. Like JPEG, GIF can reduce the filesize of some images by a huge amount with no loss of quality. However, because GIF can handle a maximum of just 256 colours, it is only appropriate for flat-colour graphics such as logos or cartoons – not photographs.

Nevertheless, GIF does have some advantages. For example, it includes a transparency feature which means it can be layered on top of other colours or images to produce interesting design effects. GIFs can also be animated in the manner of a simple cartoon. In fact, this remains a popular use for the GIF format, as seen in many animated banner-ads on the web.

With regard to production, the same variety of image editing and graphics programs used to produce JPEG, can be used for GIF.

PNG

Finally, a few words about an emergent image format called PNG (Portable Network Graphics). PNG is a 'lossless' image format released in 1996 as a replacement for GIF. PNG offers all the advantages of GIF but with much better compression, improved transparency and other features. Unfortunately, the rollout of this format has been obstructed because many user agents still do not display it correctly. However, this is slowly changing and the use of PNG is expected to intensify in coming years.

As may be predicted, the standard array of image editing and graphics programs used for JPEG and GIF can also produce PNG.

Multimedia

Multimedia (video and audio) has long been a key draw on the World Wide Web and is now beginning to emerge as a leading driver of new content. In 2002 it was estimated that 50% of internet users had the capability to receive some form of video or audio[38]. This has swelled rapidly in recent years due to the growth in broadband and web-enabled mobile devices. Indeed, in the autumn of 2003 the Yahoo!® website alone handled some 1.6 **billion** video downloads[39]!

What is interesting is that the vast majority of such activity is facilitated by just five brands of software. These are:

Real®

Real was an early innovator in multimedia and enjoyed a great deal of success in the mid to late 1990s. The software product RealPlayer® continues to be widely used for the presentation of video and audio, based on the proprietary Real Media (RM) format. While RealPlayer is available free of charge from the internet, it does not come preinstalled on most computers. Real is getting around this by concluding agreements with mobile phone and PDA manufacturers, e.g. Nokia®.

Microsoft Windows® Media® Player

Windows Media has the advantage of being built into all computers that run the Microsoft operating system (though this may change due to court proceedings). It can also be downloaded for free from the web. Media Player relies on its own proprietary formats WMV and WMA. In recent times it has also started to make inroads into the mobile computing market.

---

[38] Jupiter Research. http://www.jupiterresearch.com/. Accessed December 2004.
[39] Morgan Stanley "Global technology/Internet Trends"
   http://www.morganstanley.com/institutional/techresearch/gsb112005.html Mary Meeker, November 2005. Accessed January 2006.

Apple® QuickTime™

Apple QuickTime is a very well established and respected multimedia format. In many cases the quality of media produced in QuickTime's MOV format is better than its peers. Files of this type can be viewed using QuickTime Player, which can be downloaded from the internet for free.

Flash Video

Multimedia is increasingly being delivered via Adobe Flash. This is largely doing away with the issue of format/player compatibility which prevents files being presented on disparate systems. All that is required is the Flash plugin, which can be downloaded for free from the Adobe website. (Flash is examined in more detail later in this chapter.)

Playerless Media

Technologies that play video or audio directly in a web browser are called Playerless Media. Companies such as Eyewonder™ and Clipstream™ lead this area. Like Flash, these technologies do not depend on a visitor having a certain media product installed. All they need is a Java-enabled user agent in order to view video or listen to audio.

Limitations of Multimedia

Despite the hype, many of the initial expectations for multimedia have yet to be realised. The main limiting factor remains the speed and reliability of internet connections. Video in particular is very bandwidth hungry and this can impact upon the deployment of such content. For example, if the target audience of a website does not have access to broadband, multimedia is not a realistic option.

Despite this, the forecast for the coming years is positive. As broadband takes hold, video and audio are beginning to appear more commonly within many sites. For example, **Podcasting** is being used by organisations such as the BBC as a means of content distribution[40]. Podcasting is a publishing technique that makes MP3 files available for bulk download to mobile devices. While Podcasting cannot be used for 'live' feeds, it does allow features such as radio programmes to be saved and listened to at any time.

A standardised solution to the many different media formats that currently exist may also emerge. MPEG-4[41] (which offers audio, video and interactivity) is a likely answer in this regard. The bundling of multimedia software with the computers used for website hosting is also making video and audio more accessible to Development Teams. This is particularly evident on intranets, which are seeing a much faster adoption of multimedia than publicly available sites.

Adopting Multimedia

Where a website makes occasional use of video and audio, it is common for the tasks of production to be sub-contracted to a dedicated media agency. However, if multimedia is planned as an integral component of content, an investment in specialised technology is recommended. This includes:

- Recording equipment, e.g. cameras, microphones, lighting, etc.

- Video editing software, e.g. special effects software (Adobe® After Effects®, from $699).

- Video optimisation software, e.g. for compression and conversion into web format (Adobe® Production Studio®, from $1,699).

---

[40] For more information, visit http://www.bbc.co.uk/radio/downloadtrial/#podcast
[41] "Moving Picture Experts Group" is a format created by an consortium of 350 universities and businesses, the most popular of which are MPEG3 (MP3) and MPEG4.

- Multimedia server, e.g. software for hosting video and audio files.

Certain expert skills are also required to produce features of a quality good enough for publishing. For example, a person with broadcasting experience may be needed to script and direct a video shoot. Similarly, skilled operators are required for sound production, as well as editing and optimisation. While these can represent a significant overhead, it is probably best to spend the money upfront. A useful knowledge base can then be built up within the organisation.

Of course, a cheap alternative is simply to buy an ordinary web camera and connect it to the internet. A **web camera** (or 'webcam') is a device that generates images on a time-phased basis. No specialist viewing equipment is required — just a web browser. However, such applications usually require Java® and may function on the basis of a Java Applet (see below). Furthermore, the quality of images tends to be poor and sound is sometimes not included[42].

Moving Vector Images (Flash)

A Moving Vector Image is an animated, interactive graphic that can be displayed in a user agent, such as a desktop browser. The overwhelming majority of Moving Vector Images are created by the software product Adobe Flash (from $699), which uses a free plugin called Flash Player™ to display its files[43]. This plugin can be downloaded free of charge from

---

[42] For example, http://www.camvista.com/england/london/london-central.php#

[43] Some Moving vector Images were also created by 'LiveMotion®', a short-lived competitor to Flash from Adobe. LiveMotion was discontinued in 2003. A new entrant in this field 'Microsoft® Expression® Interactive Designer' is due for release in 2007.

the internet and it is claimed that over 97% of all desktop browsers now have it installed[44].

Flash created something of a sensation when first released in 1996. It appealed to many Designers because it was both relatively easy to author and allowed vibrant, animated content to be delivered over low-bandwidth connections. This meant a multimedia-like experience could be created for website audiences on dial-up internet accounts.

Unfortunately, very few of these early adopters used Flash in a suitable manner. For example, it was commonly deployed in the form of animated 'welcome' messages or such like. These were often very poorly thought out and incorporated strange psychedelic music or crude illustrations[45]. Flash became so synonymous with poor design that in 2000 the internet usability guru, Jakob Neilsen, described it "99% bad"[46].

Rehabilitation of Flash

Happily, recent years have seen something of a rehabilitation in its fortunes. Adobe (formerly Macromedia) has invested heavily to overcome the main drawbacks of this format, such as poor support for printing and accessibility. In fact, Flash has now advanced to the stage where it can be used to develop complex applications for Transactional websites[47]. It can also be installed as a plugin on many PDAs and mobile phones.

Yet, although it is certainly possible to develop full websites in Flash, it is still rare for this to occur. For example, research by User Interface

---

[44] Macromedia. "Macromedia Flash Player Penetration"
http://www.macromedia.com/software/player_census/flashplayer/penetration.html
Accessed January 2006.
[45] To see just how bad, visit http://www.skipintro.nl/skipintro/skipintro98.htm
[46] Alertbox October 29, 2000. http://www.useit.com/alertbox/20001029.HTML Useit.com, the website of Jakob Nielsen. Accessed April 2005.
[47] For example, www.adobe.com/store

Engineering[48] suggests that the best use for Flash remains as a supplementary content format within a standard HTML-based site. Their recommendations for the appropriate use of Flash include:

- To illustrate an event that occurs over time, e.g. an interactive animation that shows how greenhouse gases contribute to Global Warming.

- To illustrate an event that occurs within a large space, e.g. the movement of power in a power grid.

- To illustrate the relationships between objects or to clarify choices, e.g. to show the configuration options on a piece of machinery.

- To deliver rich media content such as online games.

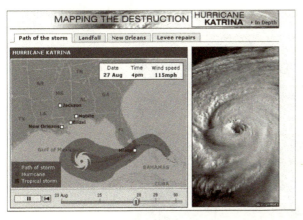

Figure 36. An example of Flash on the BBC website used to illustrate the path of a hurricane.

Finally, a Development Team Leader needs to be aware that while basic Flash functionality is easy to learn, advanced interactivity requires considerable skill. In this regard, Developers with expertise in the

---

[48] User Interface Engineering. "Making the best with Flash" 2001. Purchase this report at www.uie.com

ActionScript™ language are essential, as are Designers with animation experience.

Portable Document Format (PDF)

Portable Document Format (PDF) is a file format developed by Adobe that allows documents created for printing to be published on the web. PDF is viewed by the free software program Acrobat® Reader®.

The main advantage of PDF is that it preserves the look of original documents while also keeping filesize to a minimum. For example, although an annual report might be created in a desktop publishing program for high-quality printing, PDF allows it to be saved to a smaller size whilst maintaining the design of the original. This can subsequently be published on the web and accessed by anyone with Acrobat Reader.

Figure 37. A PDF file.

As a result, PDF is now used for the distribution of documents that must maintain a designated appearance. This includes items such as application forms (e.g. for state benefits) and marketing literature (such as whitepapers). PDF also includes security features that prevent documents being modified. This is useful for official publications that must not be open to challenge regarding authenticity, e.g. government reports.

Creating a PDF

The process for creating a PDF requires the purchase of Adobe Professional® (from $449). However, many other technologies include features that allow content to be saved in this format. For example, some WCM Systems allow text and images to be output as PDF. This is achieved using eXtensible Stylesheet Language Transformations (as explained on page 189).

Of course, the ease with which PDF can be made could give rise to the temptation to use it instead of ordinary web pages. However, this should be avoided. Evidence suggests that website visitors do not like switching between different technologies when reading online content[49]. Similarly many items that are published as PDF would look far better as plain text, simply because they could load faster and be easier to read. Finally, plain web pages can be easily presented in many user agents (e.g. mobile phones, PDAs), whereas PDF is usually optimised for large computer screens only.

Shockwave

Shockwave™ is a powerful development tool (somewhat like Flash) for creating applications that mimic the appearance and functionality of desktop programs. In this way it can be used to build rich animated environments, e.g. online games. However, because of its abundant capabilities, filesizes tend to be very large – thus rendering Shockwave all but inaccessible to visitors with a slow web connection.

---

[49] Useit.com "PDF: Unfit for Human Consumption"
http://www.useit.com/alertbox/20030714.html Accessed July 2003.

Figure 38. Adobe Shockwave logo.

For that reason Shockwave is primarily intended for use offline, e.g. on DVDs and CDs (or over high-speed broadband). As with Flash, a special plugin is required to view Shockwave. The content itself is authored within a program called Director™ from Adobe (from $1,199).

Java Applets

Java Applets are small programs that run independently within ordinary web pages. Content of this type is written using advanced programming languages, usually Java (not to be confused with JavaScript, which is examined in the next chapter). Java Applets are quite versatile and when used well, can deliver some powerful functionality, e.g. online games, animation, video (via a webcam).

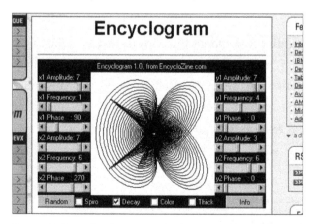

Figure 39. Example of a Java Applet from http://javaboutique.internet.com

138

Unfortunately, they are also considered to be the bad boys of the web and are blamed (often correctly) for crashing many computers. This is because some user agents cannot run programs of this type. For that reason the best use for Java Applets remains on corporate intranets or similar environments, where device compatibility is strictly controlled.

Other Content Formats

As well as the formats we have already explored, it is customary to come across other types of content while browsing the web. Some of these take the form of specialist 'training' or 'interactive' software that has been created for a particular purpose. A couple of examples include Captivate™ from Adobe[50] and Personal Navigator™ from OnDemand[51]. However, it is sometimes discovered that such features are actually based on more common formats, e.g. HTML or Flash. The authors have simply added-on a few extra functions in order to sell them as proprietary products.

Notwithstanding this, useful new content technologies do emerge from time to time. One example is that of the 'eBook'.

eBook

An eBook is a publication created for distribution in electronic format. Although many Developers choose PDF (explored above) as their default solution in such circumstances, other arrangements are possible. Two of the most popular include the Open Electronic Book Package (OEBP) and Microsoft Compressed HTML Help (CHM).

---

[50] http://www.macromedia.com/software/captivate
[51] http://www.ondemandgk.com

OEBP is a system for creating eBooks that can be browsed in a similar way to a physical document, i.e. by flicking through pages[52]. This format also allows multimedia elements to be included if desired, e.g. sound, video.

In contrast, **CHM** is a far simpler system that is built in the same format as Microsoft Office 'Help' files. CHM is preferred by some Editors because of its small filesize, inbuilt index and the fact that it can be packaged as a single file. However, low end presentation capabilities means only a very basic visual design is possible.

Figure 40. An example of an eBook in OEBP 'FlipViewer' format.

Finalising Production

As content production begins to slow down and items are ticked off the site inventory, it is worth noting that some features may not yet be ready for publishing. This is because several types of content need to be converted into additional special formats before going online.

---

[52] The product FlipViewer® can be used to view such files, www.flipviewer.com. Another example is Desktop Author, www.desktopauthor.com

For example, plain text must be transformed into the coding language HTML prior to being placed on the web. Indeed, content that is destined for Dynamic or Transactional sites requires even more attention. This is because of the many ways in which it could be manipulated. For example, a piece of text on an eCommerce site (such as a customer's name) may need to appear as:

- A personalised welcome notice, e.g. "Welcome back, John Williams"

- A message that confirms when tickets have been bought on an airline website, e.g. "Thank you, John Williams. You have purchased tickets to the value of $150.00".

- An error warning on a webform, e.g. "John, don't forget to include your billing address!"

The task of actually pulling all this together belongs in the first instance to Designers. It is their job is to build the visual templates that are required for the effective communication of content. The phase within which this occurs is called **Website Design**.

Step 3
Website Design

Design is "the process of originating and developing a plan for an aesthetic and functional object, which usually requires considerable research, thought, modelling and iterative adjustment"[53]. With regard to the web, this involves the transformation of Goals and Deliverables into graphical models that can be used to produce a site.

For many years Website Design seemed to represent all that was new and exciting about the internet. Young technophiles quickly adapted to the new medium and began creating wonderful pieces of digital art posing as websites. No one really cared that these sites were practically unusable, because they looked cool!

Today, Website Design is considerably more restrained and precise. It no longer serves solely as a creative outlet for digital artists, but is recognised as a significant contributor to competitive advantage. The

---

[53] Wikipedia http://en.wikipedia.org/wiki/Design Accessed April 2005. Copyright GNU Free Documentation Licence.
http://en.wikipedia.org/wiki/Wikipedia:Text_of_the_GNU_Free_Documentation_Licen se#VERBATIM_COPYING

volumes of material that have been written about concepts like usability, accessibility and emotional design illustrate just how seriously it is taken. For example, some of the ways in which good design can add value to a site include:

- By facilitating a visitor's online experience, e.g. through clear navigation and an intuitive structure.

- By communicating information, e.g. through diagrams and charts.

- By transmitting brand values, e.g. by using corporate colours.

- By creating or reinforcing a desired emotional response, e.g. through an appropriate use of imagery, colour and other elements.

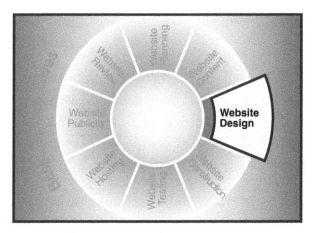

Figure 41. Website Design as a phase of the Website Development Cycle.

Because the scope of these activities is so broad, this book cannot hope to delve into too many specifics. However, what we can do is review the steps from which the design process is composed and explore the skills, technology and other resources needed to organise and equip a team.

The Website Design Process

As mentioned in the previous chapter, Website Design is composed of several distinct disciplines, each of which embraces a range of skills. The sequence in which these are deployed tends to follow a given pattern on many projects (especially during the development of a new site). This allows an outline **Design Process** to be suggested — one that encompasses the following steps:

- Information Architecture

- Interaction Design

- Interface Design

- Navigation Design

- Information Design

- Visual Design

It should be noted that there is no clearly defined point of separation between these activities. In fact, some of them occur in parallel. For example, Interaction and Navigation Design handle a very similar set of challenges, i.e. how to move through a website. As such, Designers in these areas need to co-operate closely on many projects[54].

Similarly, the design process itself is often quite circular. While many developments begin with Information Architecture and end at Visual Design, some problems may have to be processed several times before being resolved. What this demonstrates is that no single discipline has the magic touch for creating a great site. They all have a role to play.

---

[54] For an extended discussion of each of these design disciplines read "The Elements of User Experience" by Jesse James Garrett (ISBN 0735712026).

Information Architecture

Information Architecture is the first step of the Design Process and is concerned with the organisation and structure of web content. The Information Architecture for any given site can typically be illustrated in the form of a tree diagram, as shown below.

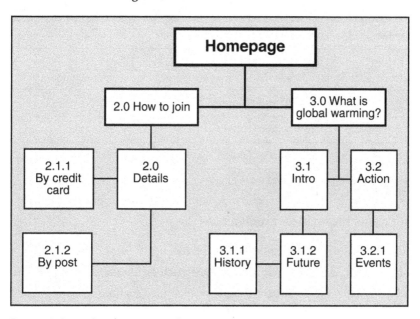

Figure 42. A simple Information Architecture.

A diagram like this is useful for demonstrating the extent of content to be placed online. For example, the architecture of a very large site may contain scores of separate branches.

The illustration also shows how content is inter-related. For instance, the tree diagram above reveals how websites are made up of clusters of information and applications, residing within an overall hierarchy. Clusters like these (as well as the hierarchy itself) are created by grouping content according to characteristics that are important to site visitors.

The process for creating an Information Architecture is relatively straightforward. It simply requires every item within a **Content Inventory** (as examined on page 116) to be organised into groups, based on characteristics that are meaningful to the target audience.

Item	Content Theme	Format(s)
Homepage	Short explanation of the website.	Plain Text.
How to Join	An overview of the joining process.	Plain Text.
Joining Details	How to join online.	Web form.
Joining Details	How to join by post	Plain Text.
What is GW	Overview of Global Warming.	Plain Text.

Figure 43. A sample website content inventory.

Creating the Information Architecture

Because an Information Architecture is the scaffolding upon which a website is built, it is critical that it be constructed to be both conceptually sound and scaleable to future needs. A usability technique called Card Sorting provides a useful way to achieve this.

Card sorting works by using all the items in a Content Inventory as building blocks within a site structure. To decide on the correct place for each block, representatives of the website audience are invited to participate in a workshop.

At the workshop customers are presented with a series of cards, each of which has the title of a piece of content on it. They are then asked to sort the cards into clusters (and into a hierarchy) based on how they think the site should be organised. Some schemes that commonly emerge from such an exercise include:

Audience-based Architecture

An audience-based architecture is appropriate when distinct visitor groups have widely different needs. This can arise due to geographic, language or business affiliations. For example, on www.dell.com content is clustered into groups based on industry types, e.g. Government, Education & Healthcare, Large & Medium Sized Business, etc.

Topic-based Architecture

This is the most popular means for structuring content on the World Wide Web. In this case, content is grouped into clusters based on the subject matter of the website itself. For example, the sports equipment manufacturer Wilson® (www.wilson.com) organises its content according to sporting interest, e.g. tennis, golf, etc. Interestingly, the content clusters displayed on Wilson's European website are different from those of the United States. While baseball and (American) football are prominent on the US site, they are missing from the European version. This is a good illustration of how different architectural schemes can be merged.

Task-based Architecture

A task-based architecture is suitable for websites whose main purpose is to deliver applications, i.e. to allow customers to 'do' something. Many online banks and intranets are structured in this way, e.g. 'View my account', 'Submit expenses', etc.[55]

While Card Sorting may sound elementary, it can be extremely effective for creating arrangements that reflect the 'mental model' of website visitors. This is because it highlights in an objective way how an audience

---

[55] Some useful research on task-based information architectures has been conducted by the web consulting group Adaptive Path, www.adaptivepath.com

thinks a site should be organised. In this manner Card Sorting is a perfect mechanism for building an Information Architecture.

When the Architecture has been completed, it can then be reproduced as a **tree diagram** (perhaps using a drawing tool such as Visio®). The tree diagram allows a site structure to be seen at a glance and the relationship between content elements to be understood.

Interaction Design

While Information Architecture attempts to match the structure of a website to the 'mental model' of visitors, it says very little about the usability of content itself. This is particularly true for applications with which users must interact, e.g. online forms. Identifying the optimal means for presenting features like this lies within the realm of Interaction Design.

Interaction Design is a system for structuring and generating actions on a website in response to user behaviour. For example, imagine you wish to book accommodation via the web and your chosen hotel has created an online form to do so. What is the first piece of information you will want to tell them? Probably the date you intend to arrive. As such, the hotel should ensure a field for "Check-in" is presented as the first step in the reservation process. In this way, Interaction Design is about matching visitor expectations to a flow of information.

However, creating interactive content that correctly matches visitor requirements is one of the most time consuming and complex tasks of Website Design. Fortunately, a huge amount of literature on this area is now available[56]. This is because the web is over 15 years old, so there has been plenty of time for techniques and conventions to have emerged.

---

[56] For example, "Defensive Design for the Web" by 37 Signals. ISBN : 0-7357-1140-X and "E-Commerce User Experience" by Nielsen, Molich, Snyder & Farrell. ISBN: 0-9706072-0-2.

Experienced designers can refer to these and to their own skills when creating such features. Two of the most widely used practices in this regard are Low-Fidelity (LoFi) and High Fidelity (HiFi) Design Modelling.

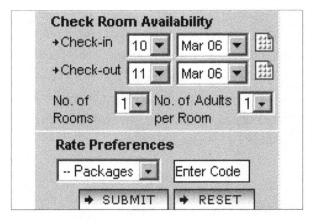

Figure 44. The reservation system on www.jurys-dublin-hotels.com

LoFi Design Modelling

A LoFi interactive design is a prototype of content (such as an online form) that has been produced in a very basic way. One of the most common means for modelling this type of application is by simply drawing it onto paper.

While a hand drawn design may not seem appropriate for developing a website, experience has shown it is a powerful way for identifying usability problems. In a LoFi test scenario, a user is asked to interact with a paper prototype as if it were a real computer. Evidence suggests that participants quickly forget that they are working with paper and become focussed on completing their assignment. As such, it is an inexpensive means of obtaining valuable feedback.

HiFi Design Modelling

After a few iterations of LoFi modelling, a HiFi design may be created. A prototype of this sort represents a much more accurate visual representation of the envisaged design.

For example, it may be created in an image editing program like Adobe Photoshop, or as a simple web page. If modelled as a web page, the design need not have all the features of the final site. This is because it is simply being used to evaluate the interactivity of content, not the overall look and feel. When the model is ready, users are invited to evaluate it and their comments are fed back into the design process.

Error Modelling

One of the key aims of this phase of design is to produce applications so good, that the possibility of mistakes is minimised. However, even after extensive modelling, Designers do not always get it right. As such, the manner in which a site is planned to handle errors deserves special attention. For example, in the event that problems do occur, contingencies should be in place to allow website visitors to understand and correct them.

For instance, imagine the user of a hotel reservation form requests a date for which no rooms are available? A good design will alert them to the problem and provide advice about how to fix it. Where possible, the design could also include clues that make such errors less likely— perhaps by displaying dates upfront for the rooms that are vacant.

Interface Design

Interface Design is concerned with the selection of web elements that facilitate interaction with site visitors. That is, an Interface Designer attempts to select features that make navigating or interacting with a website as easy as possible. Such features generally encompass the standard set of interactive elements seen on most sites, e.g. text entry fields, radio buttons, check boxes, etc, as well as ordinary hyperlinks. For example—taking the instance of an online reservation form—there are several ways in which a hotel website could allow visitors to select their preferred dates of arrival or departure (two of which are shown below).

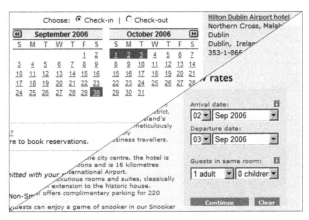

Figure 45. Visitors to www.hilton.com select their check-in and check-out dates by clicking hyperlinks. Customers of www.radissonsas.com use drop-down menus for the same task.

Interface Design is about selecting the most appropriate features to allow the completion of a task. It is common for Interface Design to occur in tandem with Interaction Design because they are so closely linked. As such, many elements of Interface Design may also be evaluated as part of the LoFi/HiFi modelling process[57].

Navigation Design

Navigation Design has always been at the heart of the World Wide Web. This is because the power of the internet lies in its ability to connect disparate information through hyperlinks.

---

[57] It is worth noting that the development program Adobe Flash provides Designers with greater flexibility with regard to systems of interface design than is found in ordinary HTML.

Navigation Design is primarily concerned with the selection of suitable systems of wayfinding. Wayfinding[58] is defined as "the process used to orient and navigate. The overall goal of wayfinding is to accurately relocate from one place to another in a large-scale space".

The most important concerns when designing such a system are to ensure that website visitors always know the answer to each of the following questions:

- Where am I?

- How did I get here?

- How can I return to where I came from?

- Where can I go from here?

A significant amount of research has been carried out in this area, from which have emerged a number of widely used systems. Among these are:

- Global Navigation

- Local Navigation

- Breadcrumb Navigation

- Index/Directory

- Contextual Navigation

- Search

- Sitemap

- Drop Down Menu

---

[58] M. Gluck (1991) Making Sense of Human Wayfinding: Review of Cognitive and Linguistic Knowledge for Personal Navigation with a New Research Direction. in: D. Mark and A. Frank (Eds.), Cognitive and Linguistic. Aspects of Geographic Space pp. 117-135, Kluwer Academic Publishers, Dordrecht, The Netherlands.

- A–Z Index

- Guided Tour

Global Navigation

Global Navigation is the primary layer of navigation on a website. Its purpose is to provide access to all major categories within an Information Architecture. The most common means for presenting Global Navigation is horizontally beneath a website's masthead (as below).

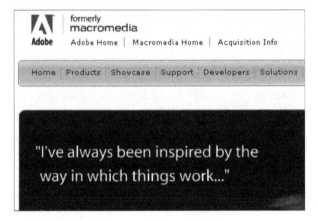

Local Navigation

Local Navigation provides access to content that adjoins or is related to the section of a website currently on view. Secondary navigation normally comes into play after a visitor has selected a category from Global Navigation.

The most popular system for Local Navigation is to place it vertically to the left (or right) of a screen, as illustrated on www.ge.com. Other systems include Flyout navigation (as used on www.adobe.com) and Doubletab navigation (as used on Apple.com).

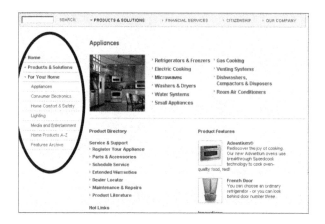

Breadcrumb Navigation

The name Breadcrumb Navigation comes from the fairy tale "Hansel & Gretel". In this story, Hansel leaves a trail of breadcrumbs behind him so he can find his way back through the forest. Despite the name, breadcrumb trails usually do not function as a way of retracing steps. Rather, they are used for illustrating the location of a visitor within a site's overall structure. Such a system is called a 'Location Breadcrumb Trail' and is illustrated below on www.useit.com.

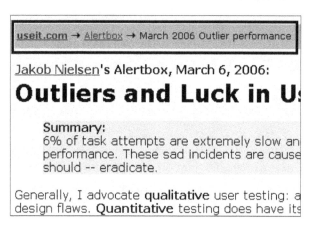

Index/Directory

This system is used on websites that contain a very large number of categories in the first level of Information Architecture, e.g. Oasis Citizens Information at www.oasis.gov.ie.

Contextual Navigation

Contextual Navigation refers to hyperlinks that are embedded in the text of a website. This system allows links to be created anywhere, as illustrated on www.wikipedia.org.

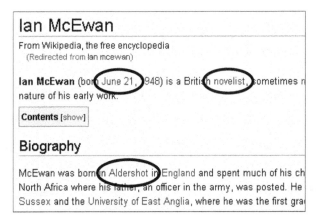

Sitemap

A sitemap provides an overview of all elements within the primary and (possibly) secondary layers of content in a site, e.g. www.amnesty.org.

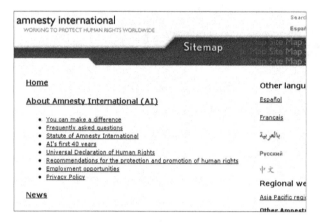

Search

Search provides access to all content on a website, via a text entry field. Results are provided based on a match between the search query and site content, as illustrated on www.hp.com.

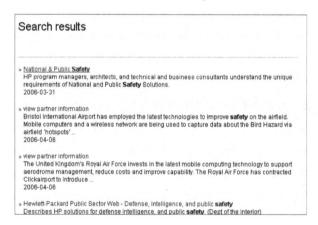

Dropdown menu

A dropdown menu enables direct access to nominated pages within a website, as demonstrated on www.gartner.com.

A–Z Index

This system uses an index of content that is organised alphabetically. This is helpful on websites with lots of information and applications, such as www.bbc.co.uk.

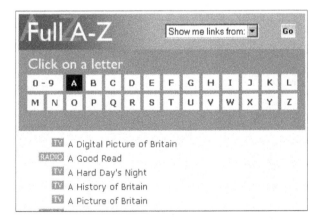

Guided Tour

This is a system that provides an overview of website content to inexperienced or first-time visitors. This is used very effectively on www.bbc.co.uk.

Other Systems

Some other navigation systems include:

Bookmarks. Also called 'My Favourites' or 'My Links', this is a feature that allows a website visitor to save hyperlinks to pages they are most interested in.

History List. This feature automatically saves a list of the top five or six pages that a visitor has accessed.

Hot Links. Hot Links combine the history lists of all visitors to create a record of the most universally popular pages.

The selection of an appropriate navigation system depends on the volume of content in a website and the detail with which it is organised. For example, a large website with a detailed Information Architecture (e.g. www.bbc.co.uk) probably requires several systems including Global and Local Navigation, Breadcrumb Trails, a Sitemap, Search, an A–Z Index, as well as a Guided Tour for first-timers. As with Interaction and Interface Design, a series of LoFi and HiFi usability tests can be used to establish the systems that are suitable.

Information Design

Information Design is concerned with the effective presentation of content on website user agents. Ongoing developments mean that more and more such technologies are being invented. This makes the task of Information Design increasingly important, as identical content must be presented in a pleasing way on a wide range of devices, e.g. PDA, desktop browser, etc.

Indeed, some user agents do not even have a display capability. For example, a Screen Reader is a software program that interprets websites for people with visual impairments. The Screen Reader reads content from web pages aloud to a visitor, perhaps via an earpiece. In such circumstances, the Information Designer must pay attention not only to the layout of the page, but to the manner in which content is ordered. This is because some arrangements (e.g. horizontal) work better for automatic reading than others (e.g. vertical).

The role of the Information Designer is to pull together the results from each of the previous phases of design in order to create unified page arrangements. The objective is to optimise communication by organising content in a cohesive and pleasing manner.

Grid Systems and the Golden Section

While almost any arrangement is possible, experience suggests that the most successful means of page layout is to assemble it in a grid-like structure. This is because a grid allows elements to be placed into rational alignments based on function and status. For example, important content can be grouped together at the top, while less important items are placed near the bottom. In this regard, grid structures based on the proportions of the Golden Section have proven particularly useful.

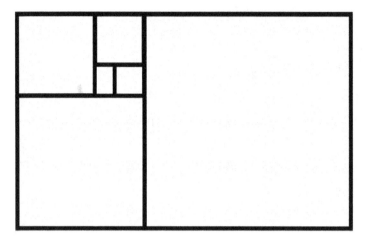

Figure 46. Golden Section.

The Golden Section is a geometric ratio of 1:1.618 (referred to as 'phi'). Research and common experience have long suggested that this arrangement is inherently pleasing to the human eye. As a result, it has been used for millennia as a basis for architecture and painting, and also forms the basis of the US 'letter' sized sheet of paper.

When applied to the web the Golden Section allows a page to be built that is aesthetically pleasing and also facilitates natural eye movement. For example, theories of Eye Tracking suggest that website visitors tend to scan pages from the top-left of the screen in a zigzag or F-shaped pattern. The Golden Section allows a very effective means of facilitating this[59]. Some examples of the Golden Section in use can be viewed on the homepages of www.bbc.co.uk and www.business2000.ie.

---

[59] Though some recent research appears to contradict this. See
http://www.newscientisttech.com/channel/tech/dn9039.html for more.

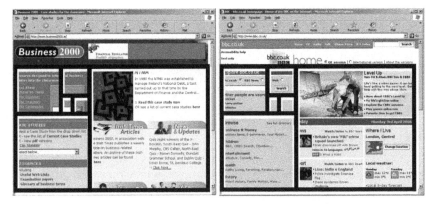

Figure 47. Examples of the Golden Section in use on www.business2000.ie and www.bbc.co.uk

Wireframe

When creating a layout of this type the principle output of the Designer is called a 'wireframe'. A wireframe is an outline drawing of a possible arrangement of web content. It is another example of a LoFi modelling technique and, as such, does not contain any colour or other visual elements. It simply shows where content could be placed for the purposes of good communication.

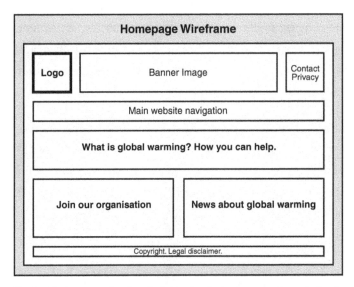

Figure 48. An example of a wireframe for the homepage of a website about global warming.

Because they are so simple, wireframes can be created in any image editing program, e.g. Adobe Photoshop, Adobe Fireworks or even Microsoft Visio. The task of applying colouring and imagery to these occurs in the final step of the design process, Visual Design.

Visual Design

Visual Design is what most people think of when they consider web design — that is, stylish sites and cool graphics being created by young trend setters. Indeed, there is a kernel of truth to this, as graphic innovation does play an important role in the design process. However, this phase of production is much too important to be left to the personal preferences of a single person[60]. Rather, a design solution must be based on the Goals of the site in question and the values of the organisation creating it.

Organisational Values

Organisational values are the set of attributes that define the personality of an enterprise. Many large organisations record their values as an accompaniment to a mission statement or corporate strategy. However, smaller companies do not have time to spend on such niceties and normally have no clear expression of their values. As a result, it is often necessary to identify them as part of the Development Cycle.

This can usefully occur during **Website Planning**, when senior stakeholders are meeting to define objectives and other matters. The approach for defining values is the same. The aim is to encapsulate in a few words the character of an organisation. These can then be used to set the tone for Visual Design.

---

[60] Especially since new research suggests that visitors can decide if they like or dislike a site within 1/20 of a second of seeing it (visit http://www.websiteoptimization.com/speed/tweak/blink/ for more).

For example, an organisation may define its values as:

- Progressive

- Unconventional

- Vibrant

To the Visual Designer these suggest a website of bright colours, decorative typography and other creative features.

However, an organisation whose values are:

- Authoritative

- Practical

- Reliable

suggests a more conservative approach is necessary.

Of course, a traditional organisation may sometimes want a site that reflects more informal values — perhaps for special marketing purposes. This can be seen in the difference between the website for the European Space Agency, www.esa.int, and a microsite it had specially created for children, www.esa.int/esaKIDSen.

As a concrete expression of organisation values, **Identity Guidelines** are used by many organisations as a means of governing online identity. The purpose of such manuals is to ensure that trademarks and logos are correctly rendered and to protect them from misuse. If such a manual is unavailable to a Development Team, interim guidelines may be needed before design can commence.

Design Conventions

Following agreement on values and identity, the creation of the Visual Design can begin. This task relies heavily on the skills of the Graphic

Designer. While this individual must have a talent for creating innovative solutions, she also has access to a legacy of tried-and-tested design conventions that can be leveraged for ideas.

Some of these include:

Graphics

Pictorial Graphics

Pictorial Graphics encompass any photographs or illustrations used in support of site content. For example, an image of a product may be placed in a prominent position alongside a description of it. Pictorial graphics can also be used standalone. For instance, cartoons feature as important elements on some websites, especially those of newspapers, e.g. The Irish Times[61].

Figure 49. 'Beautiful smiling people' being used to sell broadband.

Special care should be taken that as few 'filler' graphics as possible are used. A 'filler' graphic is one that illustrates a concept unrelated to website content. Unfortunately, these are endemic on the web and

---

[61] http://www.ireland.com/cartoons/turner/

usually take the form of a 'beautiful smiling person' who is placed on a site as eye-candy.

Graphic Devices

Graphic devices typically consist of small images that are used for decorative purposes, though they may also be used to suggest aspects of functional performance. For example, the graphic device shown below is used to indicate that clicking a link will open a new browser window. The use of purely decorative graphics should be minimised as far as possible.

Figure 50. Illustration of graphic devices for external links[62].

Graphic Text

This occurs where plain text is replaced by an image that contains a desired phrase. Care should be taken to ensure the typeface chosen for graphic text is appropriate for the website in question, e.g. sans-serif typefaces suggest modernism, whereas serif suggests traditionalism. As a rule-of-thumb as little graphic text as possible should be used due to concerns of accessibility and download time.

---

[62] Reproduced from Wikipedia, http://en.wikipedia.org/wiki/Design April 2005.

165

Figure 51. Graphic text is used on the website of Harvard University within (1) the logo, for (2) navigation and as a (3) headline on featured content.

Information Graphics

These consist of diagrams and charts that are used to illustrate or reinforce concepts, e.g. a bar chart, a pie chart. These can be used standalone or as a support for other content.

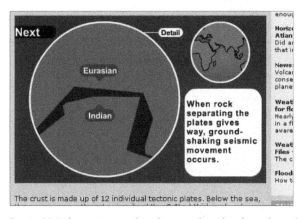

Figure 52. Information graphic about earthquakes from the website of the BBC[63].

---

[63] The full image can be viewed at
http://news.bbc.co.uk/2/hi/science/nature/4126809.stm

Colour

Colour Palette

Until about the year 2000 an (informal) upper limit on the number of colours that could be used on the web was in force. Termed the 'Web Safe Palette', this allowed a maximum of 216 colours to be employed. The reason for this limit was that many screens could not display more than this number of tones. Furthermore, outside this limited range, colours could not be guaranteed to look the same across the many different screens in use.

However, developments in technology since then mean that almost any colour combination is now permissible (with the exception of mobile phones and PDAs where colour screens are only now being widely adopted.) Nevertheless, care must still be exercised to ensure the chosen colour palette matches that stipulated in an organisation's identity manual.

Colour Model

Designers should attempt to match colours to the basic conceptual model of human colour perception. For example, in this model bright colours suggest fun and grey colours suggests soberness.

Highlighting Elements

Colours should be used for a purpose, not just for decoration. For example, bright colours are known to attract the eye. As such, colours such as red and yellow may be reserved for important content elements.

Legibility/Readability

The Designer must ensure that a colour palette allows sufficient contrast for the legibility of text and minimal eye-discomfort. The best colours for legibility are black text on a white background. Colour combinations that clash, such as red on a blue background, should be avoided.

Quantity

It should be remembered that not every colour in the palette must be used! A judicious amount of white-space is always good. As a rule of thumb a maximum of three or four colours per page is enough.

Text

Typeface

The most important consideration for the selection of typeface is whether it is commonly available on the user agents of website visitors. This is because only those typefaces that come preinstalled on such devices will display correctly. In this regard, the most commonly used fonts include Verdana, Arial, Times New Roman, Trebuchet, Georgia and Helvetica. In general, no typeface from outside this list should be selected.

The next consideration for typeface is legibility. Research suggests that the most legible typefaces for reading from a screen are Verdana, Arial and Georgia. In fact, these typefaces were specially designed for reading online. The use of such typefaces is even more important where mobile devices are concerned, due to the challenges of reading from a small screen.

A final consideration is the default size of text as it appears on-screen. While many designers love tiny fonts, the most easily readable minimum size is 10 point. As such this should be chosen as default. The visitor must also be allowed to increase the size of text on screen if desired. This functionality is key for creating sites that are accessible to people with visual impairments.

Quantity

To avoid visual confusion, no more than two typefaces should be used on any website.

Selecting a Visual Design

In most cases, a Graphic Designer will be required to create two or three templates to demonstrate options for the visual presentation of a site. These designs are typically created in image-editing programs such as Adobe Photoshop or Adobe Fireworks. It is from these that Website Management (assisted by the Development Team) must select the design that best supports the Goals of the site.

When a Management Team is evaluating Visual Design, it is crucial that analysis remain as dispassionate as possible. While everybody has colour preferences, they are usually not relevant to the process of fulfilling website Goals. As such, individual likes and dislikes should be left to one side. Instead, managers should call on the expertise of the Graphic Designer to understand the merits of each potential solution.

Having said that, some type of debate is probably inevitable, simply because Visual Design is often the most sensitive phase of all site development. The challenge for the Team Leader is to keep deliberations focussed and prevent a battle emerging over colours or images.

In this regard, it is worth emphasising that the opinions of the Designer should be paramount. This is because only she has the training, skills and experience necessary to determine what does and does not work visually on the web. Based on this advice the Management Team can then select their preferred solution.

Following this, the construction of the website itself can begin.

Step 4
Website Construction

At last! After lots of planning and preparation, all the groundwork needed to allow site construction to proceed is finally in place. This is the moment your Developers have been waiting for—the 'real' work of coding can now commence!

But wait.

Are you 100% sure what your Developers are about to produce? While they may be able to build a site that looks the same as the design templates supplied to them, how will it be made? For example:

- What coding languages will they use?

- What user agents will the site be compatible with?

- What guidelines for web accessibility will they refer to?

Without definite guidelines on aspects like this you are in danger of being delivered a site that is a mélange of different preferences.

Therefore, before Developers are asked to start construction, a set of principles to direct their activity must be agreed. The purpose of these is to steer construction and ensure the site conforms as closely as possible to business requirements.

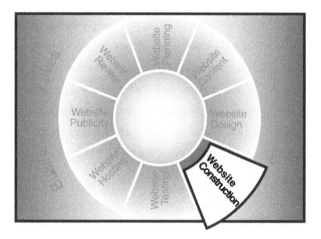

Figure 53. Website Construction as a phase of the Development Cycle.

In this section, we will explore the parameters that are relevant to this area and look at options for the technology needed to support production. To begin with we will learn about one of the most important advances in construction practice in recent years—the rise of Web Standards.

The Rise of Web Standards

Web Standards are a set of preferences for site development based on the recommendations of the World Wide Web Consortium (W3C®)[64]. The W3C is a non-profit, collaborative organisation that has it origins in the invention of the web by Tim-Berners Lee in 1989. The mission of the W3C is "to lead the World Wide Web to its full potential by developing protocols and guidelines that ensure long-term growth"[65]. This is

---

[64] Note, Web Standards are not the same as a Website Standard. A Website Standard is a document that sets out the approach of an organisation to all aspects of Website Management. This is an issue we will look into in more detail in the next chapter.
[65] W3C. www.w3c.org Accessed April 2005.

achieved through the creation of recommendations (in consultation with market participants and other organisations) that guide web activity.

The recommendations produced by the W3C cover everything from coding standards to multimedia protocols and, although non-binding, exert significant influence. This is because Web Standards are a set of rules to which everyone in the industry can refer, e.g. user agent manufacturers, Website Developers, etc. By adhering to Web Standards, Developers and manufacturers can make sure all sites are readable by every type of user agent, including desktop computers, PDAs and mobile phones.

Non-Standard Coding Techniques

However in practice, things are not as straightforward as this might suggest. For example, until recently most manufacturers modified W3C recommendations to suit their own needs. For example, a company like Microsoft or Netscape® might adopt some aspects of a recommendation, ignore others and throw in their own ideas for good measure.

For Developers, this meant trying to build a website that conformed to Web Standards **and** looked the same in all user agents was a thankless task. They could never be sure how the finished site would be displayed[66], e.g. a Microsoft web browser could present content quite differently to one from Netscape. For most organisations such visual inconsistency was not acceptable.

As a consequence, the vast majority of web Developers dumped W3C standards in favour of coding techniques that skirted around these issues. While such non-standard techniques worked well for design, they were a disaster in terms of portability. They resulted in websites that

---

[66] Indeed, this is still the case for many aspects of Web Standards, as illustrated in the Acid Test created by the Web Standards Project, http://webstandards.org/act/acid2/

were either optimised for display in one user agent only, or included reams of special coding to ensure they looked the same in all devices. This meant bloated pages, larger file sizes and slower loading times — which in turn required increased expenditure on bandwidth.

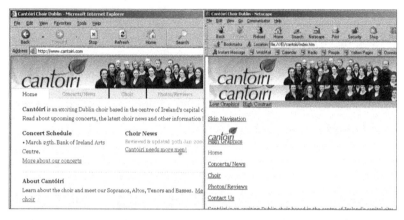

Figure 54. A comparison of the homepage of www.cantoiri.com as displayed in Internet Explorer version 5.0 (left) and Netscape Navigator version 4.7 (right).

Thankfully, this sorry situation is now being remedied, thanks in part to the efforts of The Web Standards Project (WaSP, www.webstandards.org). WaSP is an initiative of US Developer Jeffrey Zeldman (www.zeldman.com) and others that is "fighting for standards that ensure simple, affordable access to web technologies for all". To a substantial degree this group has been successful. The latest (or soon to be released) versions of most browsers are now built for compliance with Web Standards. As such, it is no longer necessary to construct sites using special coding techniques. Web Standards offer a better, cheaper and faster way to achieve the same outcome.

MarkUp, Presentation and Interactivity

The W3C recommendations that are central to the notion of Web Standards are those governing languages for the structure and presentation of web content, as well as the control of interactivity. These are:

MarkUp

The composition of a webpage is controlled using a **MarkUp language**. A MarkUp language contains information about the structural meaning of a document. That is, it defines the purpose of each element in a page. For example, it is MarkUp that determines which bit of text is treated as a headline, which is a paragraph, which is a link, etc. Some common MarkUp languages include **HTML, XHTML** and **XML**.

Presentation

The appearance of web content (e.g. layout, colours, typefaces, etc.) is controlled using a **Presentation language**. The Presentation language used for the web is called **Cascading Style Sheets**, abbreviated to CSS or **StyleSheets** for short.

Document Object Model (DOM) and ECMAScript

Lastly, interactivity is controlled using a feature called the standard **Document Object Model (DOM)**. DOM is a template that defines the way in which elements in a web page can be modified and how they relate to one another. For example, a Developer could allow the text colour of a paragraph to be dynamically altered from red to blue using the DOM. The vehicle that facilitates such manipulations is called **ECMAScript**. (ECMAScript is the standard version of JavaScript®.)

We will now look in detail at each of these and explore the options a Development Team has for defining its own Website Construction preferences.

MarkUp Languages (HTML, XHTML and XML)

HTML (Hypertext MarkUp Language) was and is the driving force behind the web. As a language that is both easy to learn and easy to use, it has been exceptionally successful at popularising the internet. For example, HTML is free and can be written using a range of simple tools. This includes everything from basic text editors, e.g. Windows Notepad®, to sophisticated WYSIWYG (What you see is what you get) authoring tools, e.g. Adobe Dreamweaver, Microsoft Expression Web Designer.

As already explained, HTML is a MarkUp language that controls the structure of a webpage and the meaning of every element in it. In this way, HTML defines the nature of all the items on a page (e.g. if text is to be treated as a link or as a paragraph) and how they relate to each other (e.g. if a link is to occur within a certain paragraph or not). A central point is that HTML has no role in describing what a web page looks like, e.g. if a link is to be red or green or blue. It is concerned only with information.

However, early versions of the language did include several features to influence the presentation of content. This included text size, colour, typeface, etc. Over time, this was seen by the W3C as a weakness and all the latest versions have had any such components removed. By the time the most recent version (HTML 4.01) was released in 1999, presentation was fully controlled by StyleSheets.

Three flavours of HTML are available depending on the preferences of a Development Team. These are:

HTML 4.01 Transitional is suitable for websites that still need to make use of some non-standards coding techniques. This might be because some people view the website with older user agents that cannot fully understand StyleSheets.

HTML 4.01 Strict is for Developers who want to be very exacting about adherence to Web Standards. This flavour of HTML excludes all presentational elements. As such, the selection of this language requires conformance to a very high standard.

HTML 4.01 Frameset allows frames (where multiple pages combined into one) to be used when creating a website. In general this is not recommended, except perhaps for some web applications.

HTML 4.01 has now been superseded by another MarkUp language that is of greater value to organisations that seek to construct robust, future proof sites.

XML and XHTML

XML is a MarkUp language like HTML—just considerably more powerful. This is because XML can be used to describe anything, not just parts of a document. For example, it could be used to describe the elements in a chemical formula or the details of a sales record (as below). In this sense XML acts almost like a database.

Description	Item
Product Name	Washing Powder
Sale Value	12.99
Currency	Euro
Location	Hamburg

In fact, XML is now used throughout the world as a means for transferring data between otherwise incompatible systems. All that is required is a set of common field descriptions. This use of XML is often referred to as 'Web Services'. Some examples include 'Legal XML' and 'FinXML'. Legal XML is a format for communicating court documents and transcripts, whereas FinXML is used for data exchange in capital markets.

XHTML

When XML was first introduced it was envisaged that a new version of HTML would be required to complement it. This is because XML is not compatible with traditional HTML, meaning no data can be transferred between them. Similarly, XML cannot be used to display information in a user agent on its own. As such, a new language was needed to allow web content to interact with XML-based applications and present data where required. The language created was called XHTML.

XHTML (Extensible HyperText MarkUp Language) is the successor to HTML. It is simply a version of HTML that has been written in XML format. Because XML can be used to describe anything, in this instance it is used to describe the structure of a document. In this way it mimics traditional HTML. However, unlike HTML, XHTML can interact with any XML-enabled device **and** display web content.

Creating a document in XHTML is relatively simple and should not trouble any experienced Developer. As with HTML, it can be written using a text editor or web authoring tool[67]. There are also three flavours to choose from:

XHTML 1.0 Transitional is useful for websites that still need to make use of some non-standards compliant coding techniques, e.g. expressing presentation in MarkUp.

XHTML 1.0 Strict is for websites that want to exclude any elements from MarkUp that refer to presentation. Such websites provide the best

---

[67] Indeed, one other means for creating XHTML (or HTML) is to convert it directly from XML using eXtensible Stylesheet Language Transformations (XSLT). However, this method is somewhat clunky and is not suitable for many websites.

integration with XML devices and are most accessible to a range of internet user agents.

XHTML 1.0 Frameset allows the use of frames, which (as already explained) is generally not recommended.

Newer versions of XHTML are also being developed. XHTML 1.1 was released in 2001, and XHTML 2.0 is in working draft as of time of writing (May 2006). These releases build on the template of XHTML 1.0 Strict and provide better integration with other XML languages. However, they are substantially more complex than ordinary HTML. As such, uptake may be slow at first until Developers become familiar with them.

Selecting a MarkUp Language

Selecting the appropriate MarkUp language (XHTML or HTML) for use on a web project depends on what is best for the development underway. This is because both HTML and XHTML can form the basis of a successful Web Standards-compliant site.

That said, XHTML is preferred because it is the nominated successor to HTML and over time will become the MarkUp language of choice. With this in mind, XHTML 1.0 Transitional is probably the best flavour to choose from. This language allows a site to be compatible both with older web browsers and new user agents. While XHTML 1.0 Strict delivers the same benefits of compatibility, it may cause rendering problems on some older devices.

Cascading StyleSheets

Earlier in this chapter we looked at the process of design. Design is about presenting a website in a graphical form to match the goals and values of the organisation creating it. The Designer does this by expressing her ideas in a series of templates that are then forwarded to a Developer for coding. The challenge for the Developer is to ensure these templates can be translated into functioning web pages, without compromising visual impact.

As we have seen, early versions of HTML could alter the presentation of web content. For example, if the text of a paragraph was to be red in colour, it was defined within the HTML itself. Similarly, if a particular content arrangement was needed, this could be achieved using HTML-tables as a layout device.

While such presentation techniques worked well in so far as matching Designers' ideas were concerned, they had several drawbacks. The greatest of these was that presentational characteristics had to be hard-coded into every page. This proved very difficult to administer on large sites. For example, a simple design change could require days of coding because it had to be replicated across hundreds of pages before taking effect. In response, the W3C began the development of a new Presentational language called Cascading StyleSheets.

Separating Content and Presentation

The purpose of Cascading StyleSheets is to allow the appearance of a site (e.g. text, colours, etc.) to be controlled using a single file, which can also be kept physically separate from MarkUp. It is this 'separateness' that provides much of the power behind StyleSheets.

This means that if a design change is needed, the alteration need only be made in one document before being instantly replicated across an entire site. This is possible because all pages use just one StyleSheet to control presentation. As a result, the development time needed to expedite visual modifications can be drastically reduced. StyleSheets have also freed HTML from any presentational obligations, allowing MarkUp to focus purely on document structure.

User Agent Support for CSS

When first developed in 1996, StyleSheets were way ahead of their time. Support was patchy and where it was in place, user agents (especially desktop browsers) interpreted them in different ways. Unfortunately, this meant Developers were unable to rely on them as a means of presentation and had no option but to ignore them.

The good news is that most browsers have now adopted a more consistent approach. With only a few exceptions, this means that the vast majority of sites coded according to Web Standards look the same across all platforms. It also means that sites can be accessed more easily from devices such as PDAs and mobile phones.

For example, if a mobile phone with an Opera® browser connects to a site, a slimmed-down StyleSheet can be used that is specially optimised for that device. When the same site is accessed using on a desktop computer, this StyleSheet is substituted for another with a fully-featured Visual Design.

Flexibility of CSS

Indeed, there are almost no limits to what StyleSheets can do in terms of presentation. It is even possible to offer different designs of the same website to a single device.

For example, many Development Teams create separate designs for people who are visually impaired. These designs may have a larger text size and higher colour contrast than a normal page. Both this and the standard design can be accessed by a browser—the user simply selects the design (i.e. the StyleSheet) she prefers by clicking a link. In this way, StyleSheets act as a powerful assistive tool for ensuring adherence to international website accessibility standards (as explored on page 199).

As we have already seen, Web Standards tend to come in threes and StyleSheets are no exception:

CSS 1. This was the first release of StyleSheets and as such could only be used for very simple presentational effects, e.g. fonts, margins, colours, etc. It could not be used to control layout.

CSS 2.1 contained all of CSS 1 as well as new elements to control layout. This meant that website designs could now be rendered using StyleSheets alone. Non-standard HTML-table based designs could be thrown out the window.

At the time of writing **CSS 3** is under development. CSS 3 includes all the features of CSS 2.1 as well as new border options, vertical text, speech formatting and more.

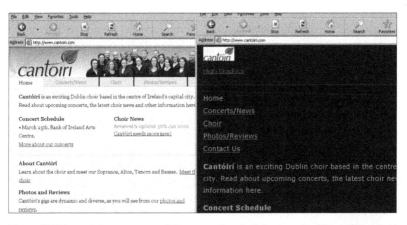

Figure 55. The website www.cantoiri.com rendered with a 'standard' StyleSheet (left) and a StyleSheet for the visually impaired (right). Note the increased text size, higher contrast and simple layout.

As a general rule, any business considering the development of a new website is strongly recommended to adhere to CSS 2.1. There are simply no longer any excuses for using outdated HTML-based presentation techniques. Even if a small number of older browsers cannot render a complex StyleSheet correctly, an alternative design can be created for them. Combining the presentational effects of CSS 2.1 with a document structure based on XHTML means a versatile and visually appealing site can be built for almost any audience.

Document Object Model & Scripting

All web users love interactivity—especially children. The more they can move things about and change colours, the better they like it. The job of facilitating such changes lies in the realm of the Document Object Model (DOM).

The Document Object Model is a description for how the elements in a web page are put together and how they can be manipulated. For example, it is the DOM that knows if text can be increased in size or displayed in a different colour.

DOM is a W3C recommendation that is hardwired (in almost complete form) into the latest desktop browsers. This means all such user agents treat interactivity in the same manner. The manner in which such interactivity is facilitated is through the use of Client-Side Scripting.

Client-Side Scripting

A Client-Side Scripting language is a relatively simple set of code that creates instructions for a computer to follow. 'Client-side' means that the processing of instructions happens on the visitor's computer, not on that which hosts the website.

ECMAScript (ISO standard 16262) is the currently accepted standard in this area. ECMAScript is the latest version of JavaScript.

In the past, DOMs and scripting languages often differed from one browser to another. For example, Netscape developed the JavaScript language for its own proprietary DOM, and in response Microsoft created JScript® and ActiveX®. This variety in languages meant that creating consistent interactivity across many browsers required all instructions to be coded in several ways. This led to the usual problems of bloated web pages and long download times.

Into the breach stepped the ever sensible W3C who responded by developing the **DOM Level 1 Specification**. This specification established a standard template to which all manufacturers could comply. At the same time the European Computer Manufacturers Association released a new version of JavaScript called **ECMAscript**.

After various false starts both of these are now taking root. The result is that it is now possible (with only a few bugs) to create interactivity that is truly consistent across a range of user agents.

Server-Side Scripting

While Client-Side Scripting can deliver a lot of attractive interactivity, unfortunately it is not capable of anything other than quite low-end functionality. For example, ECMAscript can change text colour on the fly, but it could never be used to collect orders on an eCommerce website. Operations like these require a far more powerful coding family called Server-Side Scripting.

Server-Side Scripting encompasses languages where the processing of instructions occurs not on a user agent, but on the computer that hosts a site. The advantage of such languages is that they are device independent, meaning they work on all user agents by default. Because of this, they are used extensively for creating applications in Dynamic and Transactional websites.

For example, a simple Server-Side Script might be used to create an online voting form that allows users to nominate a favourite piece of music. A more complex application could be programmed to administer a discussion forum.

In practice, Server-Side Scripting is often used in combination with Client-Side Scripting to produce complex functionality. For example, an eCommerce website might use ECMAscript (Client-Side) to validate the format of a credit card number before it is submitted for payment. A Server-Side Script is then used to process the order itself.

Variety of Server-Side Scripting Languages

A wide range of Server-Side Scripting languages are available. While each is capable of delivering highly interactive content, the choice of language is normally driven by the preference of an organisation's Technical and Development teams. Some of the more popular languages include:

PHP (Hypertext Pre-processor)

PHP is an Open Source scripting language that can be downloaded and installed for free from the web (www.php.net). Open Source means it has no licensing costs. Because it is contributed to by many autonomous web programmers, PHP is heavily used by independent design firms.

ASP® / ASP.NET® (Active Server Pages)

ASP and ASP.NET are the Server-Side Scripting languages developed by Microsoft. ASP is not free but comes bundled with Microsoft technology.

JSP (Java Server Pages®)

JSP is a scripting language (based on Java®) developed by Sun Microsystems. JSP is not free but is sold together with technology from firms such as IBM.

PERL™ (Practical Extraction and Reporting Language)

PERL was the main scripting language in the early days of the web. Development in PERL has declined as PHP and ASP have grown in use. As with PHP, PERL is Open Source and is free to use and distribute (www.perl.com).

Databases

It is normally the case that the information manipulated by Server-Side Scripting is stored in a database. This is because databases can hold a huge number of records and conduct complex queries. Indeed, it is this synergy of Server-Side Scripting, Client-Side Scripting and databases that underlies much of the power of the web.

Some of the most common databases currently used in website construction include:

MySQL®

MySQL is an Open Source database management system that is available for free download from the web (www.mysql.com). MySQL is regularly used in conjunction with PHP and is noted for its speed and flexibility.

Microsoft SQL Server®

SQL Server is the database product from Microsoft and is typically used in conjunction with ASP.

Oracle®

Oracle is the world leader in database technology. Its products can be used in conjunction with many scripting languages.

Web 2.0

Before leaving the area of Web Standards, it is worthwhile exploring a development that is beginning to transform many of the core practices of Website Construction.

Web 2.0 is the name given to a concept that is said to represent the next 'great leap forward' for the internet. Although there is considerable disagreement about what Web 2.0 actually means[68], it seems to incorporate many of the following attributes:

- Websites that incorporate very rich functionality, e.g. Google Maps.

- Websites that engender a co-operative relationship with visitors, e.g. del.icio.us.

- Websites that encourage users to modify and improve applications by making source code publicly available, e.g. Flickr.com.

- Websites that syndicate both information and applications, e.g. Google Maps.

- Websites that engage in an endless cycle of development to improve the quality of the online experience, e.g. Amazon.com.

- Websites that are loyal to Web Standards, e.g. Blogger.com.

While a quick overview of these attributes might not suggest anything new, the difference is that sites based on Web 2.0 are forging a new type of online experience.

For example, think of Google Maps and the attractive manner in which it renders images. In many ways, this site is closer to a desktop software

---

[68] Refer to http://www.oreillynet.com/lpt/a/6228 for a good discussion about Web 2.0.

program than to the type of website we have been used to for the last 10 years. Similarly, Google Maps allows itself to be combined with other websites in order to create new, even more useful applications, as on www.housingmaps.com[69]. This goes some way to explaining how transformational Web 2.0 may yet become.

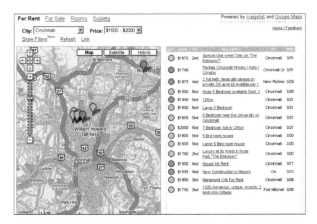

Figure 56. Housingmaps.com showing how information about room rentals can be layered onto Google Maps to create a 'mashup'. (Go to page 269 for more about 'mashups'.)

While the concept of Web 2.0 itself may be difficult to grasp, what is clear is that many of the practices within it are being powered by a set of emergent technologies. Some of the most important of these (as well as others not yet widely adopted) are reviewed below.

AJAX

AJAX is the name of a development practice for creating web applications with highly engaging interactivity. AJAX is an acronym derived from 'Asynchronous JavaScript And XML' as coined by the respected website consulting firm, Adaptive Path in 2005[70].

---

[69] Sometimes called a 'mashup'. Turn to page 269 for more.
[70] Adaptive Path "Ajax: A New Approach to Web Applications"
http://www.adaptivepath.com/publications/essays/archives/000385.php Accessed February 2005.

AJAX is a technique for building applications that are much more interactive and responsive than those produced by other coding methods. For example, Google Maps (maps.google.com) and the photograph sharing site, Flickr (www.flickr.com) use AJAX extensively within their operations.

The advantage of AJAX is that complex applications can be made to work with almost no delay when rendering results. This is seen most effectively on Google Maps, where visitors can drag images around their screen while the map continues to update. Such a responsive interaction is not possible from ordinary Server-Side Scripting. This is because each action, e.g. dragging a map, would require a web page to refresh first — meaning the visitor has to wait before they see the result. AJAX bypasses this through its 'AJAX Engine'.

The AJAX Engine is a page of JavaScript that is in continuous communication with the computer that hosts a website. This page is constantly updated and, as such, can also continuously change the user's screen — which means no more waiting around for pages to refresh. Furthermore, all the information output by the AJAX Engine may be expressed in Web Standards compliant MarkUp. As a result, it can be presented on any internet user agent, e.g. a desktop browser, PDA, mobile phone.

Although development is still in the early days, some useful aspects of AJAX functionality are beginning to appear on major websites, e.g. Amazon.com, del.icio.us.

Ruby on Rails

Ruby on Rails (often called RoR) is a web application framework based on a programming language called Ruby. In this sense, RoR is similar to Server-Side Scripting languages such as PHP and PERL, just somewhat less powerful. However, it does have one big advantage — it is much easier to learn and deploy. This means applications can be developed very easily and in a short timeframe. It also includes features whereby code can be reused and repeated as circumstances demand, particularly within AJAX.

Ruby on Rails is Open Source which means it can be downloaded for free from the web (from www.rubyonrails.com).

eXtensible Stylesheet Language Transformations (XSLT)

eXtensible Stylesheet Language Transformations (XSLT) is a scripting language (based on XML) that can be used to alter the presentation of an XML document. Essentially XSLT is a stylesheet for XML, in the same way that CSS is a stylesheet for HTML. However, XSLT also allows the format of content to be changed, not just its appearance. As such, XSLT enables an XML document to be presented in almost any manner imaginable, including HTML, XHTML, plain TXT and even PDF.

In fact, this is how some Website Content Management (WCM) Systems work. The content in WCM is stored as XML. When it is required for publishing, it is transformed into HTML or PDF by way of XSLT.

Even though XSLT has many uses, it is generally not suitable as a means of directly authoring a website. A site can be built much more easily in plain XHTML. However, XSLT is useful in application development, where data is stored in XML (as demonstrated by the AJAX development technique).

XSLT 2.0 was released as a candidate recommendation by W3C in November 2005.

XForms

As we saw in the section about Interface Design, web forms are the principal means for enabling interactivity on the web. Forms allow users to submit data using radio buttons, check boxes and text fields.

However, Designers have regularly complained that these forms are limited in how they allow interactivity. For example, they do not include certain interface controls that are common in other software, e.g. sliding scales. Furthermore, they do not render well in user agents other than desktop browsers.

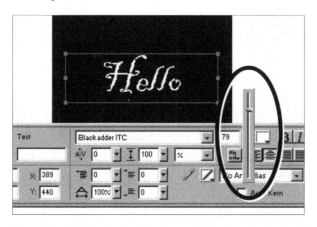

Figure 57. A Sliding Scale control for adjusting text size in the Adobe product, Fireworks MX. Such Sliding Scale controls will be available in XForms.

XForms are the nominated W3C successor to web forms and include many more options for both presentation and interactivity. For example, while web forms often use scripting languages to validate entries, this functionality is largely built into XForms. XForms also allow many other types of input, not only of plain text but also feeds from digital devices such as cameras or microphones. Similarly, Visual Design is easier because XForms are fully integrated with StyleSheets. This means presentation on multiple devices can be controlled without difficulty. In essence, XForms provide a much more powerful way for facilitating interactivity. However, because they are more complex than simple HTML, it may take some years before they start to appear on the web.

The W3C Recommendation for XForms 1.0 was released in 2003 and version 1.1 is under development. XForms will also be bundled with the next version of XHTML, version 2.

Scalable Vector Graphics

Scalable Vector Graphics (SVG) is an XML language for two-dimensional images that can described mathematically. Most non-photographic images such as logos, maps and architectural drawings fit this model.

Essentially, SVG offers a means for creating such images using MarkUp. This means a logo no longer has to be created as a GIF or PNG image, but can be rendered directly by code in a user agent! SVG also has many other advantages in terms of low filesizes, inherent accessibility and interactive possibilities.

SVG is still very much in its infancy and widespread adoption is not expected for some time. SVG is governed by W3C Recommendations SVG 1.1, SVG Tiny (for mobile phones) and SVG Basic (for PDAs).

By now it should be clear that by making sure Developers adhere to Web Standards, the construction of a high quality site can be made significantly more likely. Not only are Web Standards extremely well documented, they represent the future of the web. Indeed, their influence is being felt across many other areas of construction practice, for example:

- Browser compatibility
- Screen resolutions
- Accessibility

- Metadata

In order to understand this impact, we will now explore some of these aspects in more detail.

Browser Compatibility

Browser compatibility is concerned with the appearance and functionality of website content across a range of internet user agents. The importance of this issue is growing all the time as the variety of web-enabled products increases in number, e.g. mobile phones, PDAs, etc.

Nevertheless, for the next few years ordinary computers are expected to remain the device of choice for the majority of web users. As a result, desktop browsers still receive most attention during the development process.

Desktop Browsers

As we have seen, until quite recently almost all desktop browsers displayed web content differently—to the great dissatisfaction of Designers and Developers. While the rise of Web Standards is at last addressing this difficulty, some substantial differences remain. This means that it is still necessary to define the browsers for which a website will be compatible before construction begins.

For a site already in operation, the best way to do this is to establish the user agents that the current audience actually employ. Information on this can be found in the logfile of the computer that hosts the site.

As we saw in Chapter Two–Website Maintenance, a logfile keeps a record of every device that accesses a site. As such, Developers can find out exactly what browsers people prefer and modify their coding practices accordingly. Where such statistics are not at hand, other sources are available.

For example, HitsLink.com is a website that provides information about global browser trends. Several other sites provide a similar service, e.g. Browser News and W3Schools[71]. An aggregate of these is a good way to measure the market share held by each product. What will normally be found is that Internet Explorer from Microsoft is overwhelmingly dominant.

Browser Wars

Internet Explorer emerged as the world's leading desktop web browser at the end of the 1990s, having vanquished Netscape during the Browser Wars.

The Browser Wars were fought between Microsoft, Netscape and others as they attempted to become the most popular means of web access. Initially, it seemed that Netscape would win, but then Microsoft began to bundle Internet Explorer with new releases of its Windows operating system. This had the effect of wiping out Netscape's advantage and launching Microsoft into first place. (It has since been ruled in both US and European courts that Microsoft abused its position in this way[72].)

However, this does not mean that no competition exists.

The launch of Mozilla Firefox™ in late 2004 and the expected launch of a Google browser are reigniting this war. Firefox in particular has attracted many converts because of its useful security features. For example, in January 2006 it held up to 9.5% of the market in the United States, with Internet Explorer falling below 90% for the first time in years[73]. The

---

[71] Browser News. http://www.upsdell.com/BrowserNews. W3Schools
http://www.w3schools.com/default.asp
[72] BBC News "Microsoft vs. US Justice Dept."
http://news.bbc.co.uk/2/hi/in_depth/business/2000/microsoft/default.stm Accessed January 2005.
[73] Market Share. Browser market share for January 2006.
http://marketshare.hitslink.com/report.aspx?qprid=0 Accessed February 2006.

response from Microsoft has been to announce development on a new version 7 of Internet Explorer, due for release in 2006 or 2007.

In summary, the variety of desktop browsers on the market is likely to remain varied for the foreseeable future. As seen in the following chart, this constitutes quite a considerable number[74].

Windows XP, 2000, NT, ME, 98, 95	Apple	Other, i.e. Linux®, Sun®, Unix®.
Internet Explorer	Apple Safari™	Firefox
Netscape	Internet Explorer (discontinued)	Konqueror™
Firefox		Mozilla
Opera	Netscape	Netscape
Mozilla™	Firefox	Chimera™
AOL Browser	Opera	

Figure 58. Common desktop browsers on popular Operating Systems.

Compatibility Testing

You may also note from this list that not only are there many different types of browser, there are different browsers for different types of computer. For example, until 2006 Microsoft produced a version of Internet Explorer for Apple Macintosh® as well as Windows. Even though these have been made by the same company, they do not always display content in the same way. As such, effective cross platform compatibility testing is essential. To facilitate this, a working copy of each browser on each operating system should be provided for the purposes of assessment.

---

[74] A comprehensive comparison of desktop web browsers can be found at http://en.wikipedia.org/wiki/Comparison_of_web_browsers

However, in smaller companies such extravagance may not be possible. In this event, there are several online services that can be used as substitute. For example, BrowserCam[75] allows the appearance of a website to be reviewed without having to invest in a suite of browsers. By subscribing to this service, a screengrab of a specified site can be captured across a wide variety of systems. These can then be downloaded for analysis.

Although this is a cheap option, it does have some drawbacks. For example, it does not allow Developers to get a sense of interaction—an important feature for identifying functionality issues. Similarly, coding timescales may be stretched because each time a change is made, it must be submitted to the internet for review. Nevertheless, a BrowserCam-type service does present an attractive alternative for teams operating on a tight budget.

Mobile Browsing

Mobile browsing encompasses PDAs, mobile phones and other devices that come equipped with web capability. As mentioned, this area is experiencing massive growth and creating huge challenges for Designers and Developers. This is because the owners of such devices are demanding more content and a better online experience. Yet, until quite recently mobile browsing was dominated by a protocol called WAP that could only present information in a quite a basic way.

WAP (Wireless Application Protocol) is a system for delivering content via a format called Wireless MarkUp Language (WML). WML is a form of MarkUp for devices with small screens, low connection speeds and low memory. Although WAP is flexible in terms of functionality[76], it

---

[75] BrowserCam. www.browsercam.com
[76] A computer program that emulates the appearance of content on a WAP enabled mobile phone is available on the web from www.openwave.com

completely failed to grab the attention of consumers. This failure has been attributed to a lack of imaginative content, inherent interface design limitations and over-inflated market expectations.

Smartphone

However, a new generation of access device called the 'smartphone' is revitalising the fortunes of mobile browsing. A smartphone is a user

agent that combines the voice capability of a phone with the computing power of a PDA. These devices also have relatively large and colourful screens that support newer versions of WML. More significantly, most smartphones can also view ordinary web pages written in HTML/XHTML.

Figure 59. (left) Opera browser on a smartphone.

What this means is that content can be rendered onto small screens using Cascading StyleSheets, without the need to convert it into WML. This permits far richer browsing than was previously possible. Such is the power of user agents like this, that mobile browsing is projected to overtake the desktop as the principle means of web access towards 2010[77].

Mobile Browsers

With regard to the browsers that are actually used to display content on such devices, no clear leaders are yet apparent. The market is currently shared between Microsoft and the Norwegian firm Opera, as well as several smaller companies, e.g. Thunderhawk™. Mozilla Firefox has also expressed interest in this area.

---

[77] BBC News Online. http://news.bbc.co.uk/ July 2004.

Overall Opera is the superior product in terms of its support for Web Standards. For example, content can be easily optimised for display on Opera's mobile browser using StyleSheets (unlike its Microsoft competitor, which relies on special coding techniques). Opera has also developed an innovative system called 'Smallscreen Rendering' for presenting non-standards compliant websites on hand-held devices.

Both the Opera and Internet Explorer browsers come bundled with devices from manufacturers such as Nokia, Dell, Siemens, etc. This is helping to increase the attractiveness of mobile computing as an alternative means of web access.

Screen Resolution

Related to the issue of browser compatibility is that of the preferred screen resolution for which a website is constructed. In point of fact, a decision on this must be made before the design or production of a site can even begin. This is because screen resolution sets an absolute limit on the amount of space a Designer can work with. This space is often referred to as 'real-estate', because every pixel is so important.

History shows that the size and resolution of desktop computer screens (i.e. the total available real-estate per page) has increased steadily over the years. For example, throughout the 1990s the majority of screens were 15 inches in size and set at the relatively low resolution of 640 pixels wide by 480 pixels high. About 2000, this was overtaken by 17" screens at a resolution of 800x600, which itself is currently being superseded by 19" screens and 1024x768 resolution.[78]

While increases in resolution allow more information to be displayed online, the essential challenge of designing within a specified limit

---

[78] As with browsers, statistics for screen resolution are recorded in server logs. Alternatively, they may be found on sites such as the W3C Schools site.

remains. If a Designer exceeds these constraints, usability issues can result. For example, designing a web application that is 900 pixels wide to run on a screen with a setting of 800 pixels, will result in horizontal scrolling — a proven interaction problem.

Liquid Layout

While it is desirable to match screen settings to those used by the majority of a website audience, designing for a single resolution may not always be optimal. If a site is designed for 800x600, someone viewing it on a larger screen will see a lot of extra empty space surrounding the content. While this has few implications in terms of usability, it does represent an inefficient use of real estate. As a result, many Designers now create sites with a 'liquid', 'fluid' or 'elastic' layout.

A liquid layout is one that expands or contracts to fill the space on a user's screen, no matter what its resolution. While such a site may be designed to appear best at one particular setting, it can also degrade gracefully at any other. For example, a website may be designed to look best at 800x600, but also look good with 1024x768.

Some websites go so far as to create entirely separate designs for different screens. For example, Microsoft.com uses StyleSheets to deliver a different homepage design to a screen with 800x600 resolution, than one at 1024x768.

Screen Resolution on Mobile Devices

The challenge of designing for various screen sizes is particularly relevant when mobile browsing is considered. For example, many handheld devices have screens of very low resolution, sometimes as small as 75 pixels wide x 125 pixels high. The limitations this imposes is forcing the creation of innovative solutions for the presentation of content in a restricted space. It also underlines the need for strict compliance to good development practice, including:

- Short and concise content.

- Small filesizes.

- Compliance with Web Standards.

Indeed, design restrictions on such user agents go beyond screen size. For example, the challenge of facilitating interactivity on handheld equipment is very tricky. This is because the normal 'mouse & cursor' combination cannot be used. As such, options like roller wheels, joysticks, stylus and wands are all being trialled. In short, this entire area of design will continue to develop in exciting ways over the coming years.

Web Accessibility

Of the many topics in Website Development that have grown in prominence in recent years, Web Accessibility is certainly top of the pack.

Web Accessibility is a principle that seeks to ensure that site visitors with disabilities can locate, navigate, read and understand web content. The main impairments covered by this are:

- Vision, e.g. blindness, colour blindness.

- Hearing, e.g. deafness.

- Physical and speech, e.g. restricted use of limbs.

- Cognitive, e.g. learning difficulties.

Various studies have found that millions of people have disabilities that affect their ability to access the web. For example, it is estimated that between 10%–20% of the population of any given country have some form of permanent web access impairment[79]. Furthermore, many other people experience temporary disabilities, e.g. a short sighted person who misplaces their spectacles may find small text difficult to read.

Paradoxically, the web is now the primary means by which people with permanent disabilities access news, information and other entertainment. However, poor design means that this is usually only possible after considerable effort. The aim of the web accessibility movement is to remove such barriers. To this end, a key development has been the creation of a set of international standards by the Web Accessibility Initiative (WAI™)[80].

Web Accessibility Initiative

The WAI is a branch of the World Wide Web Consortium (W3C). Tim Berners Lee (the inventor of the World Wide Web) has expressed particular interest in this topic as he sees "access by everyone regardless of disability" as an essential aspect of the web.

The WAI carries out work on five levels:

- Ensuring that web technologies support accessibility.

- Developing guidelines.

- Improving tools to evaluate and repair web accessibility.

- Conducting education and outreach.

- Co-ordinating research and development.

---

[79] Dr. Barry McMullin. Research Institute for Networks and Communications Engineering (RINCE). Dublin City University. http://eaccess.rince.ie/white-papers/2002/warp-2002-01/warp-2002-01.HTML Accessed April 2005.
[80] Web Accessibility Initiative. www.w3c.org/wai/

WCAG 1.0

In May 1999 the WAI formally published its first set of Web Content Accessibility Guidelines 1.0 (WCAG 1.0) to explain how website content can be made accessible to persons with disabilities. The guidelines also indicate how an existing website can be graded to establish its level of accessibility conformance. Three levels of conformance are now in use. These are:

- Level A or Priority One

- Level AA [double-A] or Priority Two

- Level AAA [triple-A] or Priority Three.

Level-A conformance indicates that a web page adheres to the lowest level (or Priority-1) accessibility guidelines. Without this, one or more groups would find it impossible to access information. The elements of Priority-1 are outlined in a checklist provided by the WAI[81]. To gain Level-A Conformance web content must satisfy each point in the checklist.

Level-AA [double-A] conformance indicates that a web page adheres to Priority-2 accessibility guidelines. Without this, one or more groups would find it difficult (but not impossible) to access information. The elements of Priority-2 are outlined in the same checklist as Level-A.

Level-AAA [triple-A] conformance indicates that a web page adheres to Priority-3 accessibility guidelines. Without this, one or more groups will find it somewhat difficult to access information in the document. Priority-3 elements are also outlined in the same checklist as Level-A and Level-AA.

---

[81] http://www.w3.org/TR/WAI-WEBCONTENT/full-checklist.html

As part of the process for promoting this area, a series of WCAG conformance logos have been created. Website owners can place one of these on their site to indicate a claim of accessibility conformance.

Figure 60. WAI conformance logos.

It is interesting to note that the use of these logos is not administered by the WAI nor does the WAI oversee the award of such claims. Conformance certification is solely the responsibility of content owners. Unfortunately, this has led to some abuses, often because inexperienced Developers misinterpret the guidelines.

WCAG 2.0

Since November 2005 a draft of a new WAI standard (WCAG 2.0) has been available for review[82]. The key difference between this and the existing version is that accessibility 'Guidelines' have been replaced by 'Success Criteria'. The success criteria defined in WCAG 2.0 are:

- Content must be perceivable by all users regardless of disability.

- Content and controls must be easily understandable.

- Interface elements must be operable regardless of disability.

- Websites must work well with both old and new technology.

The hope is that this change will simplify the development of accessible websites.

The other major change is that non–W3C technologies may also be used in accredited sites (as long as they are made accessible). This means that

---

[82] Available at http://www.w3.org/TR/WCAG20/

for the first time, content formats such as PDF and Flash can be legitimately certified as conforming to a WAI standard.

The final release of WCAG 2.0 is expected sometime in late 2006 or early 2007.

National Developments

As well as efforts by the WAI, advances in accessibility at the level of national government have also occurred. The now famous Section 508[83] of the United States 1998 Disabilities Act sets the benchmark that other governments attempt to match. Section 508 is a legislative instrument designed to "eliminate barriers in information technology, to make available opportunities for people with disabilities, and to encourage development of technologies that will help achieve these Goals". As a result all federal agencies in the US must now ensure their sites are accessible.

In Europe, the United Kingdom's Disability Discrimination Act (1995) is also having a strong impact by compelling both public and private companies to produce accessible web content. Other European countries that have implemented some form of guidelines include Denmark, Finland, France, Germany, Italy, Portugal and Ireland. Australia, Canada, New Zealand and Japan have also been active in this area.

Market Response to Web Accessibility

In general, websites have been slow to respond to the demand for accessibility. For example, a study in Ireland in 2002[84] found that of the

---

[83] Section 508. www.section508.gov
[84] Dr. Barry McMullin. Research Institute for Networks and Communications Engineering (RINCE). Dublin City University. http://eaccess.rince.ie/white-papers/2002/warp-2002-01/warp-2002-01.HTML Accessed April 2005.

top 214 Irish websites, 94% failed to meet WCAG 1.0 Level-A standard, with 100% failing to meet Level-AA.

However, since then the situation has improved steadily. This change is being driven by a number of factors, including:

Market Realisation

There is a realisation that people with disabilities represent a disproportionately large web audience and many firms are seeking to capitalise on this. Further, it is clear that many design changes brought about by the need for accessibility, e.g. resizable text, can also assist other users — notably older people.

Web Standards and Technology

Many simple website construction and design techniques can achieve excellent results for accessibility. The growth of web standards and the inherently accessible nature of sites built in this way is assisting this. Similarly, Website Content Management Systems are a useful support because they can automatically generate accessibility compliant content.

Increased Awareness of Disability

Many non–governmental organisations are promoting debate on the area of accessibility and lobbying business to cater for disabled users.

Legislation and Litigation

More legislation about web accessibility will arise in developed countries in the short to medium term. Litigation could also speed up this process, depending on the development of case law.

It is increasingly obvious that any business developing a site must at least adhere to the Level-A standard, as a matter of good practice.

Governmental or state funded websites may be further compelled to conform to the higher Level–AA benchmark.

Metadata

Metadata is a set of descriptive (usually short) information about a piece of content. It typically encompasses details such as:

- Who created it

- When it was created

- A short description

- Copyright ownership

While metadata can be applied to any format of information (including images, video, Flash, etc.) it is through its application to HTML that most Developers come into contact with it.

Dublin Core Metadata Initiative®

The format for most of the metadata used in HTML is based on the recommendations of the Dublin Core Metadata Initiative[85] (DCMI). The DCMI is "an open forum engaged in the development of interoperable online metadata standards that support a broad range of purposes and business models". Essentially, the DCMI defines the metadata that can be included in web pages and how it should be formatted. While the full set of DCMI metadata is extremely lengthy, some elements that are commonly used include:

- Title

- Author

---

[85] Dublin Core Metadata Initiative, www.dublincore.org. Note: 'Dublin' in this case means Dublin, Ohio—not the home of Guinness.

- Keywords (these may be taken from a taxonomy if one is available)

- Description

- Date created

- Copyright

These are then placed within the code of a HTML page, as follows:

```
<META NAME="DC.Creator.Corporatename" CONTENT="Company
name, Address.">
```

```
<META       NAME="DC.Language"       SCHEME="ISO639-1"
CONTENT="en">
```

```
<META NAME="DC.Title" CONTENT="Company name">
```

```
<META NAME="DC.Description" CONTENT="Our company is
the world's leading supplier of high quality widgets">
```

Full templates and other advice regarding the creation of metadata are available on the Dublin Core website, http://dublincore.org/.

Character Set

Of all the metadata placed in a web page, one of the most important is that of Character Set. For example, imagine that a website written in English is suddenly required to be localised into Russian. After the content has been translated and republished, it is noticed that the text is not displaying correctly. The most likely reason is that the wrong Character Set has been specified.

A Character Set is a piece of code that matches the alphabet of a spoken language to that of a computer language. Character Sets on the web are based on Unicode™. Unicode is a system that provides a unique number to identify all the symbols in every language used for electronic communications. The manner in which Unicode is interpreted is based on the Character Set employed. For instance, some sample character sets include:

- ISO-8859-5 for the Russian Cyrillic alphabet: `<meta http-equiv="Content-Type" content="text/html; charset=iso-8859-5">`

- ISO-8859-1 for the Roman alphabet: `<meta http-equiv="Content-Type" content="text/html; charset=iso-8859-1">`

- ISO-2022-jp for Japanese characters: `<meta http-equiv="Content-Type" content="text/html; charset=iso-2022-jp">`

By selecting the right Character Set, a Developer can be sure that published content will display with the correct script. In cases where languages are mixed or are expected to change, the safest choice is UTF–8 (8–bit Unicode Transformation Format).

- UTF–8: `<meta http-equiv="Content-Type" content="text/html; charset=utf-8">`

UTF–8 allows all languages to be represented in their common written form. This is particularly important for Bi-Directional languages such as Hebrew or Arabic, where text is written right-to-left but may also include some right to left terms[86]. Issues of this nature are explored by the Internationalisation committee of the W3C whose Goal is "proposing and co-ordinating any techniques, conventions, guidelines and activities ...

---

[86] For example on www.bbc.co.uk/arabic

that allow and make it easy to use W3C technology worldwide, with different languages, scripts, and cultures."[87]

Taxonomy

In the early years of the web, the placement of metadata in web pages was popularised as a means for improving Search Engines rankings. This is because metadata was used for identifying suitable targets.

Although this practice has declined to some extent, metadata still plays an important role in Website Development. For example, it provides a means for administering the categorisation of content within a site's taxonomy.

A taxonomy is a system for classifying objects into an ordered hierarchical structure that indicates natural relationships. A well known example of taxonomy is that of the animal kingdom, i.e. Domain, Kingdom, Phylum, Class, Order, Family, Genus.

On the web, taxonomy is frequently used as a basis for organising information and in this sense is much like Information Architecture. However, it differs from Information Architecture because a taxonomy does not have to be based on the needs of a website audience.

For example, a book retailer who wants to create a structure for organising his collection may choose the **Dewey Decimal Classification®** **System** as the basis for his taxonomy. The Dewey Decimal System (DDS) is a comprehensive means of library classification that includes categories and sub-categories based on subject matter, e.g. technology, literature, history, etc.

---

[87] W3C Internationalisation http://www.w3.org/International/ Copyright 1999 W3C (MIT, INRIA, Keio), All Rights Reserved.
http://www.w3.org/Consortium/Legal/2002/copyright-documents-20021231

If the vendor then decides to sell his books online, he must create an Information Architecture (i.e. a structure) for the intended site. This may be different from the taxonomy (the DDS) because it is the website audience that usually defines an architecture, not the site owner. (Read more about making an Information Architecture on page 145.)

In this sense, the audience might think it is easier to find to a book when the collection is organised by author name, price, bestseller lists, etc, rather than by the DDS.

However, references to taxonomy can still be usefully included in the metadata of each page. For example, when our retailer creates HTML to describe each book, he can include its place in the DDS taxonomy as an element of metadata. This could help him track books of a similar nature even if they are placed in different sections of the site. It could also be used as a fall-back system of navigation or search for expert users.

For example, the book 'Atonement' by Ian McEwan might be found in two places in the Information Architecture:

- Under "Mac" in an alphabetical list of author names.

- Under a list of Booker Prize winning authors.

The HTML metadata in that book's web page would also indicate its place in the Dewey Decimal System, i.e. English literature (823).

```
<META      NAME="Dewey     Decimal     Classification"
CONTENT="823.212">
```

Folksonomy/Social Tagging

An interesting development known as 'folksonomy' or 'social tagging' is beginning to merge elements of taxonomy and architecture into a novel system of navigation.

A folksonomy is a means of categorisation that uses keywords to group information. The central point is that a folksonomy is created by a website audience using keywords they have chosen—not those of the Development Team. Furthermore, no constraints are imposed on the type of descriptions that can be used.

So far, folksonomies have been adopted by large sites that are host to substantial online communities. A good example of this is the photograph sharing site Flickr (www.flickr.com).

On Flickr, whenever a community member uploads a photograph he or she is asked to describe it in some way. For example, a holiday photograph could be termed "Holiday" or "Rome" or "Italy", or anything else. Flickr tracks all these keywords and presents a list of the most frequently occurring labels. This is referred to as a 'tag cloud'. In this tag cloud, commonly occurring words (cameraphone, family) are displayed larger in size than less common words (animal, bird)[88].

All time most popular tags

amsterdam animal animals april architec beach berlin bird birthday black b california cameraphone china christmas church city clouds cc europe family festival fireworks fl

Figure 61. A tag cloud on Flickr.com

The advantage of a folksonomy is that it reflects the mental model of a website audience more accurately than a taxonomy. However, the lack of

[88] http://www.flickr.com/photos/tags/

a structured or managed approach to classification means that valuable content could be lost or overlooked.

Semantic Web

An emerging concept in the area of metadata that will strongly influence the future of the internet, is that of the Semantic Web. The Semantic Web is a project instigated by the inventor of the World Wide Web, Tim Berners-Lee, as a means for allowing the exchange of information between diverse sources. This exchange is achieved by applying a kind of extended metadata to documents, called an 'ontology'.

An **ontology** is a concept that links taxonomies together by establishing relationships between the elements within them. Take the following example:

Amazon.com is an instance of a *Transactional website*. Transactional sites (along with Dynamic and Basic sites) are members of a taxonomy called *'Types of Website'*.

Amazon.com also resides on the *World Wide Web*. The World Wide Web (along with email, FTP, Gopher, etc.) belongs to a taxonomy called *'Internet Services'*.

As such, we have now made a connection between two taxonomies — *'Types of Website'* and *'Internet Services'* — based on the shared element *Amazon.com*.

Taxonomy 1 'Types of Website'	Taxonomy 2 'Internet Services'
Transactional ⟶ Amazon.com ⟵ World wide web	
Dynamic	Email
Basic	FTP

Figure 62. An example of an ontological link between two taxonomies.

The idea is that ontologies which do this on a global scale could allow information to be pooled between different systems in a machine readable- rather than a human-readable format (as is the case with the current web). The aim of the Semantic Web is to encourage the adoption of such techniques, thereby opening up information repositories around the world to opportunities for data sharing. Indeed, the Semantic Web is a key principle underlying the concept of Web 2.0.

One anticipated benefit of the Semantic Web is that the quality of results received from search will improve. This is because well structured ontologies will allow Search Engines to better interpret the content of documents. Methods like this are already being used by the online shopping application Froogle™, which uses concepts derived from the Semantic Web to encode information.

Website Construction Tools and Software

Because of the ease with which HTML/XHTML can be written, it is hardly surprising that many websites are built with nothing more than a basic text editor. Yet, other more sophisticated products are also available. This includes Adobe Dreamweaver (from $399), Adobe GoLive® (from $399) and Microsoft Expression Web Designer ($n/a).

The advantage of such tools is that they incorporate WYSIWYG (What you see is what you get) interfaces that allow a site to be created simply by dragging and dropping elements onto a screen. The programs themselves generate all the necessary code (which can then be edited by hand if necessary). These tools also provide other facilities, including libraries of JavaScript and other elements, e.g. Flash files, etc.

While WSYIWYG tools are useful for many construction projects, expert Developers eschew them in favour of advanced text editors. Programs like this allow code to be written directly in MarkUp, while also providing libraries of common elements. BBedit™ (from $199), Adobe Homesite™ (from $99) and EditPlus™ (free) are three of the most common of these. Other tools known as Integrated Development Environments (IDE) are sometimes used for authoring Server-Side Scripting languages, e.g. Microsoft Visual Studio® (from $2,400) and Eclipse™ (free).

It is the experience of many Developers that text editors are preferable when an exact compliance with Web Standards or accessibility guidelines is required. This is because Dreamweaver, GoLive and Web Designer sometimes create bloated MarkUp that is neither standards compliant nor accessible.

However, many of these issues are now being overcome. As a result, good clean code is gradually becoming more commonplace. Furthermore, some WYSIWYG programs also incorporate mechanisms that can test pages for compliance to such standards.

In fact, it is precisely this type of site evaluation that occurs during the next phase of the Development Cycle, **Website Testing**.

Step 5
Website Testing

Website Testing is a process for evaluating the conformance of a site to an agreed set of guidelines. The purpose of testing is to ensure a website is capable of operating to a minimum acceptable standard in order to meet the Goals that have been set for it.

Unfortunately, some organisations view this phase of development as an unwelcome delay that can prevent their project finishing on time. Judging by the number of sites that are launched with such basic errors as broken links or missing images, second-rate testing appears to be the norm. This is in stark contrast to the often rigorous sign-off procedures that are followed for other media.

For example, no business would ever dream of issuing a printed brochure before thoroughly checking it for errors in spelling, imagery or layout. Yet, many websites are launched after only the most cursory of testing. It is simply taken on trust that everything will be OK. The trouble with this is that site visitors are left to pick up the pieces when things go wrong. Inevitably this can damage the perceived trustworthiness of an organisation.

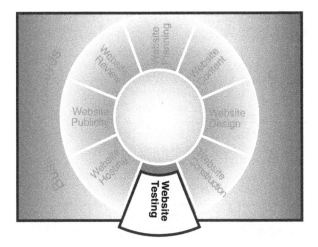

Figure 63. Website Testing as a phase of the Website Development Cycle.

What is needed is a change in mindset—away from one that sees testing as an obstacle, towards one that sees it as a facilitator of site Goals. A possible way to achieve this is to demonstrate the value that testing can add to a site. For example, the web guru Jakob Neilsen has established that by spending 10% of a project budget on usability testing, the quality of a visitor's online experience can improve by up to 135%[89]! Imagine applying this to a website whose revenue relies on credit card transactions, e.g. Amazon.com. The easier the site is to use, the more money can be collected.

The Website Testing Catalogue

Yet, usability is only part of the story. Website Testing encompasses many other areas—ranging from simple spell checking to full security reviews. For convenience, these can be grouped into a catalogue that lists all appropriate methodologies.

---

[89] Useit.com "Return on Investment for usability!
   http://www.useit.com/alertbox/20030107.html January 2003. Accessed December 2005.

Test Method	Description
Code Testing	This tests that all languages conform to accepted code standards.
Design Testing	This tests that all pages conform to the website's preferred layout and design.
Spelling Testing	This tests that HTML and other code has been inserted in an optimal manner.
Hyperlink Testing	This tests that all links to all documents and assets resolve correctly.
Page Weight Testing	This ensures that all pages conform to the maximum allowed page weight.
Browser Testing	This tests that the website displays correctly across target browsers and Operating Systems.
Usability Testing	This ensures that the website conforms to appropriate practice in the area of usability.
Accessibility Testing	This ensures that the website conforms to the stated level of accessibility outlined in the organisation's Web Accessibility Policy.
Security Testing	This tests that the website operates with minimum risk in a secure environment.
Functional Testing	This tests that the website operates as expected under normal and error inducing conditions.
Performance Testing	This tests the responsiveness of the website to user actions.
Website Standards Review	This reviews the website against the organisation's Website Standard.
Operational Monitoring	This puts in place procedures for the ongoing monitoring of the site.

Figure 64. Website Testing Catalogue.

The overall co-ordination of these activities is the duty of the Development Team Leader. On her shoulders rests responsibility for ensuring everything is in proper working order. She may also carry out various aspects of testing herself, notably the Website Standards Review.

However, in most circumstances testing is performed by specialists from within the Development Team.

The Skills and Resources Needed for Testing

For example, Functional Testing may be undertaken by Developers, and Performance Testing by technical personnel. Where a team is large enough, it is advisable to get hold of staff who have not been directly involved in a project and ask them to carry out such assessments. This ensures familiarity does not lead to errors being overlooked.

It may also be desirable to seek external assistance for specialist disciplines like Accessibility and Security. This is particularly necessary where in-house skills are not good enough. Some areas of testing may even entail the participation of site visitors, e.g. usability, where data about user experience is important.

Finally, the procedures of site testing themselves require an assortment of technology in order to occur. This can include anything from simple office stationery (pen and paper) to specialist evaluation software. The degree to which these are needed depends mainly on the scale of the site to be assessed. For example, a large Transactional website is likely to need more technology than a small Basic Site. Of course, budget constraints also set limits to what can be provided.

Now that we understand what is needed for Website Testing, we can start to explore the processes and procedures by which it is carried out.

Code Testing

As the first task in the assessment catalogue, Code Testing ensures that the basic components of a site are in conformance with accepted standards. This includes:

- MarkUp (HTML/XHTML)

- StyleSheets (CSS)

- Client-Side Scripting (ECMAscript/JavaScript)

- Server-Side Scripting (PHP, ASP, JSP, PERL, etc)

An assessment like this is required because improperly authored code can lead to problems of presentation and functionality on some user agents, notably smartphones and screen readers.

Several tools are available to assist this review. For example, the W3C provides an online validator for assessing MarkUp and StyleSheets. To use this validator:

- Select the address of the page you wish to validate

- Visit http://validator.w3.org

- Insert the address of the web page you wish to validate and click 'check'

The page is then checked against the appropriate standard. If it fails to comply, a list of issues is displayed that can then be used for correcting errors. In circumstances where the file you wish to evaluate is offline (i.e. it has not yet been published on the internet) it can be checked by uploading the code to the validator.

Needless to say, this method of page-by-page assessment can be very tedious when a large website is involved. Thankfully, many of the Quality Assurance tools reviewed in Chapter Two (page 48), provide functionality that speed it up. For example, WebQA from Watchfire and Website Monitor from HiSoftware include modules for evaluating compliance with Web Standards. Similarly, the authoring tools Adobe Dreamweaver and Expression Web Designer contain reporting functions for validating MarkUp.

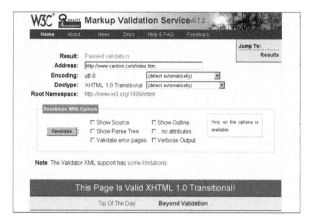

Figure 65. The MarkUp validation service from W3C.

The assessment of Client-Side and Server-Side Scripting languages require more specialist programs. Known as Integrated Development Environments (IDE), these are used to identify and fix bugs. Two popular examples are Microsoft Visual Studio and Eclipse.

Design Testing

The purpose of a Design Test is to ensure that each page on a website is in conformance with the templates agreed for it during development. This includes Information Architecture, Navigation, Interaction, Interface, Information and Visual Design. The basic procedure is to review a site and try to locate unplanned changes in structure or appearance, e.g. distended layout, missing images or inappropriate colours. These can then be corrected as necessary.

The execution of a Design Test is intensively manual, simply because it requires every page to be analysed individually. Technology is no match for the human eye in this regard!

That said, some technology (in the form of user agents) is needed in order to mimic the experience of site visitors (desktop computer, smartphone, PDA, etc). By employing such devices a Designer can be sure that she is viewing a site in the same way as an ordinary user. This means that any observations can be considered accurate (notwithstanding the issue of browser compatibility which is explored below).

Spelling and Grammar Testing

Nothing on the web appears more amateur than carelessly written text. As such, a detailed focus on language is essential for maintaining a professional appearance.

The bulk of responsibility for this activity lies with the Website Editor. As seen in Chapter Two, the resources needed to assist this task include dictionaries, thesauri and grammar guides. Word processing programs such as Microsoft Word also provide useful functionality. As a result, it is usually possible to prevent poorly written content going online.

However, no process is flawless and bad spellings can sometimes escape notice. In this case, website Quality Assurance tools like those created by HiSoftware or Watchfire (page 48) can be useful. These include spell checking capability, as do many Website Content Management Systems. By scheduling a regular review with such a device, any errors that were overlooked can be corrected.

Hyperlink Testing

The humble hyperlink is probably the main reason for the overwhelming success of the World Wide Web. For example, the ease with which fragmented information can be linked together has revolutionised knowledge sharing. Yet, while hyperlinks are a cause for celebration, they can also be a source of considerable frustration when they point to pages that no longer exist!

Fortunately, a substantial array of Quality Assurance software is available to help detect such faults. Many of these were explored in Chapter Two (page 48). In addition, several web authoring programs (e.g. Adobe Dreamweaver) and Website Content Management Systems have similar capability. In fact, because of the technology used within WCM, manufacturers claim it is impossible for broken links to arise. This is because a WCM system can automatically detect and delete links to pages that have been removed.

Page Weight Test

A Page Weight Test seeks to ensure that anything placed online conforms to a maximum allowed filesize (usually expressed in kilobytes). For example, the maximum recommended weight for any page primarily used for navigation on the web (e.g. a homepage) is 60 Kilobytes (kB). This limit is based on the time it takes to download a file of this size over a standard 56.6 Kilobits-per-second (kilobit/s) modem connection[90]. 60kB takes about 8 to 10 seconds, which research has shown is the limit of patience for the majority of web users[91].

Non-navigation pages, such as those with paragraphs of text, can safely extend up to 100kB. This is because visitors can begin to read a long page while the rest of it is loading. As the uptake of high-speed broadband grows, this limit will gradually increase.

It should be noted, however, that the figure for page weight must be calculated from all the files being viewed – not just the basic HTML. As such, a web page consisting of a 45kB HTML file, two images of 15kB each and a StyleSheet of 3kB, has a total weight of 78kB.

---

[90] 56 Kilobits (56×10^3) equals about 56,000 bits.
[91] Useit.com "The need for speed". http://www.useit.com/alertbox/9703a.html Accessed January 2006.

As with many aspects of Website Maintenance, page weights can be measured using Web Quality Assurance software. Similarly, Content Management Systems can also set restrictions on the size of files permitted to be published.

Browser Compatibility Test

As previously discussed, browser compatibility remains an active issue because of the variety of devices that now come with web capability. Indeed, the diversity of internet enabled user agents is forecasted to increase dramatically in the coming years as more and more gadgets go online, e.g. GPS systems, video game players, iPods, etc. The purpose of Browser Compatibility Testing is to ensure that a site can display and function in a useable way on all such appliances. At present, this mainly encompasses desktop computers and (increasingly) mobile devices.

To assist Browser Compatibility Testing, some organisations create 'Test Labs' in which a variety of user agents can be assessed. These user agents are chosen to reflect the devices that are preferred by website visitors. This might include desktop computers like a Microsoft Windows PC, an Apple MAC and a Linux machine (and perhaps even a UNIX or Sun OS box, if a technical audience is targeted). The lab may also contain a range of PDAs, smartphones and Web TV, Playstation or Xbox devices. Each of these is then loaded with the browser software used by visitors.

The following list shows the range of devices and browsers that could be included in such a lab.

Windows XP, 2000, NT, ME, 98, 95	Apple	Other, i.e. Linux, Unix, Sun, PDA, Mobile Phone, Web TV.
Browsers include: Internet Explorer Netscape Firefox Opera Mozilla AOL browser	Browsers include: Apple Safari Internet Explorer Netscape Firefox Opera Camino	Devices & browsers include: Firefox Konqueror Mozilla Netscape Chimera Opera Smartphone/PDA Internet Explorer PDA Thunderhawk PDA Blackberry™ Web TV Windows Ultra-Mobile PC Playstation® Xbox® Jaws® Screen Reader

Figure 66. Equipment to be included in a compatibility test.

Because many organisations cannot afford such comprehensive test suites, other help has become available. For example Openwave.com has downloadable software that allows mobile devices to be mimicked and tested on a desktop computer. Similarly, we have already learned about Browsercam.com (page 194) which allows the appearance of a website to be evaluated on many different platforms via the internet. Facilities like these are very useful when development resources are restricted.

The procedure of compatibility testing itself involves a review of site content for conformance against a set of design and functional specifications, across all selected browsers.

As this takes place, it may be noticed that content is presented well on some systems, but poorly on others. That is, a site may appear exactly as planned in the Mozilla Firefox browser, but be less than optimal in Internet Explorer. While the challenge for Developers is to ensure a consistent online experience, this is not always possible. As such, a mechanism that allows a site to 'degrade gracefully' is required.

'Graceful degradation' is a concept that declares as long as a visitor can read content and use applications properly, the lack of pixel-perfect layout may be overlooked. In this sense, browsers that are planned for 'graceful degradation' should be those that are least used by visitors.

Usability Test

A Usability Test is the measure of the quality of a visitor's experience when interacting with a website. The web guru Jakob Neilsen has defined usability as encompassing five factors. These are[92]:

- Ease of learning

- Efficiency of use

- Memorability

- Frequency of errors

- Personal level of satisfaction

Because of the variety of issues involved, there is no single test that can be defined as **the** usability test for a website. Rather this area

---

[92] Useit.com "Usability 101: Introduction to Usability" http://www.useit.com/alertbox/20030825.html August 2003. Accessed July 2005.

encompasses a range of assessment techniques that together seek to improve overall performance. We have already become familiar with some of these. For example, Card Sorting (page 146) is a usability technique for building an Information Architecture.

It should also be clear that usability testing does not commence only when the construction of a website is complete. Rather, it occurs in tandem with the Development Cycle itself. Some of the most common procedures used during production are explored below:

Website Planning Phase

Expert Review

An expert review engages an experienced usability consultant to assess a website against the parameters of good design practice. Expert Reviews are often used as a starting point when initiating a redesign project. Such a review might also be undertaken when a website is created for the first time. In this circumstance, the focus is on competitor sites, in order to gather lessons about what makes them so successful.

Personas

As we have seen, a Persona is a profile of an imaginary user who encompasses all the characteristics of a target audience. If several audiences exist, several Personas may be needed. For example, the Personas for a business listed on the stock-exchange may include professional investors, as well as ordinary customers. Personas are a proven way of keeping a Development Team focussed on users' needs.

Survey

A survey is a useful way of gathering opinions from a website audience about their expectations for a site. A survey can also be used to collect views within a business for an intranet development project.

Focus Group

A focus group uses many of the same techniques as a survey, though an invited audience takes the place of a random sample.

Hallway Surveys

A Hallway Survey is a technique used for evaluating intranet designs within an organisation where the target audience is collected together. In this method, a design is displayed in a public area, e.g. a canteen, under the supervision of a manager. Passing staff are then asked to participate in simple task assessments or asked for their opinions based on a series of preplanned questions.

Design Phase

Card Sorting

As we have seen, card sorting is very effective for building an Information Architecture. Not only can it be carried out without any technology, it is also useful with small groups who are representative of a wider audience.

LoFi Task Assessment Exercise

A LoFi task assessment exercise is a technique for evaluating design assumptions. In this method, an outline Website Design is created on paper and presented for assessment by users, e.g. wireframe.

HiFi Task Assessment

A HiFi assessment mimics the approach of a LoFi assessment, however the design is presented in a more sophisticated manner, e.g. as full colour graphics or in simple HTML. As with the LoFi assessment, the objective is to ensure that planned tasks can be successfully completed.

Final Expert Review

A final expert review of a website may be conducted to identify any last minute usability improvements that can be made.

Usability Lab

Many of the resources required for usability testing are very cheap. For example, both Card Sorting and LoFi assessments require nothing more than pen and paper. The most expensive resource in such circumstances is the time needed to host the sessions. However, more sophisticated techniques require additional expenditure. Indeed, some large organisations choose to invest in specialised usability labs explicitly for this purpose.

A usability lab is a room that comes equipped with all the facilities needed to carry out comprehensive usability testing. This normally includes several internet user agents, a video camera (to record user experiences) and observation points where design staff can watch tests without interfering in them.

Usability software from firms such as TechSmith® (from $200) can assist the monitoring of such tests. Programs of this type track mouse movements on-screen via video. This allows user actions and expressions to be evaluated together. It also means that sessions can be recorded and played back at any time.

For organisations where usability is a key aspect of success, e.g. an online bank, a lab like this represents a sensible investment.

Web Accessibility Test

The evaluation of a website for accessibility is relevant only if this feature was stipulated as a Deliverable at the site planning stage. However, given everything that we have learned about Web Standards, the law and the benefits of accessibility, this should be treated as given.

The purpose of an Accessibility Test is to evaluate the compliance of a site to established standards. These standards may be expressed in law (as in the UK and USA), or refer to international guidelines like those of the WAI. The actual task of evaluation is carried out by Developers, though there are significant advantages to employing specialist evaluation firms for this work.

Specialist Accessibility Assistance

For example, as we saw on page 201, WCAG 1.0 is self-accrediting. That is, you decide for yourself if your site is compliant or not. Needless to say, this can lead to the temptation to award compliance even if some issues have been missed. Similarly, the methodologies by which accessibility is assessed are constantly evolving. Only experts in the field can know which are acceptable to the disabled community. Finally, some aspects of evaluation require specialist tools to be implemented effectively. A dedicated service provider is much more likely to have such resources at hand.

Although the cost of hiring an accessibility specialist may be prohibitive, independent confirmation can be taken as proof that your organisation is serious about supporting users with disabilities[93]. This in itself may be useful as a marketing tool.

Accessibility Review Process

However, even if the work of evaluation is implemented externally, it is still worthwhile understanding the process to be followed. In this regard,

---

[93] The Irish utility company ESB validates compliance with WCAG 1.0 by employing an independent evaluator, http://www.esb.ie/main/home/accessibility.jsp

the recommendations of the WAI are particularly beneficial. While these are only intended to ensure adherence to the WCAG 1.0 standard, they are useful for a general review.

Step 1. Identify the standard with which the website aims to comply

For the WAI, this means compliance with WCAG 1.0 Level A, Level AA or Level AAA (though the standard might also be stipulated in law, as in Section 508 or the UK Disability Discrimination Act).

The specific criteria to be adhered to are available as a series of checkpoints that can be used by Developers when constructing a site. The checkpoints for WCAG 1.0 are available online at www.w3c.org/WAI.

Step 2. Identify the pages that will comply with the standard

Sometimes it is not feasible for an entire website to be compliant with an accessibility standard. For example, legacy content may be very expensive to convert. In this regard, the WAI allows sections to be excluded from compliance, as long as such exclusions are clearly notified to website visitors.

Step 3. Use an automatic evaluation tool to gauge compliance

Some of the most widely used accessibility evaluation tools include Bobby from Watchfire, Wave from WebAIM and A–prompt from the University of Toronto. In general, these work by trawling a site and assessing each page against the WAI standard. This includes text equivalents (alt tags) for images, the coding of data-tables and document declarations. Watchfire also includes aspects of Bobby technology in the Quality Assurance suites WebXM and WebQA. In addition, the web authoring packages, Dreamweaver from Adobe and Web Designer from Microsoft incorporate basic accessibility reporting tools. Some Content Management Systems can also be configured to check for compliance.

Step 4. Undertake a manual evaluation of website content

Several aspects of website accessibility are quite subjective, meaning that tools such as Bobby can incorrectly label good content as inaccessible. As such, a manual review is necessary before compliance can be finally certified.

A manual review requires the use of a user agent, such as a desktop web browser. The purpose of the review is to mimic the experience of a visitor with a disability. For example, older people find small text hard to read. Therefore, a simple check of accessibility is to establish if text can be increased in size.

For those with more profound impairments, e.g. blindness, a more thorough evaluation is required. In this case, the computer screen could be turned off and the mouse unplugged. The objective in this case is to establish if it is possible to navigate and read the website in the same way as someone with no vision. To assist this, it is also necessary to invest in a screen reader.

A **screen reader** is an assistive technology that allows people with visual impairments to browse the web. A screen reader works by dictating text on a web page aloud to visitors. JAWS by Freedom Scientific (www.freedomscientific.com) is a leader in this area.

When evaluating a website with a screen reader, the aim is to establish if it is possible to navigate and read the site by using aural clues and keyboard movements alone. This is because a person with blindness cannot use many of the tools or clues available to sighted persons, e.g. a mouse. Some of the items to be checked for include:

- Is information presented in a meaningful order when spoken, e.g. are headlines presented before body text?

- Is it possible to navigate and input details to a web form without recourse to a mouse?

- Are plain text descriptions provided for all images that are central to the understanding of content?

- Do suitable titles appear for hyperlinks that change the onscreen environment, e.g. that open a new window or application?

- Does the website still work when scripting is disabled in the browser? (This is because some screen readers cannot interpret Client-Side Scripting.)

Once any issues have been rectified, a final review of the site against the guidelines of the WCAG 1.0 can be completed. If all the requirements have been met, the site can be awarded compliance status and the appropriate logo displayed.

Of course, new content must also comply with this standard. As such, it is recommended that a complete website accessibility assessment be carried out at least every six months.

Security Test

A key threat to the ongoing development of the World Wide Web is concern about online security. An endless series of viruses and data infiltrations have caused significant disruption to the internet, as well as increased costs for development and hosting. This is because of the extra security equipment that is now necessary. Yet, the most serious consequence of all this activity is that it is undermining public confidence in the web.

As we saw earlier, trust is a key factor for determining the success or failure of an online venture. The same holds true at a global level — if the public do not trust the internet as a secure means of communication, they will not use it. This is particularly problematic for Transactional sites that depend on credit card payments. For example, one-third of consumers say they would increase their online spending if they felt more secure about privacy[94]. As such, safeguarding the notion of trust and maintaining good security need to be top priorities for any Development Team.

Although web security encompasses a wide variety of disciplines, the fundamentals that underlie it can be expressed in just three concepts. These are:

- Confidentiality

- Integrity

- Availability

A website that fails to uphold each of these not only threatens its own business, but also exposes customers to risk.

Confidentiality

Confidentiality is the idea that information should only be available to those who are authorised to use it. For example, visitors may be given permission to download information from a website, but not upload it. The most common means for controlling such access is a 'Firewall'.

A **Firewall** is a software program that regulates traffic between 'zones of trust' on a computer network. For example, the internet is considered a zone of 'zero trust' because of the many viruses and other security problems that originate from it. In contrast, the computer upon which a website resides is 'high trust' because it can be tightly managed by a Technical Support Team. A key aim of website security is to allow connections between both these zones while also minimising risk.

To achieve this, a Firewall can be configured to limit the type of traffic that is acceptable, e.g. uploading or downloading.

---

[94] Forrester Research "Online Privacy Concerns: More than Hype". March 2004.

Yet, there may be instances where it is desirable for access to be extended. For example, a bank may wish to grant customers the ability to manage their accounts online. The challenge in this instance is to open the Firewall, whilst also limiting entry to approved persons only. In most cases this can be facilitated by some form of 'access control'.

Access Control

Access control means restricting the right of entry to a network to a limited audience. For example, a website that contains valuable research may only allow people who have paid a subscription fee to see their information. The most common means of doing so is via a Username/Password combination.

A Username/Password works by requiring two matching pieces of information to be entered into a site. These can then be compared against a database record. If they agree, access is granted.

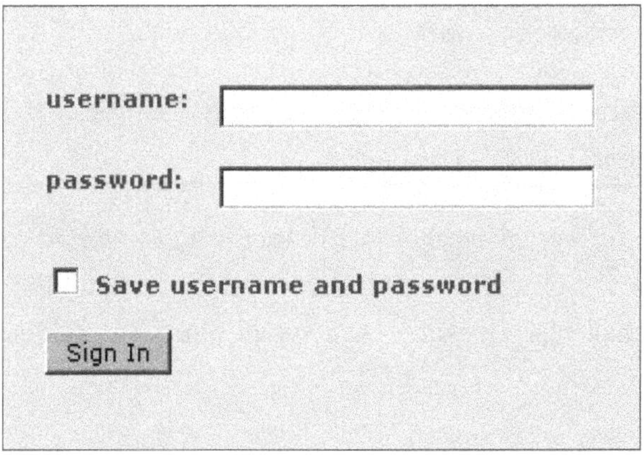

Figure 67. Access control on www.gartner.com

However, this simple combination may not always be enough. Criminals know that most people use terms like their children's names as passwords, and that more complex words are often written down as memory aids. Such carelessness is a leading cause of identity theft.

Identity Theft

Identity theft occurs where a criminal obtains data about an individual and attempts to pass themselves off as that person for fraudulent purposes. In 2005, 55 million Americans were exposed to identity theft[95].

While the eradication of identity theft is probably impossible, some simple rules can minimise its impact. For example, website users should not enter personal details into a site about which they have any doubts. Similarly, they can be advised to avoid passwords based on personal or family history, and not to share them with anyone. Other helpful guidelines include:

- Select passwords of at least eight characters.

- Include a mix of alphabetic, numeric, special (e.g. asterisk or hyphen) and uppercase characters.

- Select a word from a foreign language.

- Deliberately mis-spell the word.

A good password could be the German word **"zeitgeist"** (spirit of the age), rendered as **"seit-gei5T"**.

In some circumstances, further levels of authentication may be needed to protect customers' data. For example, a website may request a secret PIN number or pose a 'Challenge Question' (e.g. your mother's maiden name) before granting access.

Physical Authentication

In extreme cases, it may even be necessary to limit access to visitors who are equipped with a physical authentication device. These are now being

---

[95] USA Today "2005 worst year for breaches of security" http://www.usatoday.com/tech/news/computersecurity/2005-12-28-computer-security_x.htm December 2005. Accessed January 2006.

used to facilitate access to corporate extranet applications and banking systems.

An authentication device (such as those manufactured by RSA Security and Vasco [96]) is a piece of equipment that generates random PIN numbers. To access a secured site, a site visitor must use the currently displayed PIN together with their own username and password. Because the PIN is synchronised with the source website, it can easily be established if the number entered is valid or not.

Figure 68. Examples of RSA SecurID Token Cards.

Hackers and Crackers

Evaluating the resilience of access controls is a key procedure for testing site confidentiality. This is because many organisations will at some stage gain the attention of a Hacker or Cracker.

A **Hacker** is someone who wishes to break into a secure system, although they generally do not wish to undertake any type of illegal activity. In fact, Hackers may often be benign and simply seek to highlight inadequate security to website owners. That said, the phenomenon of Hacktivism can result in a site being penetrated in order to deface or vandalise it — perhaps for a political purpose.

A **Cracker**, on the other hand, has malicious intent and may attempt to steal or corrupt data.

---

[96] RSA Security, www.rsasecurity.com. Vasco, www.vasco.com

The Open Web Application Security Project is an organisation "dedicated to finding and fighting the causes of insecure software". In pursuit of this they maintain a list of the 'Top Ten Most Critical Web Application Security Vulnerabilities[97]' commonly exploited by Crackers. This list is compiled by a variety of security experts and represents a consensus on the most critical issues facing Developers. As of June 2006, these included:

- Unvalidated Inputs

- Broken Access Controls

- Broken Authentication and Session Management

- Cross Site Scripting (XSS) Flaws

- Buffer Overflows

- Injection Flaws

- Improper Error Handling

- Insecure Storage

- Denial of Service

- Insecure Configuration Management

Testing these vulnerabilities must form part of any security assessment. Additional tests for website confidentiality include ensuring authentication software is correctly configured and that all known loopholes are closed. Some firms go so far as to hire professional Hackers to conduct 'Penetration Tests' on their sites. These reports can be used as a means of tightening up access.

---

[97] The OWASP Foundation, "The Top Ten Most Critical Web Application Vulnerabilities." Copyright Open Web Application Security Project (OWASP) http://www.owasp.org/documentation/topten.html Accessed March 2006.

Specialist security review software is another useful tool for assessing possible vulnerabilities[98]. Packages like AppScan™ from Watchfire and Web Vulnerability Scanner from Acunetix can test for many of the issues on the OWASP list (where product cost is dependent on website scale).

Finally, the website of the Computer Emergency Response Team (CERT®) is an excellent resource for monitoring general internet security developments. CERT (www.cert.org) is a US government-funded institute that publishes advisories and incident reports about online threats.

Integrity

"Integrity" is a concept that seeks to prevent data being interfered with in an unexpected way, especially when being transferred over a network.

On a closed network, e.g. an email system within a university, the risk of unauthorised interference is low because all users are known to the Technical Support department. However, no such certainty is available on the internet. This means transferring details like credit card numbers over the web is inherently more risky. In such circumstances, the best way to manage the integrity of data is by way of encryption.

Encryption

Encryption is a system that uses mathematical algorithms to modify data so that it is unintelligible to anyone without a decryption key. Secure Sockets Layers (SSL) is the currently accepted standard for encrypting web transactions and can be used to protect data to a strength of 128 bits.

A bit is a unit of information, i.e. 0 or 1. As such, a 2-bit encryption key has four possible values: 00, 01, 10, and 11. As the number of bits

---

[98] For more visit, http://www.watchfire.com/securityzone/product/appscansix.aspx

increases, the amount of possible permutations grows exponentially. This means a 128 bit key has over **300 trillion trillion** combinations. If a Cracker attempted to decipher such a code, it could take years of work on the world's most powerful computers to find the right answer. Therefore, to all intents and purposes, SSL transactions are fully secure.

All the latest desktop browsers come preconfigured with 128 bit SSL capability. Such browsers also display various visual clues to help internet users find out if a page they are visiting is secure. For example, Microsoft Internet Explorer displays a 'padlock' symbol. The address of the web page also changes from 'http' to 'https' – the 's' indicates that the page is secure.

Figure 69. Close-up of Internet Explorer browser version 7 (Beta) showing address bar and 'padlock' symbol indicating a SSL secured webpage (from www.lulu.com).

Creating an SSL encrypted website is quite straightforward. All that is required is a certificate of identity and an encryption key from an approved vendor, for example Verisign or Thawte. SSL can then be enabled by the Technical Support Team.

Quantum Cryptography

While 128-bit encryption is adequate for current needs, the demand for even safer means of communication is growing all the time.

Developments in cryptography are advancing to the point that, in the near future, it may be impossible to decode certain exchanges. 'Quantum Cryptography' as it is termed, involves encoding information onto particles of light. The laws of physics ensure that if such data is interfered with, any attempted intrusion can be detected. Quantum cryptography may start to be introduced for video transmissions by 2007.

The most common test procedure for site Integrity, involves checking that all SSL certificates are up-to-date and that the host computer can handle secure transactions in the correct manner. This is especially critical for Transactional sites that rely on credit-card submissions for revenue.

Availability

The concept of availability requires information to be available to those who want it, when they want it, without interruption. For most sites this translates as a need for content to be up and running 100% of the time. Such high availability is particularly important for sites that engage in eCommerce. This is because online retailers are unable to collect revenue whenever a site is down. In this regard, one of the biggest threats to Transactional sites is the so-called Denial of Service (DoS) attack.

Denial of Service Attack

A DoS attack occurs when a site is bombarded with traffic from a malicious source. In such an event, the infrastructure of the website is unable to cope with such high levels of activity and effectively shuts down.

Unfortunately, these attacks are increasingly common simply because they are so easy to carry out. They have even been used as a means of extorting money[99]. For example, several online gambling firms have been threatened with a DoS attack if they did not pay blackmail to a criminal gang. For many sites, it proved cheaper to pay the money than to suffer the loss of revenue that would result from a security incident.

While such attacks are difficult to prevent, some basic screening can be carried out to block traffic from suspicious sources. However, even such fundamental measures can be ineffective because it is so difficult to distinguish between legitimate and criminal activity on the internet. The only fallback for most sites is to continuously monitor traffic and disconnect suspicious visitors before (or as) an attack occurs. To assist this, software known as an Intrusion Detection System (IDS) can be useful for screening visits and highlighting unusual goings-on, e.g. unexpected surges. Some well known IDS programs include Cisco Systems® Secure IDS and Top Layer IPS 5500 (licence cost is dependent on the scale of a website).

Of course, it should be realised that not every surge in traffic constitutes a DoS attack. It may simply be that many legitimate customers are visiting the website at once – perhaps as a result of a promotional campaign. As such, before taking any action, unusual instances should be checked to ensure that they really are a threat.

In general terms, the procedure for testing the availability of a site is to implement software for continuous monitoring. Options in this regard are explained below in the test process 'Performance Testing'.

Other Security Issues

Alongside such software issues, the security of website hardware should not be overlooked. The basic assessment procedure here is to ensure

---

[99] For example, BBC News Online "Online Service Foils Ransom Plot" http://news.bbc.co.uk/2/hi/technology/4579623.stm Accessed May 2005.

hardware is stored in a secure location—perhaps in a locked room to which only approved individuals have access. Many hosting companies provide such services, with the promise that their facilities are protected against destruction by vandalism, fire, flooding, etc.

However, if the worst does happen and a physical infrastructure is compromised, it is sensible for a standby solution to be in place. Some website hosting companies also provide this as part of their service.

(An organisation that manages its own infrastructure needs to have a similar set-up. Options in this regard are explored in Chapter Five—Website Infrastructure.)

Functional Test

Functional Testing is a process for evaluating whether a website can operate as expected under normal and error-inducing conditions. That is, does a site do what it is supposed to, even if a visitor makes a mistake when interacting with it?

For example, if the objective of a website is to allow people to book a hotel room, can such transactions be completed successfully? If errors occur, are they recoverable or is all information lost?

Everything else being equal, the only way to establish whether a site is functionally sound is to test each step of every application and record the outcome. Inevitably, this can be incredibly time consuming for a website that includes many features.

Fortunately, experienced Developers can write scripts that automate such tests. Furthermore, some Website Quality Assurance tools include the ability to record and run assessments, e.g. Web QA from Watchfire. Additional services are available in more advanced 'Performance

Management' software from companies like Keynote Systems, BMC Software and Mercury.

As well as testing if applications work correctly, it is also necessary to see how a site reacts when things go wrong. For example, if an online form to book a hotel room includes a field for credit card numbers, what happens if a user attempts to submit a wrongly formatted number? If the application has been well designed, the form should display an error message advising of the problem and indicating how it may be resolved.

HTTP Errors

Another common test is to consider the effect of a visitor entering an address for a page that does not exist, or to which they do not have authorised access. In such circumstances, a system generated error message should appear. The most common examples of such pages include:

"HTTP 404. Page Not Found"

This page appears where a user enters an address for a standard HTML page that does not exist. For example, if I am looking for
www.website.com/products.HTML
and I mistype it as
www.website.com/prodcts.HTML
I will receive a HTTP 404 message.

"HTTP 500. Internal Server Error"

This error appears where a user enters an address for a Server-Side Scripted page that does not exist. For example, if I am looking for
www.onlineshop.com/dvd-pricelist.php
and I mistype it as
www.onlineshop.com/dvd-priceleest.php
I will receive a HTTP 500 message.

"HTTP 403. Unauthorised Access"

This page appears where a user attempts to enter an address to which they do not have authorised access.

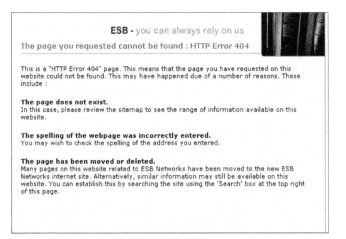

Figure 70. A customised HTTP 404 error message (from www.esb.ie).

Because these pages are automatically generated, the error messages they contain are usually not very helpful. As such, it is recommended that a series of customised messages be shown in their place. While the normal HTTP 404 page may merely state what has happened in a very general way, the customised page could include text that directs the visitor to a Search Engine or sitemap. It could also be wrapped within the site's design template.

Performance Test

The purpose of a Performance Test is to gauge the responsiveness of a website under normal and exceptional operating conditions. For example, on an average day a small website may receive a few hundred visitors. But what happens if a promotional campaign attracts thousands more? Will the Website Infrastructure be able to cope with the increase in load, or will it crash?

Performance Testing aims to establish the 'happy values' within which a site can operate. Many aspects of such testing can be accomplished by executing scripts that mimic real life scenarios. These include:

Load Testing

This is a test that mimics standard activity on a website and identifies the limits of acceptable performance. That is, based on an average number of visitors, do response times remain within acceptable limits?

Load testing can also consider contingencies in the event that activity on a website increases dramatically. For example, can additional processing power be made available if traffic increases over time? If not, users may experience a poor response which could damage the business. Typical recommendations for spare capacity range from 25% to 50% of average loads (bearing in mind that traffic peaks are often three times greater than average figures).

Stress Testing

As the name implies, Stress Testing pushes a website to the edge to establish how well it reacts in extreme circumstances. A test of this nature could be used to determine the maximum number of visitors a site can handle at any one time. It can also allow a Technical Support Team to plan how it would respond in circumstances where heavy traffic is received (perhaps by prioritising some traffic over others).

Endurance Testing

This test evaluates what happens in the event that heavy loads are sustained for long periods. Can the computer that hosts the site continue to deliver content effectively, as well as manage its own internal systems, e.g. memory caching? If not, what mechanisms are in place for reducing activity in a measured way, e.g. by deliberately cutting-off some visitors?

Spike Testing

Finally, Spike Testing can be used to establish what happens in the event of a sudden dramatic increase in activity that lasts only a few seconds. Will the website crash or can it be configured to process requests in an orderly manner?

The tasks of Performance Testing are carried out by a Technical Support Team, sometimes with the support of software from companies like Keynote Systems, BMC Software and Mercury Interactive (licence cost is dependent on website scale).

Website Standard Review

This review seeks to evaluate a site against the guidelines in a Website Standard. A Website Standard is a document that details an organisation's approach to every aspect of site management and construction (see page 298 for more).

The evaluation process involves comparing each item in the Standard against the site (in the manner of a checklist) and ticking them off as necessary. The main items to focus on are those that encompass development practices specific to the organisation itself.

For example, a Development Team may have its own preferences for the naming of files, linking to external websites and the use of pop-up windows. Because these rules can change from organisation to organisation, they need to be tested for prevailing circumstances.

Signing Off Successful Website Testing

Once all testing has been completed, the Team Leader is in a position to decide if the site can go live. Such a decision is essentially a judgement about whether she believes the site conforms to a minimum acceptable standard.

If it does, then there is no need to delay—the site can go live immediately.

However, most Website Testing will uncover at least a few problems that require attention. Of these, there may be a small number that cannot be resolved in time for an agreed date. The challenge for the Team Leader is to determine whether to launch the site as it is (complete with errors) or insist on a delay to allow remedial action.

Needless to say, any decision of this type is inherently thorny. For example, going live too early could result in bad press if some key applications do not work properly. Yet, delaying a launch could antagonise stakeholders who want the site to be made public.

Show Stoppers versus Nice to Change

To allow a Team Leader to arrive at a sensible conclusion, it is useful to categorise problems into one of four groups. These are:

- **Show stopper.** This indicates a problem that could seriously impede the integrity of the site, e.g. a security review finds that the Firewall is intermittently failing, leaving the site open to attack.

- **Highly disruptive.** An error of this kind implies that a core design or development requirement has not been satisfied. For example, a key application may have failed a Functionality Test.

- **Somewhat disruptive.** This category encompasses problems that are not considered overly serious. For example, a Discussion Forum that does not accept postings containing HTML.

- **Nice to Change.** Issues in this category typically include incidental suggestions that may improve the general performance of a site, e.g. marginal results from a series of usability tests.

By labelling problems according to the disruption they cause, these categories provide an objective means for assessing the impact on site quality. They can then be used by the Team Leader to arrive at a sensible decision. For example, problems classified as 'Show Stoppers' or as 'Highly Disruptive' usually mean the site cannot golive until a fix has been put in place. In such circumstances, a renegotiation of a launch date will be necessary.

In contrast, problems classified as 'Somewhat Disruptive' or as 'Nice to Change', indicate it is probably OK to release the site — even though some minor issues may arise.

Ongoing Assessment

Once the site is live, the Development Team Leader (in conjunction with the Maintenance Team) should set out a programme for continuous Operational Testing. A programme like this indicates when various activities of the Website Testing Catalogue need to be repeated. For example, the calendar might specify that 'Link Testing' should be reviewed each week (as seen in Chapter Two–Website Maintenance), whereas Accessibility Testing may only be needed twice a year. The benefit of such a schedule is that it ensures a site can continue to conform to the high standard achieved when first released.

Step 6
Website Hosting

The moment has finally arrived. All testing has been completed and any repairs to the website have been made. You are ready to go live!

Well, nearly.

Two final tasks remain. That is, to choose a suitable Domain Name for the site and select an infrastructure upon which to host it. Although these activities may be thought of as somewhat technical in nature, they are critical for achieving business goals. This is because getting a Domain Name is about more than just submitting a registration—it is a brand investment that is central to business identity. Similarly, the provision of good hosting is key for determining the levels of performance to be experienced by site visitors.

To help you arrive at a favourable outcome for both of these, an overview of the parameters to be considered is outlined below.

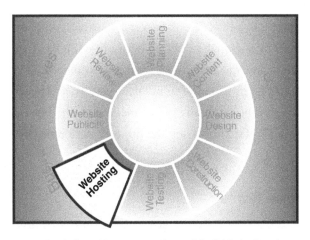

Figure 71. Website Hosting as a phase of the Website Development Cycle.

Domain Names

In Chapter Two (page 62) we saw how every device on the internet has a unique number called an IP address attached to it, e.g. 123.456.789.012. However, strings of numbers are difficult to remember, so a parallel system is also available. This allows addresses called 'Domain Names' to be created from alphabetical characters.

A Domain Name is simply a textual label that corresponds to a numerical IP address. In fact, either can be used when visiting a website. For example, to visit the BBC online you could use the Domain Name 'bbc.co.uk' or the IP address '212.58.224.88'[100]. A service called the Domain Name System (DNS) links them together. The DNS is simply a database that records the relationship between these two types of address and ensures that requests are always routed to the right location.

---

[100] A handy service for matching Domain Names and IP addresses is available at http://www.hcidata.co.uk/host2ip.htm

A small number of computers called 'Root Servers' (currently 13) are used to manage the DNS at a global level[101]. These are supported by numerous regional servers, and the amount of information they hold is quite staggering. For example, in 2005 the number of web IP addresses rose by 17.5 million to 74.3 million overall[102]. This made 2005 the busiest year ever for internet growth—far surpassing the dot.com period of 1999 and 2000.

The Format of Domain Names

Typically, Domain Names are expressed in the form 'NAME.SUFFIX', e.g. website.com. When prefixed by 'www', they may also be referred to as 'Web Addresses', e.g. www.website.com. In actual fact, many variations on the format of a web address are possible.

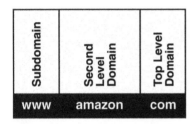

Figure 72. The three main elements of a domain name.

For example, the unusually named http://del.icio.us[103] is a perfect example of a site that has been named for special marketing purposes. This type of configuration is possible because a web address is composed of several different parts. These are:

- Subdomain

- Second Level Domain

---

[101] For a full list of Root Servers visit http://en.wikipedia.org/wiki/Root_nameserver
[102] Netcraft. July 2005 Webserver Survey.
   http://news.netcraft.com/archives/web_server_survey.html Accessed August 2005.
[103] Incidentally, the prefix 'http://' is not part of the address. It indicates the protocol that is used to transfer the information over the internet. Other protocols include 'https' & 'ftp'.

- Top Level Domain

Subdomain

The subdomain is the 'www' bit that prefixes the main part of a web address. 'www' indicates that an address is pointing to the World Wide Web. However, 'www' is merely a convention and there is no technical reason why it could not be different.

As we have seen, some organisations (like del.icio.us) change the subdomain for marketing reasons. Another might use it to identify content that is specific to a particular geographic region. For example, a subdomain called 'sverige' could correspond to Sweden (http://sverige.website.com).

Second Level Domain

A Second Level Domain forms the core of a web address and usually reflects the title of the business venture for which the site has been created. Although your imagination is free to run riot when dreaming up a Second Level Domain, several rules need to be applied.

For example, a Second Level Domain can only start with a number or a letter and cannot include any special characters other than a hyphen (-). Furthermore, it cannot be longer than 63 or shorter than 2 characters in length[104]. Although Multilingual Domain Naming in languages such as Japanese and Korean is possible, support for the standards that underlie this area are sparse as yet[105].

The registration of Second Level Domains is administered by a number of authorised organisations who also control the allocation of Top Level

---

[104] Note that the total permitted length of a web address, including the Subdomain, the Top Level Domain and the '.' separators is 255 characters.
[105] For more about multilingual domains go to footnote 115 and visit
http://www.w3.org/2000/Talks/0717-mldns/Overview.html

Domains, e.g. .com, .org. etc. (The registration process is explained in more detail below.)

Top Level Domain

The Top Level Domain is the final part of a web address and is literally meant to reflect the 'domain' or realm of activity within which a site operates. For example, the domain '.edu' is supposed to be used by educational institutions only. Other well established Top Level Domains include:

- **.com**: This was initially intended for commercial businesses but may now be used for almost anything. The .com domain represents 47% of all globally registered Domain Names[106].

- **.org**: This is intended for the use of non-commercial organisations, e.g. the web address for the United Nations is www.unitednations.org

- **.net**: This was originally intended for organisations such as Internet Service Providers (ISP)

- **.mil**: This is for the use of the military, e.g. the web address for the United States defence department is www.defenselink.mil

- **.gov**: This is for the use of government websites, e.g. the web address for the United States government is www.firstgov.gov

The creation of Top Level and Second Level Domains is controlled by ICANN (Internet Corporation for Assigned Names and Numbers— www.icann.org). ICANN manages the distribution of Domains to ensure

---

[106] Verisign. Domain Name Industry Brief.
http://www.verisign.com/Resources/Naming_Services_Resources/Domain_Name_Ind ustry_Brief/page_002553.html Accessed August 2005.

each web address is unique[107]. However, the allocation process itself is subcontracted to numerous licensed resellers.

New Top Level Domains

While traditional Top Level Domains continue to be very popular, a large number of other Domains have recently been created or are recommended for approval by ICANN. These are intended to reflect particular types of online activity or are planned for use by special interest groups. For example, some of the most up-to-date include:

- **.int**: This is for the use of international organisations, e.g. the web address for the European Union is europa.eu.int

- **.eu**: This is for the use of organisations or individuals based within the European Union.

- **.biz**: This is intended for business purposes only.

- **.info**: This is intended for any organisation that wants to publish informational content.

- **.museum**: This is for museums.

- **.name**: This is for Personal names.

- **.pro**: This is used for various professional organisations or individuals.

- **.coop**: This is for the use of genuine co-operative organisations.

- **.aero**: This is for the use of the aviation industry.

- **.jobs**: This is proposed for use in the recruitment industry.

---

[107] It is worth noting that as of March 2006, China has signalled its intention to create its own set of Top Level Domains, including Cantonese character versions of .china, .com and .net. This would have the effect of creating a completely separate internet outside the control of ICANN. This move is being driven partly by political reasons and partly by frustration with the predominantly English-language basis of the internet.

- **.travel**: This is proposed for use in the travel industry.

- **.post**: This is proposed for use in the postal industry.

- **.mobi**: This is proposed for use in the mobile phone industry.

- **.asia**: This is for the use of organisations in the Asian region.

- **.mail**: This is proposed for the creation of a spam free email zone.

- **.tel**: This is proposed to allow telecommunications companies to register telephone numbers as domain names.

Submissions for additional Top Level Domains are often made to ICANN, although it is by and large quite conservative in its approach.

Registering a Domain Name

Domain Name registrations can be processed by any one of a huge number of vendors, many of which also operate as Website Hosting companies. Indeed, it is recommended that all the registrations of an organisation be co-ordinated through just one supplier, preferably its chosen host. This makes the upkeep of names much easier.

In most circumstances, Domain Names are distributed on a "first come, first served" basis (excepting cases where there are mitigating factors, such as theft[108]). For a fee, registration can then be made for a period of between one and ten years, depending on the conditions laid down by ICANN. The typical price for a standard '.com' Domain is about $10 per year.

To submit a Domain application, simply visit a reseller's website and complete an online form. All that is usually required are some contact details, including a name and email address. These are then logged with

---

[108] A Domain Name Dispute Resolution Service is operated by the WIPO Arbitration and Mediation Centre in cases of disputed ownership http://arbiter.wipo.int/domains/

ICANN. (Before making a submission you may also wish to check that your desired name is still available by checking the ICANN website.)

Country Level Domains

The objectives of some organisations means their activities must remain confined to certain countries of operation. For example, a civil organisation supported by the government of Finland has jurisdiction within the territorial limits of that state only. As such, a generic Top Level Domain like '.com' or '.net' may not be appropriate.

To cater for this, an alternative system of 243 Top Level **Country Domains** is available alongside the standard Top Level Domains. In 2005, these represented 35% of all globally registered names.[109]

As well as governmental organisations, addresses of this type are also used by local firms and big multinationals. For example, a large part of the marketing effort of a global company like Unilever is segmented along national lines. This helps create the impression of allegiance to each individual territory. Although the main website for Unilever is www.unilever.com , the addresses for some local sites include:

- **Canada**: www.unilever.ca

- **Finland**: www.unilever.fi

- **Russia**: www.unilever.ru

Other sample Top Level Country Domains are[110]:

- **.de** for Germany

- **.lb** for Lebanon

---

[109] Verisign. Domain Name Industry Brief.
http://www.verisign.com/Resources/Naming_Services_Resources/Domain_Name_Ind ustry_Brief/page_002553.html Accessed August 2005.
[110] A full list may be found at http://www.uwhois.com/cgi/domains.cgi?User=NoAds

- **.ar** for Argentina

- **.us** for the United States

- **.za** for South Africa

The allocation of such Domains is not handled by ICANN but by local agencies, often appointed by government. Furthermore, the rules for allocation at this level tend to be stricter than for ICANN. For example, to purchase an '.ie' (Ireland) Domain, a registered business name or proof of identity must be provided.

Incidentally, the Pacific nation of Tuvalu was paid $50 million in 2001 to lease its Top Level Domain ".tv" for commercial purposes over the next 12 years. This was driven by the commercial value of this sequence of letters, as illustrated in its uptake by broadcasters such as the BBC, www.bbc.tv and CNN, www.cnn.tv.

Website Hosting

Website Hosting refers to the service that allows a site to be stored on and accessed from the internet using established protocols. For most organisations there are only two options in this regard: invest in a self-made infrastructure or find an external host.

While a small website with expert staff could probably undertake its own hosting, most customised infrastructures are created for busy Dynamic or Transactional sites. This is because these sites are driven by a desire to retain total control of everything they do. (Learn more about internal hosting in Chapter Five–Website Infrastructure.)

As such, the only realistic option for the vast majority of firms is to seek the support of an independent Website Hosting company.

Website Hosting Companies

As already mentioned, Website Hosting companies number in the thousands. Yet, even a cursory review will show that they are not all the same. Some offer excellent value in terms of disk space, but have very poor service. Others have highly knowledgeable staff, but are undermined by bad technology. How can you identify the company that is right for you?

In such circumstances, the best thing to do is shop around. This simply means that the offerings of each Host should be evaluated and compared against those of its peers.

To help you undertake such a review, the following guides for **Selecting a Service Plan** and **Selecting a Website Host** may be of use.

Selecting a Hosting Service Plan

The first thing that becomes clear when searching for a Website Host, is the sheer variety of services available. A multitude of deals are available from hundreds of firms — each of which are branded with a dazzling array of titles. However, a closer look reveals that many of these are quite similar and can typically be grouped into one of five types. These are:

Free Space Plan

Many Website Hosts offer free space. In fact, if you already access the internet via a telecoms company, chances are that you are entitled to free hosting. However, such packages are primarily intended for personal use and are not suitable for commercial purposes. For example, customer service tends to be of low quality and most accounts come with preset addresses that cannot be changed, e.g. businessname.webhost.com.

Basic Plan

Plans of this type are aimed at clubs, societies or small businesses that have a Basic (HTML/XHTML) site and expect low traffic volumes. The cost of such deals varies between $100–$200 per year, with a few email addresses and other services thrown in.

Business Plan

A Business Plan is one aimed at small to medium sized organisations that want to deploy a substantial Dynamic site, but do not intend to engage in activities like eCommerce. Such plans typically include the provision of Server-Side Scripting and database facilities, as well as unlimited email accounts. They generally cost around $250–$500 per year.

Enterprise Plan

An Enterprise Plan is suitable for a business that foresees significant use of its website and plans to roll out a wide range of technologies, including eCommerce. Hosting for Transactional sites of this nature generally starts at $600 per year, but can rise steeply depending on traffic and services deployed.

Dedicated Server Plan

Also known as 'colocation', a Dedicated Server Plan occurs where a business buys and installs its own hardware and software at a Website Host's facility. This provides many of the advantages of a customised infrastructure, whilst ensuring maintenance is handled by the service provider. Although the costs of colocation start quite low (at about $1,000 per annum), it can grow quickly if more technology is added.

Selecting a Website Host

Having identified the type of service that is required, the next step is to select the company with whom to do business. In simple terms, the best Website Host is the one that has the right infrastructure and expertise to meet your needs.

The following process can be used to identify suitable candidates:

Step 1. Collect References

Because of the huge number of Hosts in the market, it can sometimes be hard to decide where to begin. The easiest thing to do may be to approach your peers (e.g. via a trade organisation) and find out how they handle their own sites. The recommendations they provide could be used to create a list of suitable candidates. Alternatively, a review of appropriate literature may highlight alternatives. For example, many internet magazines conduct regular reviews of local Hosting companies.

Step 2. Initial Screening

The objective here is to narrow down the field of candidates to a manageable list. One way of doing so is to contact selected Hosts by email, outlining your requirements. Any company that fails to respond within a timely period can be eliminated. Such a failure indicates that their customer service culture is not satisfactory. Similarly, any Host that does not provide a response of adequate quality can also be dropped.

Step 3. Detailed Screening

Having selected a shortlist (perhaps three or four), they can then be invited to submit a tender. When writing the 'Invitation to Tender' document, as much detail as possible should be included to allow the candidates to recommend the service they believe best suits your needs. For example, information about the 'scale' of your site should be made available (the concept of Website Scale is explored in Chapter Two, page 14), including:

- The size of the website (in this case in Megabytes).

- Complexity, e.g. Basic, Dynamic or Transactional.

- The volumes of traffic expected, e.g. hundreds or hundreds of thousands per week?

- Any additional requirements, e.g. video, audio, etc.

Of course, the tender document should also ask detailed questions about the Host's infrastructure and service commitments. This can be used to assess the quality of their operation. Some important aspects include:

A. Site Hosting and Connectivity

A reliable and speedy connection to the internet is the principle requirement of a Website Host. Without this, visitors could experience difficulty accessing information, which may lead to lost business. Other essential elements include:

- What technology is utilised for web-hosting, both hardware and software?

- What percentage availability can be expected, e.g. 99.9%? (It is important to note any difference between scheduled and unscheduled downtime. The important figure is cumulative downtime.)

- Are scheduled downtimes kept to a minimum and will they inform you about these in advance?

- What degree of responsiveness can be expected? For example, if 1000 people access the site at once, will it slow down?

- What percentage reliability can be expected, i.e. how many failures per year are tolerated?

- In the event of a failure what backup is in place?

- Are there any limits on data transfers to or from the internet, i.e. the amount of data downloaded or uploaded to the site? (Note, a site with a lot of multimedia will need a higher quota of data transfer. This is usually expressed in Gigabytes per month.)

- What operational maintenance activity is undertaken, including back-up of site content and maintenance of log files for analysis?

- How is maintenance/publishing access to the website controlled?

- How scaleable is the infrastructure? Is it possible to ask for more servers in the event of a significant traffic increase?

B. Site Security

The Website Host must demonstrate they have appropriate security in place to safeguard the property and good name of your business.

- What virus control package and other measures do they operate?

- Does the host keep up to date with internet security issues and install all necessary patches on a regular basis?

- Where are servers physically located? Is the location secured against interference and/or theft?

- Following any incident, how is service restored and in what timeframe?

C. Customer Service

Can the host demonstrate that their service is easy to use and that knowledgeable responses can be expected?

- Is a control panel available for monitoring the website?

- How can issues about the website be logged, e.g. via email or telephone?

- What is the escalation procedure?

- What level of responsiveness to problems is provided?

- Are there refunds for falling below agreed service levels?

Evaluation and Decision

Having considered all these aspects, a decision can then be made. This step is mainly about balancing benefits and risks. The question to answer is "Can this company meet our organisation's needs, now and in the future". If the answer is 'yes', the decision has been made and final negotiations can begin.

Service Level Agreement

Although price will form a key part of such discussions, the conclusion of a Service Level Agreement (SLA) must also be given attention. An SLA is a contract that stipulates commitments about the quality of service a Host will provide.

In Chapter Two–Website Maintenance (page 74), we looked at some of the most important aspects to include in a website SLA. These were:

- **Availability**: At least 99.9% should be demanded as a minimum, though up to 100% is offered by many hosts. (Note: 0.1% equates to about 9 hours downtime per year.)

- **Reliability**: At a maximum, no more than 1 or 2 unplanned outages should occur per year, i.e. the site should not be falling over every day.

- **Responsiveness**: There should be no decline in the speed of the website below a certain agreed number of concurrent visitors, e.g. 1000.

Such an agreement may also identify means of redress in the event that stated levels of service are not achieved. For example, if the availability of a website falls below 99.9% in any month, the vendor may agree to refund the hosting charge for that period. This charge is justified because for each moment a site is unavailable, business cannot be conducted. In the event of a continuous failure to meet contract terms, a new hosting company may be needed. Ultimately, such a decision is the responsibility of a Website Management Team (see Chapter Four–Website Governance for more).

As soon as a contract has been concluded, the website can be loaded onto the Host's infrastructure. It is then ready to be offered to the world.

Now the real work begins.

Step 7
Website Publicity

"Build and they will come!"

Such has been the cry of many failed web developments. Indeed, it is a basic truth of the internet that your site is just one of several million vying for the attention of a selective and impatient audience. Standing out from the crowd needs more than just beautiful design — it requires the support of some serious publicity.

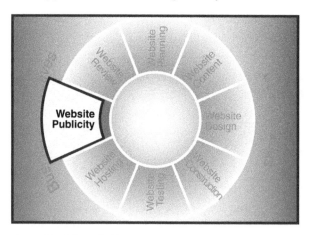

Figure 73. Website Publicity as a phase of the Website Development Cycle.

In this section we will learn about a number of promotional techniques — both online and offline — that can be used in this regard. To begin with we will explore a concept that defines how these may be combined to maximum effect. This is referred to as the 'Communications Mix'.

Communications Mix

The Communications Mix describes the way in which a promotional budget can be allocated among different media. For example, the Communications Mix for a common household product, like washing powder, could include:

- TV advertising: 60%

- Billboard advertising: 15%

- Magazine/journal advertising: 15%

- Other promotional techniques, e.g. free samples: 10%

In this example we see a heavy reliance on mass marketing channels. In contrast, the mix for a more specialised product, e.g. a website, could be quite different:

- Online advertising: 45%

- Magazine/journal advertising: 30%

- Search Engine Optimisation services: 20%

- Other promotional techniques, e.g. email newsletter: 5%

That said, there is no magic solution for creating the right mix for a website. The type of media to be deployed depends both on the availability of finance and, particularly, on the audience being targeted. In this sense, the use of Personas can prove helpful for arriving at a good solution.

Personas

Earlier in this chapter we saw how a Persona named "Sally" could be used to identify content that is suitable for a website about Global Warming. The same Persona can be leveraged to develop a promotional campaign aimed at attracting people to this site. To do so, two questions must be answered:

- What marketing messages are likely to attract Sally to the site?

- What channels are most effective for communicating these messages to her?

The task is to ensure that the desired messages connect with the target audience, through an appropriate mix of channels.

"Sally is 25. She attends college where she is studying engineering. She is interested in the environment but has only a limited understanding of Global Warming. However, if made more aware of the issues, she would like to get involved somehow. Sally feels intimidated by the variety of ecological organisations and is not sure how to contribute."

Figure 74. "Sally", the Persona for a website about Global Warming.

As mentioned, the assortment of media that is chosen will be heavily constrained by the availability of finance. For example, TV advertising is so expensive that it is usually only an option for the very biggest of organisations, e.g. government.

Nevertheless, there remain many other cheap (and often free) means for publicising a website. Several of these can be extremely effective at attracting traffic and are heavily used by many sites. The most popular of these are explored below.

Online Publicity

Online Publicity encompasses promotional activity that occurs over the internet.

#1 Choose a short, easy to remember Domain Name

In the previous section, Website Hosting, we learned that the selection of a good Domain Name is essential for site branding. To improve the chances that the chosen name will stick in people's memory, the following guidelines should be referred to:

- Make the name as short as possible. However don't use abbreviations or hyphens unless the Domain is very long or unusually formed.

- Use natural words, i.e. do not use 'made up' words that can be easily misspelled.

- Register common misspellings of your Domain Name. For example, if the Domain 'Business.com' is chosen, also register 'Buisness.com' and point it to the same site.

- Register a sensible array of Top Level and Country Level Domains, e.g. .com, .net, .org, .de, .co.uk, etc.

Of course, many sites debunk these rules by choosing strange names that somehow embed themselves in the public consciousness, e.g. del.icio.us.

#2 Use email to inform customers about a website launch

This technique entails sending an email to all existing customers informing them of a website launch. While this can be very effective at attracting initial attention, care must be taken to avoid being perceived as a 'spammer'. Legislation in many countries stipulates severe penalties for those who send unsolicited electronic communications. As such, messages should only be sent to individuals who have 'opted-in', i.e. expressed an interest in being contacted in this way[111].

#3 Create reciprocal linking agreements

In many early websites it was common to find pages that contained long lists of arbitrary links. While such features are now less widespread, complementary linking remains a useful way to generate traffic. Agreement can normally be easily reached with non-competing sites to feature shared links in predetermined locations.

#4 Offer syndicated content to other websites

An excellent means for generating traffic is to offer free content to other websites. In return, a link can be inserted that points back to the original source. While this can easily be done using normal HTML, the advent of Really Simple Syndication (RSS) has hugely popularised this as a marketing technique.

Really Simple Syndication (RSS)

RSS is a means of publishing based on XML. As explained on page 176, XML is a language that can be used to describe any type of data. In this case it is used to describe information such as 'news headlines' or 'recent updates'. Because all items in the RSS file point back to the original content, whenever a link is clicked, the visitor is redirected to that site.

RSS can be plugged directly into a website as an extra content element, or viewed on its own using software called a News Reader. A News Reader operates like a browser and pulls together RSS files from all over the internet. This makes it is possible to see updates on many sites without having to visit any of them. RSS is now used extensively by large content

---

[111] The 'opt-out' method allows emails to be sent to anyone who has not indicated they do not want to receive marketing email. Countries differ as to which rule is in force.

publishers, for example the BBC, Reuters, CNN, etc. News readers are also being incorporated into many standard desktop browsers, e.g. Firefox and Internet Explorer.

Figure 75. Content the BBC News website that has been syndicated and reproduced on www.greenol.co.uk using RSS.

Web 2.0 and Mashups

While RSS is useful for distributing plain information, a new method for sharing interactive content between sites is emerging from the concepts of Web 2.0 (as discussed on page 186). Referred to as 'Mashups', syndication of this type is based on the circulation of Application Programming Interfaces (API).

An API is a protocol that allows requests to be made by one website against another, and for data to be exchanged between them. When APIs are shared in this way, completely new types of content can be created. Among the leaders in this area is Google Maps.

A good illustration of a mashup based on Google Maps can be seen on the real-estate website Housingmaps.com. Housingmaps uses a Google API to layer its own information about rental and sales properties directly onto an interactive map.

The benefit of this mashup to Housingmaps.com is that development costs can be kept very low. The advantage for the API provider is increased recognition of its brand and extra revenue (if a license fee is charged).

#5 Create a subscription based email newsletter

Email newsletters are a successful means for generating traffic. In fact, it is common experience that whenever a newsletter is published, readers often follow up by visiting the source website for further information.

Many professional systems are available to manage promotion of this type, including VerticalResponse.com and Newsweaver.ie. The functionality provided by such tools includes email management (bounced emails, html vs. text) and response measurement (open rates, click-thrus, unsubscribes, etc).

#6 Write clear and concise content

The production of clear and concise content helps Search Engines to identify the subject matter of a website. This makes them much more likely to direct traffic to it.

#7 Write metadata and keep it up to date

Good metadata increases the confidence of a Search Engine that a site is well managed and is therefore a good bet for traffic. (Go to page 205 for more about metadata.)

#8 Submit the website address to an internet directory

An internet directory is an edited list of websites that is sorted by category. The two most popular examples of this type are the Open Directory Project (www.dmoz.org) and Yahoo!, which both contain hundreds of thousands of sites.

A directory differs from a Search Engine in that it only lists websites that have been reviewed by an editor for quality and relevance. In contrast, a Search Engine crawls the entire World Wide Web looking for results.

To add a website to a directory, visit Yahoo! or DMOZ and click the link 'Submit a site' (usually displayed at the bottom of the page).

While it is possible to have a website listed in a directory for free, submissions may take many weeks or months to be processed. This can sometimes be short-cut by paying an upfront fee, which guarantees a listing in about seven days. Some companies also offer a service whereby website details can be entered into many directories (and Search Engines) at once, e.g. www.submit-it.com.

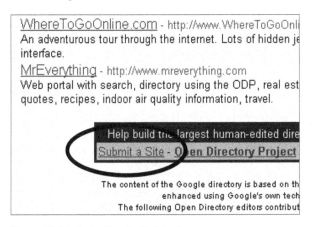

Figure 76. The 'submit a site' link in dmoz.org

#9 Use Search Engine Optimisation (SEO) services

Part dark-art, part science — an entire industry has emerged for ensuring links appear in the first page of results from a Search Engine. Some common SEO techniques include repeating key phrases and using both the singular and plural forms of a word in one page.

Websites like Google respond to such manoeuvres by constantly tweaking their algorithms to negate these effects. Google's logic is that

SEO manipulates search and does not always work in the interests of visitors. For example, many businesses (called 'black hats') use dishonest techniques to attract traffic to their sites. When found out, this can lead to a delisting[112]. As such, while SEO makes it possible to get a good listing on Google for a short time, guaranteeing this long-term is almost impossible.

#10 Pay for online advertising

After a serious collapse in revenues in 2001, online advertising has grown strongly in recent years. This has been driven in large part by the success of contextual advertising, as pioneered by Google AdWords™ and Yahoo! Web Ads (formerly Overture).

Contextual advertising is a technique for displaying ads that are directly related to the behaviour of online visitors. For example, a search for "printers" in Google will only display ads related to that topic. The logic is that such notices are not distracting, but add value because they point to useful resources. Advertisers also benefit because announcements of this type are only payable when a visitor actually clicks them. This makes contextual advertising a cost effective means of publicity.

Other traditional means of graphical online advertising such as banner ads, 'skyscrapers' and interstitials also remain in use. Flash animation and even Flash-video are now being used in such formats as well. However, research consistently shows that messages of this type are not very effective and are generally unpopular with visitors[113].

---

[112] As happened to BMW Germany in 2006.
http://news.bbc.co.uk/2/hi/technology/4685750.stm
[113] For example, read "The most hated advertising techniques", Useit.com
http://www.useit.com/alertbox/20041206.html

Offline Publicity

Offline publicity encompasses promotional activity that does not occur primarily over the internet.

#1 Include your web address on all company stationery and literature

This simple measure ensures the website name is always visible to potential customers.

#2 Invite the media to review a website

Following the launch of a website, relevant journals and magazines can be invited to review it. This is a useful means for gaining free publicity (provided the site is of sufficient quality!)

#3 Engage a public relations company for standard advertising

An advertising campaign could encompass TV, radio, newspapers and billboards. However, 'above the line' promotion like this is generally very expensive. Indeed, millions can be spent on flashy television campaigns and newspaper adverts with little discernible effect. Think of the vast sums expended on half-time advertising during the NFL Superbowl each year!

Nevertheless, there are many similar—though less expensive—means of advertising that can be leveraged in order to attract attention to a site. For example, given the right audience, a marketing campaign that combines subtle humour with a careful selection of communications channel (both online and offline) can generate tremendous interest, even on a small budget. This type of promotion is commonly referred to as Guerrilla Marketing.

Guerrilla Marketing

Guerrilla Marketing is a system of publicity that employs unconventional, low-cost tools to produce highly effective results. A subset of Guerrilla Marketing known as 'Viral Marketing' is one of the most popular techniques in this regard.

Viral Marketing was coined in 1997 to describe a 'word of mouth' or 'word of web' system of publicity. The critical feature of Viral Marketing is to make members of the public the unwitting salespersons for a featured product or service. The idea is that the recipient of a viral message is so entertained and compelled by it, that they will share it with their friends. These people react similarly and forward it on again. The cycle continues until a huge number of people have been exposed. Techniques like this have been successfully demonstrated in many campaigns, most famously by Hotmail.com and John West Salmon.

Hotmail® is the free online email service from Microsoft. The Viral Marketing technique used by Hotmail was to include the tag line "Get a free email address from Hotmail.com" in every mail generated by its system. Because this message was visible to all mail recipients, it generated significant return at no cost. As a result, the number of subscribers to Hotmail grew from zero to almost 12 million in the first 18 months after its launch. Incredibly, only $50,000 was ever spent on standard advertising, e.g. newspaper ads.

Similarly, a television advertisement for John West Tinned Salmon was leaked onto the internet in 2000. This humorous ad, which featured an angler wrestling a Grizzly Bear, caught the imagination of internet users. The video was subsequently emailed millions of times and did more to raise the profile of John West than any other campaign.

Since then, many companies have attempted to emulate the achievements of these campaigns with varying degrees of success.

However, it is difficult to 'manufacture' a winning viral campaign because audience tastes are so fickle. Nevertheless—in comparison with the small fortunes that can be spent on TV advertising—it remains an attractive option.

Intranet Publicity

Inevitably public-facing websites receive the vast majority of attention (and budget) when it comes to promotional activity. This is because the very existence of a business may depend on how well its site is recognised by customers.

Even so, many organisations maintain substantial intranets that contain a lot of important business content. Yet, it is frequently the case that the scope or utility of these sites is not well understood by staff, simply because they are not aware of the extent of services available. A program of Intranet Publicity may be necessary to counteract this. Such a campaign could be justified on the basis that it enhances Return-on-Investment in web technology.

While the full range of techniques described above may not be appropriate for intranet promotion, several ideas can be leveraged, including:

- **Posters.** Colourful and informative communications can be placed on staff noticeboards to highlight aspects of site functionality.

- **Staff newspaper.** Regular feature articles in a staff newsletter can be useful for promoting new applications or content.

- **Attended kiosks.** The intranet Maintenance Team Leader can perform informal training for staff by attending a kiosk in a staff area, e.g. a canteen. In this way staff can ask questions, learn about intranet content and provide useful feedback on design and construction.

- **Daily email**. If permitted, a daily email could alert staff to content that has been added or changed on the site.

And that is it! Your site is now live and being actively promoted to an audience who (hopefully) find it a useful and engaging resource.

Although you are entitled to a short period of celebration, the tasks of Website Maintenance (as explored in Chapter Two) come into play almost at once. These activities are essential for ensuring a site remains operationally sound and responsive to customers.

Yet, no matter how well these tasks are carried out, it is almost inevitable for a gap of some sort to eventually open up between the visitors' experience of a site and the Goals that were set for it. Although this is natural, it can become dangerous if allowed to develop for too long. As such, a regular system of site review is required to keep things on track.

The activities encompassed by this are explored in the next and final phase of the Development Cycle, **Website Review**.

Step 8
Website Review

In Chapter Two–Website Maintenance, we learned how the success of a site can be determined by comparing it against a series of Key Performance Indicators (Kpis). Kpis are the targets that have been selected by management for evaluating operations. For example, an important KPI for a website like Amazon.com (a Transactional eCommerce site) could be the value of weekly sales. Over the short term Kpis like this can be used to highlight the tactical changes that are needed to improve immediate business fortunes.

However, such measures say very little about the strategic accomplishments of a site. That is, they do not reveal if high level targets are being met. Because of this a different and more in-depth method of review is needed. The purpose is to establish if Website Goals are being achieved and, if not, what corrective action is needed.

The strategic nature of such an investigation means it is usually led by a Website Management Team (WMT). As outlined in Chapter Five, a WMT is the senior authority in charge of a site. It alone can decide how frequently to undertake this activity — though annually or semi-annually is usually enough. As regards the process of review itself, the first step is to gather evidence against which the Goals of the site can be assessed.

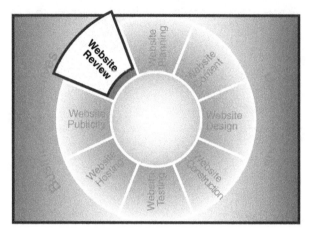

Figure 77. Website Review as a phase of the Website Development Cycle.

Review of Website Goals

In the first phase of the Development Cycle, Website Planning, we learned about some common Website Goals. For example:

- "Our website will generate at least $1,000,000 revenue by 2006 by selling more tickets for our airline to budget travellers."

- "Our extranet will reduce the workload on students at our university by 2 hours per week."

- "Our intranet will reduce HR administration costs by 15% for our European office."

We also discovered that such Goals must be SMART, that is Specific, Measurable, Achievable, Realistic and Timely.

Fortunately, Goals that have been formulated in this way include clear quantitative targets that aid the task of measurement, e.g. revenue earned, time saved, etc. In this way, they provide a dispassionate means for evaluating **Return on Investment** (ROI). For example, if it costs $250,000 to build and operate a website that generates an extra $1,000,000 in sales — ROI is 400%. Other metrics commonly assessed for ROI include:

- How many extra sales leads have been obtained via the website?

- Has the number of 'abandoned carts' decreased as a result of a redesign?

- By what amount have administration costs decreased as a result of allowing customer self-service via an extranet?

Evaluation of Visitor Feedback and Opinions

Other types of Goal are more difficult to judge. For example, a site that seeks to "increase awareness about Global Warming", might identify visitor numbers as a key performance measure. Yet, a busy website does not necessarily imply that the objective of 'awareness' has been achieved. For example, visitors may be coming to the site but finding it very difficult to understand.

In circumstances like this (i.e. where qualitative factors such as feelings, opinions and beliefs are important) primary research may be needed in order to evaluate success. For instance, a website about Global Warming may have to conduct a survey of users to see if they have a better awareness of the subject as a result of their visit.

Visitor opinions and feedback are particularly important during a review because of the influence they have on the Development Cycle. Unhappy customers could easily decide to ignore a website that offers a poor online experience. This would be disastrous for an organisation that wants to use the internet as a means of reducing cost or earning revenue.

SWOT Analysis of a Website

Where feedback is consistently unfavourable, it may indicate that a more formal site assessment is necessary. A valuable approach in this regard is to use a SWOT analysis. A SWOT analysis is an appraisal technique that relies on four categories to evaluate a business or website. These are:

- **Strengths**: What is the website good at, e.g. navigation design, infrastructure performance?

- **Weaknesses**: What should it be good at, but is not, e.g. responding to feedback monitoring, writing good content?

- **Opportunities**: What is happening outside the business that could prove beneficial to the website, e.g. growing broadband penetration?

- **Threats**: What is happening outside the business that could undermine the site, e.g. new security threats.

The most impartial means of applying a SWOT analysis is to contract an independent expert to conduct the review.

An **Expert Review** (as outlined in the section about Website Testing) evaluates the usability, content and other aspects of a site against a series of industry standards. If the results of this audit match the negative tone of visitor feedback, it strongly suggests that some rework is needed.

Among the aspects that could be included in such an audit are:

Design Evaluation

- **Information Architecture**: Does the site structure reflect the mental model of visitors?

- **Navigation System Design**: Do the systems in use support the tenets of knowing where I am, where I can go, where I came from and how to return?

- **Interaction/Interface Design**: Are interfaces intuitive and do they follow a logical sequence?

- **Information Design**: How well does the basic page layout reflect good design practice?

- **Look and Feel**: Are the values of the users and business reflected in the visual design?

- **Branding**: Are branding guidelines for identity/logo followed?

- **Graphics**: Are appropriate graphics being used, e.g. Pictorial Graphics, Information Graphics, Graphic Devices, Graphic Text?

- **Colour Palette**: Does colour match the palette stipulated in branding guidelines?

- **Colour Model**: Do the colours match the human colour-model? For example, grey suggests soberness, blue suggests efficiency, bright colours suggest fun, pastels suggest romance.

- **Highlighting Elements**: Does colour attract the eye to correct content, e.g. are bright colours (yellow, red) used for important messages?

- **Legibility/Readability**: Does colour allow sufficient contrast to allow legibility and enhance readability?

- **Quantity**: How many colours are used? More than four or five colours are too many.

- **Typeface**: Is the typeface chosen for plain text content legible at small sizes?

Content Evaluation

- **Appropriateness of Content**: Does content match expectations for subject matter?

- **Quantity of Content**: How much content is there?

- **Quality of Content**: Is the content authoritative, comprehensive and accurate? Has it been written according to web writing guidelines? Has it been edited?

- **Creative Content**: Is creative or surprising content used to make a more fun or enjoyable user experience, e.g. games or other?

Construction Evaluation

- **Web Standards**: Does the site adhere to Web Standards?

- **Technology**: What technologies are used, e.g. plain text, Flash, JavaScript, video, audio, other? Are they used appropriately?

Evaluation of Website Processes and Procedures

However, it would be a mistake to think that the only things that can go wrong on a website are design and content. Failure could also be due to inadequate management or supervision. For example, perhaps the Maintenance and Development Teams are being forced to work on a shoestring budget, which is having an effect on site quality.

As a result, an examination of management procedures can form another useful component of review. An assessment of this type could reveal areas of administration that require enhancement, including:

- An incomplete editorial process that results in substandard content.

- Inadequate testing that fails to identify functional errors.

- Insufficient change control mechanisms that cause conflict in maintenance schedules.

An improvement in each of these would considerably improve the ability of a site to achieve its Goals.

Assessment of Website Goals

Once all facts have been gathered, an assessment can be made about whether the website's Goals are being achieved.

If they are, congratulations!

If not, an investigation into the reasons for failure and the potential for corrective action is required. For example, the SWOT analysis could have found that environmental threats or other business changes have thrown the site off course. As a consequence, a reappraisal of the suitability of current Goals may be needed.

Environmental changes are those that occur at a global level and are beyond the influence of all but the biggest organisations. Changes of this type include things like new technology and the law. All that can really be done for such aspects is to monitor any trends and react to them. For example, the advent of new legislation may require increased spending on security. This reduces the ability of a site to achieve its Goals because less money is available for other developments, e.g. new content.

Similarly, the **dynamics of an organisation** can affect the ability of a site to perform well. If a business experiences a period of disruptive change (e.g. a takeover or merger) the original expectations for its site may no longer be relevant. In this event, the only option is to reformulate the website's Goals to reflect the new reality.

The Need for Ongoing Assessment

Even if a site's Goals are being achieved, it is still recommended that they be revisited on at least an annual basis. For instance, it could be found an organisation has been overly conservative and that more demanding targets can be set. Furthermore, the business may discover that the manner in which its site is being used is also evolving. This could mean that Goals need to be reshaped, to keep pace with changing visitor tastes and expectations.

For example, in Chapter Two we learned about Flickr.com and how it started life as a forum for online gamers. Overtime, the owners of this site found that visitors were beginning to use it mainly as a platform for sharing photographs. Following a review, they sensibly decided to update their Goals to take account of this shift in demand.

In this way, we see how a Website Review can drive and re-energise site development. For example, if Goals are modified in response to evolving business or user expectations, site content must also be updated. In turn, this prompts the need for planning, design, coding, testing, etc.

And so the Development Cycle begins to turn once more[114].

---

[114] For reasons of posterity, it is worthwhile saving a copy of a website onto optical disk before any radical change is undertaken. This is to ensure a history of online activity remains available. Several firms offer such archiving services, e.g. SiteImprove.com. A free web service is also operated at http://web.archive.org

Chapter 4
Website Governance

The Constitution. The President. The House of Representatives.

The Mission Statement. The Chairman. The Board of Directors.

The FA Rule Book. The Referee. The Linesmen.

It is difficult to think of any collection of people or type of activity that is not underpinned in some way by a system of governance. There seems to be a basic human condition that craves structures for the organisation and management of our collective affairs. The purpose of such structures is to provide the rules by which participants (citizens, employees, players) can conduct themselves, as well as a higher authority to which they can refer for guidance or redress.

Unfortunately, little thought is ever given to such ideas when it comes to the activities of Website Management. In fact, some firms seem to believe that the only governance they need is a part-time 'web guy' who will take care of everything.

Yet, an approach of this type can easily end in disaster. What usually happens is that the 'web guy' is forced to rely on the goodwill of colleagues in order to get things done, instead of on the authority of his own position. As a result, political forces come to dominate and website goals are ignored.

The Purpose of Website Governance

The purpose of Website Governance is to avoid this mess by putting structures in place for managing a site in a controlled and orderly way. The principal benefit of good Governance is that a clear set of rules and a strong central authority are created to direct all aspects of operations. This means team members can remain focussed on their tasks, instead of wasting time in political debates about what is or is not allowed.

Happily, the method by which Website Governance may be implemented is quite straightforward. It does not require a huge and unwieldy bureaucracy, just some plainly written guidelines and clear executive oversight. These can then be used by the Maintenance, Development and Technical Teams as a reference when planning their work.

Unfortunately, a good many websites (as well as many intranets and extranets) lack any such mechanism. The inevitable result is a blurring of goals and a significant degradation in overall performance. Sites like this can be recognised in a number of ways:

They typically exhibit wide disparities in design

With no-one to curb their creative enthusiasm, every manager thinks he is a designer. As such, a website can quickly become a mess of different styles. This is especially evident on intranets.

They display a lack of focus in content

The quality of governance on a site can be determined by a quick examination of its homepage. For example, the homepage of a site with good governance usually contains a small amount of highly focussed content. In contrast, a site with no system of oversight will be a mess of disparate information and applications. This betrays the internal rivalries that are being played out over the web.

They use 'bleeding-edge' technologies

Developers are often keen to experiment with new web authoring techniques. Indeed this is welcome as a means of exploring possible content options. However, the unfettered use of technology can spell disaster for site visitors. For example, 'cool' website features remain invisible to many users simply because they cause their computers to crash!

The essential problem on such sites is that no-one is appointed to oversee development at the highest of levels. Furthermore, no mechanisms are in place for ensuring standards are adhered to.

The purpose of this chapter is to help you avoid such a fate by explaining the fundamentals of good governance. As we will now see, the first step is to appoint a group with overall responsibility for site administration.

Website Management Team

A Website Management Team (WMT) is the senior authority in charge of a site. It is responsible both for setting a site's high level Goals (as seen in Chapter Three) and for ensuring they are achieved. The principle means it has for doing so are:

- By directing strategic development

- By organising and resourcing all teams

- By creating and policing adherence to standards

In truth, the only real requirement for the successful operation of a WMT is that it has confidence in its own authority. Yet, an assurance like this is only possible where the group has been established as the result of a senior management decision. A WMT that merely constitutes a collection of interested middle managers is unlikely to have much leverage, no matter how good their intentions.

In contrast, one that is appointed by (and is accountable to) a board-level Director is automatically invested with significant power. The higher up such an appointment is made, the better things are in terms of legitimacy.

The Composition of a WMT

The members of a WMT typically include stakeholders from departments for whom the website constitutes an important asset. For example, areas like Marketing/Communications are normally represented, as well as large functional areas with a significant presence, e.g. product divisions.

The delegates themselves are frequently senior department managers or nominees empowered to make decisions on their behalf. Representatives from the teams charged with the actual management of a site are also present, i.e. the Maintenance Team Leader, Development Team Leader and Technical Support Team Leader.

In summary, a typical WMT might reflect the following composition:

- A Chairperson

- Delegate from Marketing/Communications

- Delegates from other business lines/divisions

- Delegate from Website Maintenance Team

- Delegate from Website Development Team

- Delegate from Website Technical Support Team

The position of chairperson can be assumed by any of these individuals (perhaps on a rotating basis) or be vested in someone directly appointed to this role. This decision is normally taken by a senior executive.

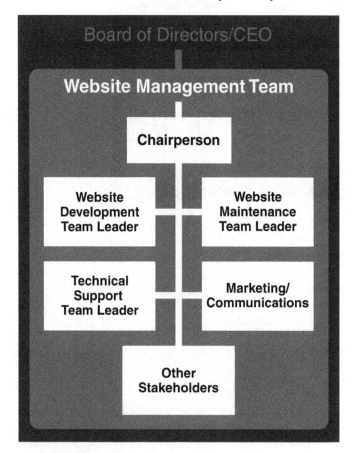

Figure 78. Website Management Team.

All the other teams involved in operations then report into the WMT via a Website Manager, i.e. a Maintenance or Development Team Leader who is also given an overall supervisory role.

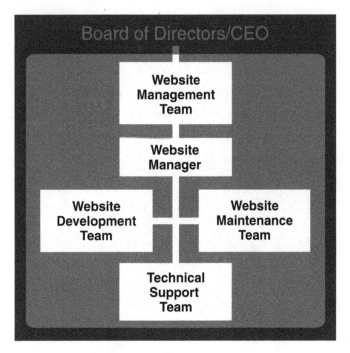

Figure 79. Overall website reporting structure.

Responsibilities of WMT

The principal concerns of a WMT are:

- Setting corporate web strategy

- Agreeing site Goals

- Monitoring overall performance

In this regard, delegates work with other team members to provide direction and enforce standards.

As a group, a WMT has little operational involvement in the sites for which it is responsible (although individual delegates often do). This is because such activities are best left to experts in the appropriate teams. However, the WMT may wish to get involved in decisions of a political or strategic nature, e.g. homepage changes, technology investments.

In order to exercise its responsibilities, a WMT is advised to meet on a regular basis. This could range from a frequency of about once a month for a busy Transactional website, to quarterly or semi-annually for a brochureware site. The purpose of these meetings is to review ongoing management and address any high-level issues that have arisen in Development, Maintenance or Infrastructure. A standard list of agenda items for such a meeting may include:

- General website review

- Development review

- Hosting review

- Resourcing review

- Governance review

General Website Review

A general review of site activity allows a WMT to monitor overall performance. For example, stakeholders may have identified a series of Key Performance Indicators (KPIs) by which they track success, e.g. traffic activity, revenue, etc. (The Maintenance Team Leader is normally responsible for the presentation of this data.)

Where KPIs fall short of expectations, it could prompt the WMT to allocate additional resources or reform procedures. Where necessary a review of site Goals may also be instigated. The purpose is to ensure that they continue to be relevant within environmental and organisational constraints (for more about this, go to page 278).

Website Development Review

It is common for a website to have several items progressing through the Development Cycle at any time. For example, an online quiz may be in planning mode, while a new Feedback Form is undergoing usability testing.

Within the terms of its responsibility for overseeing development, a WMT should be presented with an update on each of these and kept appraised of any issues. It must also have the opportunity to review and signoff on major changes before they go live, e.g. a new homepage. Where approval is needed between scheduled meetings, a single delegate (usually the chairperson) may be given signoff authority.

New Content Proposals

A Website Development Review also provides stakeholders with an opportunity to debate new proposals for site content. In fact, all ideas for new information or applications must be approved by a WMT before work commences. This is to ensure content remains in support of site Goals and to prevent costly 'solo-runs'.

In order to get a development approved, a proposal must be submitted and a collective decision made about whether it is suitable for the site (perhaps based on advice from the Editor). In cases where new technology or other significant changes are required, the guidance of industry experts may be required before a decision is made, e.g. first use of multimedia, adoption of eCommerce, etc.

Website Hosting Review

As seen in the last chapter (Website Development), hosting has many implications for a site—particularly the levels of performance to be experienced by visitors. In this regard, Website Performance encompasses measures for Availability, Reliability and Responsiveness. That is:

- Is the website available when customers want it?

- Is it fast enough?

- Is it reliable, i.e. what is the mean-time between failures?

Figures for these are probably stipulated in some form of Service Level Agreement and can be provided by the Technical Team Leader. Reviewing them allows a WMT to gauge how well the chosen solution is operating and whether it continues to be appropriate to business needs. Where such an analysis reveals a consistent inability to deliver on promises, the WMT may decide that a new host is necessary.

Website Resourcing Review

As discovered in Chapter Three–Website Development, not only must Website Goals be achievable, they must also be realistic. For example, it is no good demanding that feedback be responded to within 30 minutes if there is no-one available to do it! In this sense, a WMT must ensure sufficient resources are provided for all operational and development activities. As time progresses, it will become clear whether these are being achieved to the desired standard.

For example, when a site is first developed, a judgement may be made on the extent of people and time needed to support it. This is based on an estimate of its 'scale'. In Chapter Two–Website Maintenance we learned that scale is a means of classifying websites in terms of:

- Size

- Complexity

- Levels of activity

(Go to page 13 for more about website scale)

Website scale also provides a useful means for calculating the resources needed for support.

For example, if initial forecasts were overstated, too many resources might have been provided meaning cutbacks are necessary. Not surprisingly, a far more common scenario is that too little resource is available. In this case, an increase in investment is required to keep the site going.

While it is easy to blame a WMT for thinking its website can be managed on a shoe-string, it might be that budgeting is beyond their control. An organisation's senior executives usually have the final say on how much money is allocated to web development. In such circumstances, the only means a WMT has of influencing their decision is via an annual **Budget Submission**.

The purpose of a Budget Submission is to estimate costs for staff, technology and all the other resources required to support the Goals of a site. Many of these are explored in other chapters and include:

Website Maintenance

- **Salary Costs**: Editor, Content Contributors, Feedback Co-ordinators, etc.

- **Cost of Technology**: Web quality assurance tools, website content management, etc.

- **Other Costs**: Hiring specialist authors.

Website Development

- **Salary Costs**: Team Leader, Designers, Developers, etc

- **Cost of Technology**: Graphic design tools, site authoring tools, website testing lab, hosting charges, software licences, etc.

- **Other Costs**: Hiring accessibility consultants, etc.

Website Governance

- **Salary Costs**: These are minimal as most members of the Governance team are existing staff members.

- **Cost of Technology**: Little or no specialist technology is needed.

- **Other Costs**: Hiring business consultants, etc.

Website Infrastructure

- **Salary Costs**: Server management, database management, Security.

- **Cost of Technology**: Computer hardware (servers), software (Webservers, Application Servers), security monitoring software, etc.

- **Other Costs**: Hiring specialists on an as-needed basis.

Where senior executives fail to provide the necessary financial support, it must be made clear that the Goals of the site will be compromised as a result.

Website Governance Review

For most of the time, a WMT is focussed on the fulfilment of site Goals. However, it is also responsible for overseeing the execution of the activities of Governance itself and for policing issues as they arise. For example, a WMT must ensure all necessary structures, processes and procedures are in place to support site management. This includes hiring (and firing) staff, as well as acting as the 'court of final appeal' for operational disputes, e.g. allocation of resources.

As a consequence, a WMT must function as the guarantor for all the documentation, standards and procedures involved in site management. This type of endorsement is vitally important as a means for establishing preferred **Organisational Practices**.

Such practices encompass the conventions that have emerged as standard for site management within an organisation. Many examples of these are referred to in other chapters, including:

- Publishing Process (Maintenance)

- Feedback Procedure (Maintenance)

- Design Process (Development)

- Construction Parameters (Development)

- Testing Process (Development)

- Infrastructure Maintenance (Infrastructure)

As part of its role, a WMT can request that these practices be reviewed at regular intervals to ensure they continue to reflect industry standards and business requirements.

Among all the documents that may be endorsed in this way, there is one that stands out due to its overriding importance. This is the document that defines the strategic approach of an organisation to all aspects of site management — the Website Standard.

Website Standard

A Website Standard is a document that details the approach of an organisation to the management of its site. In some ways, a Website Standard is like a 'constitution', because it lists all the conventions by which activity is regulated. For example, such a document could include rules on things like:

- The coding languages to be used

- The security systems that must be implemented

- The file formats that can be used

- Preferred usability testing methods

- The screen dimensions the website must be designed for

- Etc.

Although it must be comprehensive, a good Website Standard should not set out in too fine a detail every aspect of operations. If it did, it would become unusably large and extremely difficult to maintain. Nevertheless, sufficient detail should be included so staff can rely on it as a practical support when carrying out their duties.

For example, imagine a Developer receives a request to build a new application in Adobe Flash. The first thing she would do is consult the Website Standard to establish if Flash is a permitted content format. If so, the document would tell her the parameters to be adhered to, including:

- The frame rate at which the file must be streamed.

- Whether sound is permitted.

- Whether it must be web accessible.

In this way, a Website Standard can act as a practical support for Designers and other staff when producing content.

Creating a Website Standard

As a cornerstone of site governance, the production of a Website Standard is the responsibility of a WMT. However, so many disciplines are encompassed within it that other teams must also be involved. This includes Website Maintenance, Development, Technical Support and Marketing/Communications.

Before these teams sit down to commence production, it must be emphasised that a Website Standard is not merely a list of aspirational rules. That is, it is not a 'discussion' document that can be ignored as desired. Rather, it must state in unambiguous terms exactly how a site **must** be managed with respect to the environmental and operational constraints of the business.

Indeed, a clear understanding of these constraints is vital before production can begin. This is because a Standard that is written in ignorance of the factors that influence site management could end up violating them — perhaps with serious consequences. As such, the first step for creating a successful Website Standard is to explore all such constraints in full.

The Constraints of Website Management

Website Management does not occur in a vacuum — but is influenced by a multitude of factors. At the highest level aspects like the law and technology play an important part, while closer to home, employee skills and budgeting are relevant. Taken together these define the limits within which Website Management can take place. They also constrain in a fundamental way the freedom of an organisation to experiment on the web.

For example, an entrepreneur who wants to develop an online dating service needs to be cognisant of the law. This is because her site will only succeed if it adheres to regulations for online privacy.

When creating a Website Standard, it is essential that the impact of such things be considered. This ensures the completed document will be as comprehensive and reliable as possible.

To aid analysis, factors that are relevant to Website Management can be grouped into a number of categories. These are:

- The Environment
- Established and Emerging Industry Practice
- Organisational Values
- Organisational Policies
- Organisational Goals and Resources

- Organisational Practice

- Website Infrastructure

The effect of these on the activities of Maintenance, Development, Infrastructure and Governance is explained below.

The Environment

'The Environment' is a term used to describe elements that shape Website Management at the highest of levels. As we will see, key drivers in this area are either set directly by government or indirectly as a result of high-level trends in society. What is interesting is that most such factors cannot be altered by any organisation alone — they are simply too big (though they may be open to influence if several firms act together, e.g. to lobby government).

Among the chief constraints on site management in this area are:

- The Law

- Politics

- Economy

- Society and Culture

- Technology

The Environment: Law

The law encompasses legislation, directives and court judgements that have the power to influence web activity. Of course, conditions in this area can differ from country to country and give rise to quite varied operating circumstances.

A famous illustration of this arose in 2000 when the US company Yahoo! was found guilty by a court in Paris of allowing the sale of Nazi material on its French site. Under local legislation the sale of such memorabilia is forbidden and a $15,000 fine was imposed for each day it continued to be available. This provided Yahoo! with a painful reminder of the need to be aware of all law relevant to its operations, particularly when operating across national boundaries[115].

Notwithstanding this, an array of common Website Management regulations has now emerged at a global level. By ensuring a site is in compliance with at least this core set of rules, a baseline of legality may be assured. These are:

- Privacy and Data Protection

- Criminal Damage

- Freedom of Expression

- Copyright

- Electronic Commerce

- Disability

- Official Languages

Privacy and Data Protection Legislation

Legislation of this type refers to the need to protect information about individuals and respect their privacy. Laws like this confer a special responsibility on organisations that process personal data, while also giving a right of access to individuals.

A common requirement is that data collected for one purpose should not be used for any other reason, without the consent of the person concerned. For example, an email address that is collected for an online newsletter should not be used as a sales opportunity.

---

[115] An interesting discussion of the issues raised by this case can be accessed on the BBC News website http://news.bbc.co.uk/2/hi/technology/4641244.stm

Many countries now offer vigorous protection to the public in this regard, with hefty fines for organisations that break the law. Complementary legislation also imposes substantial constraints on the use of unsolicited email or spam. The US state of Virginia has gone so far as to practically ban emailing where more than 10,000 recipients are involved[116]. Furthermore, the United States has enacted specific legislation to safeguard the privacy of children (Children's Online Privacy Protection Act, 2000), as they are considered a particularly vulnerable group.

Criminal Damage Legislation

Criminal damage in the context of the World Wide Web refers to the effect a visit to a website may have on a person's equipment. For example, it may happen that a site unknowingly hosts a virus in one of its downloadable files that causes irreparable damage to a visitor's computer. If a case of this type is proven, the website owners may be found liable for injury through neglect and be compelled to pay damages. If this were to happen to thousands of visitors, the potential costs are enormous.

This type of legislation also encompasses the instance of a website's infrastructure being cracked for the purpose of attacking another system. For example, a Cracker may invade a site and (unbeknownst to the owner) use it to launch a malicious assault on another organisation. This is referred to as a 'zombie' attack[117]. Despite the fact that consent was not given, a court may find that the cracked company was negligent by not having appropriate security in place to prevent it.

---

116 BBC News. "Virginia Books Anti-Spam Laws"
  http://news.bbc.co.uk/2/hi/americas/2988207.stm Accessed October 2005.
117 For example, BBC News "Zombie PCs target vulnerable sites"
  http://news.bbc.co.uk/2/hi/technology/4625304.stm Accessed January 2006.

Legislation Limiting Freedom of Expression

As seen in the Yahoo! case, many countries have prohibitions that limit the right to publish on the web. Though nations like the United States have a liberal attitude in this regard, other countries are more circumspect. Typical categories covered by such preclusions include adult entertainment (pornography) and political literature (hate politics).

In fact, some limits may be self imposed due to the difficulties posed by **libel and privacy laws** — particularly in the UK. For example, despite the fact that it may be legal in this country to publish a piece of content, it could result in a court case to claim damages. Even though the courts may eventually dismiss the claim, the fact that it has to be legally tested first means it is too expensive to pursue.

Nations with **strong religious traditions** or an **authoritarian regime** present a particular set of challenges. For example, countries like Saudi Arabia and China are known to completely block access to many websites because of the content they contain. China also requires domestic sites to register with its local communication authorities to ensure no subversive or illegal content is published. The dilemma for companies that operate within such territories is to remain in compliance with local law, even when it is distasteful. In recent times this has been a cause of embarrassment for several international firms. For example, Google and Yahoo! have been accused of an over willingness to bow to pressure from the authorities in Beijing and elsewhere[118].

Copyright Legislation

A state of copyright is established by the act of creating an original work. For example, anyone producing a new painting, video or book is protected by law the moment it is made. The essence of such law is to

---

[118] BBC news "Hi-tech firms censured over China"
http://news.bbc.co.uk/2/hi/technology/4541524.stm Accessed December 2005.

give the owner sole rights for distribution and to protect their work from unauthorised copying. Because of this, the freedom to reproduce original material is constrained to some degree in most countries.

In the United States the concept of 'fair use' allows excerpts from copyrighted material to be used for the purposes of commentary only. In this sense, a website may reproduce a short extract of text or video as part of a feature about it—but not in a way that makes it unclear who the owner is.

Such flexible rules do not exist everywhere. In the European Union the 2001 Copyright Directive imposed very tight restrictions on the use of original material. In part, this was prompted by the ease with which text, images, multimedia and code can be illegally reproduced on the web.

Indeed, the growth of online music and video piracy has led to a surge of enforcement in this area. Many influential movie studios have given their backing to the concept of **Digital Rights Management** (DRM) in order to limit how their assets are used. DRM is an umbrella term for any technology that restricts or prevents file copying. The main threat as the studios see it comes from Peer-to-Peer (P2P) file sharing networks, across which thousands of unlicensed reproductions are transferred daily.

P2P file sharing allows a user at one location to access another computer over the web and copy files from it—usually music or video. The popularity of this technology is so strong that in 2004 it accounted for over 60% of all internet traffic[119].

The famous Napster website was the original P2P network, though it was eventually shut down by court order. Furthermore, in June 2005 the US Supreme Court found that file sharing services are responsible for what

---

[119] Morgan Stanley "Global technology/Internet Trends"
http://www.morganstanley.com/institutional/techresearch/gsb112005.html Mary Meeker, November 2005. Accessed January 2006.

users do with their software, i.e. they are liable for supporting breach of copyright. This means that many other P2P networks such as Gnutella and Morpheus are likely to be driven off the web in short order.

In opposition to this trend of enforcement, one online initiative called Creative Commons is trying to find a more flexible way for sharing content.

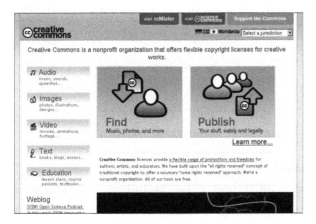

Figure 80. The website of Creative Commons.

Creative Commons (www.creativecommons.org) involves a system of voluntary licensing that allows authors to indicate whether they consent to their work being reproduced. Authors can stipulate several types of licence. For example, allowing the reproduction of images or text for non-commercial purposes. Despite the fact that this system has no strict basis in law, it is proving popular as a new way for sharing content on the web[120].

---

[120] A similar UK-only initiative has been commenced by BBC, Channel 4 and others for the distribution of audio-visual material within their archives. For more, visit http://creativearchive.bbc.co.uk/

Electronic Commerce Legislation

eCommerce is defined as the purchase of goods and services over the World Wide Web by means of a secure connection. As a well established part of the economic landscape, Business to Consumer (B2C) and Business to Business (B2B) eCommerce accounted for almost $2,575 billion worth of spending in 2004[121]. In a significant way such an intensity of activity is only possible because of the legislation that has been introduced to govern online transactions.

In the early days of the web it was found that the laws regulating contracts, advertising and other business functions were not flexible enough to cope with such a new technology. Inevitably, this had a detrimental effect on electronic trading because—without well established rules—many enterprises were unwilling to take the risk of going on the internet.

In response, a flurry of law reform took place in the mid to late 1990s. Some common types of legislation enacted during this period include:

- Agreements made via the internet are legally binding.

- Electronic signatures have the same standing as written signatures.

- Web transactions are liable for tax (in compliance with international agreements).

- Consumer rights are protected when purchasing goods online.

The purpose of these changes was to create an atmosphere of trust between consumers, retailers and government by allowing online

---

[121] IDC. International commerce marketing model, version 8.3.
http://www.libdirectory.idsc.gov.eg/cas/articles/commerce/commerce2.pdf
International Data Corporation. 2004. Accessed December 2005.

business to be conducted securely. As the rise in eCommerce clearly indicates, these laws have been mostly successful.

Disability Legislation

In previous chapters, we discovered how strong the concept of accessibility has become on the web. A key driver of this success has been the enactment of appropriate legislation. The most influential instrument in this regard is Section 508 of the United States Rehabilitation Act 1998.

Section 508 stipulates that all US government agencies must make electronic information accessible to everyone, regardless of disability. The most important consequence of this was that it shifted the onus of legal compliance onto Developers. So successful has Section 508 been, that it has served as a model for similar laws in many other countries.

In the United Kingdom, for example, from October 2004 the Disability Discrimination Act has required all businesses to make their websites accessible. Australia has also been quick to move in this area. Much of the impetus for this came from a case brought against the website for the Sydney Olympic Games. The site was found to be inaccessible and as such in violation of the Australian Disability Discrimination Act 1992. As a result, the Sydney Olympic Organising Committee were fined $20,000 and forced to implement an upgrade.

Language Legislation

In countries where more than one official language is recognised, legislation may create a duty to cater for all of them, e.g. Finland, Canada, Ireland. While this does not normally apply in the private sector, public or publicly-funded organisations usually have to comply.

The Environment: Politics

There is hardly a government in the world that does not have some form of policy about the World Wide Web. Most nations have long since recognised the opportunities provided by the internet and are eager to ensure their citizens realise its potential. Because of this, governments are investing millions in internet awareness programmes. Yet, a key problem that has yet to be overcome is the Digital Divide.

Digital Divide

The Digital Divide is a euphemism for the difficulty many marginalised socio-economic groups have when trying to access the web. These groups often lack the finance, training or other resources needed to go online. As such, they are in danger of being left behind.

A variety of initiatives to address this issue are now being introduced in many countries. For example, in 2005 the UK government announced a plan that involves schemes such as[122]:

- The rental of laptops and PCs to students.

- The expansion of training to help adult learners learn about the web.

- The encouragement of broadband take-up in poorer areas.

Other common measures include the provision of free internet access to schools and libraries, as well as focussed awareness programmes for marginalised communities. Is addition, some US cities (e.g. Philadelphia) are going so far as to provide wireless internet access as a free public service[123].

---

[122] BBC News "Digital divisions tackled head on"
http://news.bbc.co.uk/2/hi/technology/4401175.stm Accessed December 2005.
[123] BBC News "WiFi Cities spark hotspot debate"
http://news.bbc.co.uk/2/hi/technology/4351400.stm Accessed December 2005.

Figure 81. A model of the $100 laptop designed by MIT (www.laptop.org).

The creation of a **low cost user agent** is also being addressed by a number of developing nations. This is because the high price of computers makes going online in these places all but impossible. As such, research into the creation of a cheaper device is ongoing. For example, Massachusetts Institute of Technology has developed a laptop costing less than $100 that can be sold to poorer nations for distribution to the public[124].

The Environment: Economy

Mention the words 'economy' and the 'internet' in the same breath and most people think of the bubble years of the 1990s. While that period of inflated stock values is now long gone, the World Wide Web itself has never stopped growing. In fact, 2005 saw the biggest expansion in the number of computers used to host sites since the Web began back in 1989[125]. Furthermore, online retailing continues to boom as more and more people discover the convenience of buying goods or services online. Sectors such as travel, clothing and entertainment lead this field.

---

[124] MIT http://laptop.media.mit.edu/ Accessed November 2005.
[125] Netcraft. July 2005 Webserver Survey.
   http://news.netcraft.com/archives/web_server_survey.html

Yet, it must be remembered that all this activity also has a direct impact on the cost of site development. For example, although strong market growth is good overall, it has the knock-on effect of increasing salaries and making staff more expensive to hire.

The Environment: Technology

While it may seem obvious to mention technology as a constraint on Website Management, it is striking how frequently this area is overlooked. Indeed, many teams have grossly mistaken assumptions about the impact of technology on their work — particularly rates of change. Unfortunately, this can lead to a gradually worsening experience for site visitors.

For example, think of a website that was released in 2002 but has not been redeveloped since. This site would probably have been built using the special coding techniques of the time (refer to Chapter Three page 172 for more). Yet, many of these practices are going out of date as **Web Standards** and technologies like Web 2.0 gain in popularity. The result is that a site which relies on old techniques is in danger of being sidelined.

In addition, we have already seen how web access via **mobile devices** is increasing in popularity extremely quickly. For instance, it is estimated that 58% of the UK population will possess a mobile device with web capability by 2008[126]. It may even happen that mobile browsing will replace the desktop as the primary means of web access by the end of this decade.

In part, this change is being driven by the growing availability of **broadband**. 3G phones with connections speeds of up to 2 megabit/s are now available. These in turn are stimulating demand for richer content. By 2008, the business intelligence firm Gartner® estimates that ten

---

[126] BBC News Online http://news.bbc.co.uk/ July 2004.

percent of all mobile phone owners will use their handsets for downloading multimedia entertainment[127]. In reaction, video that is specially optimised for handheld devices is already being produced. For instance, Fox® has created 'mobisodes' of its popular thriller series "24" exclusively for smartphones[128].

What this means is that every website owner must have a strategy for ensuring they can keep pace with emerging technology.

The Environment: Society and Culture

While the effects of the 'internet revolution' may be overstated at times, there is no doubt that society in general has adapted well to the new technology. Web guru Jakob Neilsen estimates that there are now **one billion people online** globally, 24% of whom are in Europe, 23% in North America[129]. Additionally, the average amount of time spent on the web in the UK is expected to grow by up to 60% before 2008[130]. Needless to say, the significance of these developments is not being lost on the content providers who are preparing to take advantage of it.

Innovative methods for attracting new online audiences are already emerging in places like Japan and South Korea. In these countries, the adoption of broadband is already very high[131], which means new services can constantly be trialled. This includes linking website content with other media, e.g. television, and allowing audiences to interact in real-time. Services are also being developed that aim to attract groups which, to date, have not been frequent internet users. Retired people are particularly popular in this regard.

---

[127] Gartner. Predicts 2005: Mobile and Wireless Technology. October 2004.
[128] BBC News Online. "24 being made for mobile phones".
http://news.bbc.co.uk/2/hi/entertainment/4002035.stm Accessed October 2005.
[129] Useit.com "One billion internet users"
http://www.useit.com/alertbox/internet_growth.html Accessed December 2005.
[130] BBC News Online http://news.bbc.co.uk/ July 2004.
[131] For example, broadband penetration is over 70% in South Korea.

'Digital Natives' and 'Silver Surfers'

While the web may seem like a realm that is most natural for the young (so-called 'Digital Natives'), a large portion of new growth is being fed by senior citizens. Referred to as 'Silver Surfers', this group represents an attractive market because of their huge spending power and large amounts of free time[132].

Yet, in attempting to entice this audience online a whole new set of development challenges are being uncovered. For example, many older people have poor vision and reduced dexterity. This means Designers and Developers must create a different type of website – one that is more suited to this kind of visitor, e.g. by using larger text and bigger buttons.

Indeed, the challenge of creating sites that are easier to use goes beyond content itself. For example, many mobile devices are so small as to be practically unusable by older people. Yet these are increasingly popular as a means for accessing web content. Consequently, the improvement of such devices (and the sites that can be viewed on them) will need to occupy an increasing amount of Designers' time into the future.

Established and Emerging Industry Practice

Industry Practice may be defined as a set of conventions that are central to the activities of a community of interest. For example, the Web Industry (as a community of interest) has a well understood set of development principles and techniques. It is these that constitute industry practice for Website Management.

Although no central registrar of such practices exists, some of the most widely accepted as of 2006 include:

---

[132] For example, BBC News Online "Silver Surfers Say Net is Vital"
http://news.bbc.co.uk/2/hi/technology/4582831.stm Accessed May 2005.

- **XHTML 1.0** as a choice of MarkUp language.

- **CSS 2.1** as a choice of Presentation language.

- **WAI Web Content Accessibility Guidelines 1.0** as a means for evaluating website accessibility.

(You will note that this list that no mention of some areas of Website Construction, e.g. Server-Side Scripting. This is because—due to historical and market factors—no single standard has emerged as dominant.)

What is interesting is how many of these practices (such as XHTML) have been around for years but have only recently been adopted. It is almost as though any new industry practice must endure a lengthy period of gestation before acceptance.

A good example of this is the image format PNG (see page 129) which has been available since 1996 but is only now starting to be used[133]. While the lack of early adoption can be explained by a lack of familiarity among Designers and manufacturers, it also highlights how new conventions must be released years before being finally accepted.

Gartner Hype Cycle

Indeed, it has been observed by the business intelligence firm Gartner how many new practices and technologies seem to progress through a 'ski-jump' lifecycle before adoption. Referred to as a Hype Cycle™, it has five stages:

- **Technology Trigger**. This is when the new industry practice is launched.

---

[133] Read more about PNG in Chapter Three - Website Development.

- **Peak of Inflated Expectations.** In this stage, over-enthusiasm sees a new practice vaunted as a panacea for all ills, though they almost never achieve such high hopes.

- **Trough of Disillusionment.** When a new practice fails to meet lofty expectations it falls into a trough.

- **Slope of Enlightenment.** Following a period "out to graze" the new industry practice begins to emerge once more, but in a more measured way.

- **Plateau of Productivity.** In the final stage of the cycle, the practice becomes widely accepted.

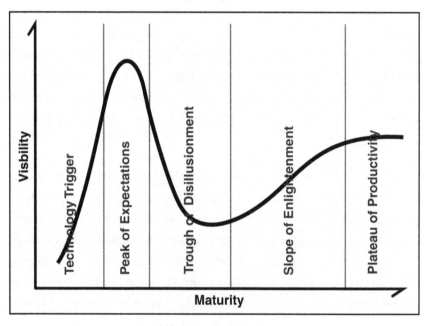

Figure 82. Gartner Hype Cycle (Copyright © Gartner).

Whenever a new web development is being planned, a business must understand where in the Hype Cycle all the industry practices it intends to adopt are located. For example, although the W3C releases new recommendations very frequently, does it make sense to begin adopting them immediately? What about aspects like design and usability where no co-ordinating bodies are available? Should a new navigation system be adopted just because one company has done so, e.g. folksonomy? (Turn to Chapter Three, page 209, for more about folksonomies.)

Experience suggests that it is safer to wait until a new practice has approached the 'Slope of Enlightenment' before planning for adoption. At this stage, it is well on its way to becoming generally accepted. Furthermore, the experience of early adopters is starting to become available in the form of advice and support.

Organisational Values

As discussed in Chapter Three–Website Development, organisational values are the set of attributes that define corporate personality. When applied to a website, they play a central role in the design process. For example, a business that lists 'fun' as a core value, may want a website that uses bright colours and imaginative imagery. In contrast, an organisation that sees 'tradition' as a central value, will want a far more sombre approach.

Yet, the influence of values goes beyond matters of Visual Design. It also has an important impact on other areas of site management. For example, an organisation that adopts 'trust' as a key value, implies that the emotional relationship it has with customers is of overriding concern. This means that safeguarding privacy must be paramount during development. As a result, a substantial investment in security equipment may be required as a means of maintaining this bond. The danger is that if customer data is ever compromised (due to inadequate protection), the impact on the organisation's image could be disastrous.

Other examples of how organisational values can affect Website Management include:

- **Accuracy**. Such a value would mean that nothing could be published on a website without being fully fact-checked. This could require a very comprehensive editorial process.

- **Reliability**. This could mean that a website should never be unavailable. This implies a robust (expensive) web hosting environment is required.

- **Progressive**. This value might imply early adoption of new technology and business processes.

As can be seen, a loyal adherence to values can create a series of (sometimes costly) obligations. However, this expenditure can be viewed as an investment in the reputation of an organisation—that it fulfils its promises.

Organisational Policies

Policies are the legal code of an organisation. That is, they are the rules by which it sets limits to the behaviour of the business and its staff. For example, a Security Policy could specify that online transactions must be protected with SSL encryption (for more about SSL go to page 237).

Yet the link between organisational policies and web activity is not always so explicit. For example, a Safety Policy may not seem to have much of an impact on web management, but it could influence publishing by blocking content that suggests unsafe work practices.

As such, organisational policies should be studied for any impact they might have on a Website Standard. Some of the most common areas to review include:

Security Policy

A Security Policy sets out the approach of an organisation to protecting the confidentiality, integrity and availability of its information and assets (as well as those of its customers). This can have a significant influence on all aspects of site management.

Privacy Policy

A Privacy Policy creates a series of rules for ensuring customer and staff information is handled in a sensitive and lawful manner. Guidelines in this area typically stipulate how data may be collected, how it is stored and for how long it may be held. Such a policy may also include procedures that describe how customers can exercise their right to access information about them. In this way, it can impose limits of the activities of site maintenance, particularly feedback and website traffic analysis.

Corporate Identity Policy

A policy of this type is often articulated in the form of an Identity Manual. An Identity Manual provides precise guidelines regarding the use of the logo and imagery of an organisation. This can have a profound impact on Website Development, especially design.

Ethics Policy

An Ethics Policy summarises at the highest possible level, the business practices that are acceptable to an organisation. While a policy of this type has no immediate effect on site operations, it does impose constraints on the behaviour of staff involved in Website Management. This could be important on a site with a blog or discussion board — so that competitive products are not made the object of ridicule.

Customer Care Policy

A policy of this type sets rules for the manner in which an organisation's relationship with customers is maintained. The policy itself might also be used as a marketing vehicle by being published in the form of a

'Customer Charter'. Such a charter could include a series of guarantees about service, e.g. the speed with which correspondence is responded to.

Safety Policy

As mentioned, a Safety Policy can influence site maintenance by ensuring no content is published that could be interpreted as supporting unsafe practices. A policy of this type is particularly important for intranets.

Equal Opportunity Policy

As with safety, an Equal Opportunity Policy aims to ensure no content that implies discrimination is published. Similar policies in this area include Sexual Discrimination and Bullying.

Organisational Structures and Goals

It is a fact that many sites operate on the basis of a very tight budget. Talk to any Website Maintenance or Development Team Leader and you are sure to hear complaints about a lack of staff or inadequate technology. The challenge these teams face is to achieve their Goals even in the face of such limits. But to have even the smallest chance of doing so, some basic structures must be in place to ensure resources are expended in a sensible way.

As we have seen, Website Goals are the targets by which the strategic performance of a site is measured. Although many businesses pay lip service to the idea of pursuing Goals, the structures and procedures needed to make it happen are nowhere to be found. For example, there may be no one with the authority to say what is or is not allowed. This means a lot of time and money is wasted arguing about and producing bad content. The result is an unfocused and fragmented site of the type we learned about at the beginning of this chapter.

In contrast, a team with a strong system of governance usually has a very tight grip on the purse strings. This means resources are allocated solely to developments shown to be in direct support of Goals. The net result is a site that is ultimately successful in achieving its potential.

Organisational Practice

As explained in Chapter Three, the Website Development Cycle encompasses all of the hands-on activities required to oversee the creation of a site. When undertaking such work, the staff involved may have a number of preferred techniques or conventions that they rely on. It is these that comprise the **Organisational Practices** to be reflected in a Website Standard (as opposed to the 'Industry Practices' discussed earlier).

Practices of this type are based on the skills of staff, company traditions and preferences for technology, e.g. Open Source versus Licensed Products. Some common areas that may be included are:

- **MarkUp**: Development may have to occur in HTML 4.01 because staff with skills in XHTML are not employed.

- **Testing**: The usability testing of new applications could be limited because the interface designer is only trained in certain techniques.

- **File naming**: The development tradition in the organisation may stipulate that all filenames be less than 8 characters long.

Rules of this type are given explicit reference in a Website Standard because of their significance to development activity. However, unlike Industry Practice, conventions of this type are more flexible and can change as new skills or techniques are introduced, e.g. by training or investment.

Organisational Website Infrastructure

The final set of constraints to be reflected in a Website Standard derive from the infrastructure that is used to host a site. Website Infrastructure encompasses all of the hardware, software and other technology needed for hosting. A variety of solutions are available in this regard and are described in Chapters Three and Five.

For example, a hosting service could be bought on the open market (from a dedicated Hosting Company, as in Chapter Three) or built in-house using staff skills (as examined in Chapter Five). It is the technology used within each solution that determines its effect on site management.

For instance, the systems used to operate a Basic website are so rudimentary that severe constraints are imposed on development. This is because such sites can only host static information—no interactivity is possible. In contrast, fully Dynamic or Transactional sites have far fewer restrictions and can provide a much wider range of content, e.g. discussion, eCommerce, etc.

Basic Website	Plain content (HTML/XHTML).
Dynamic Website	Content generated from a database.
Transactional Website	Fully transactional content, e.g. eCommerce.

Figure 83. The Three Levels of Website Complexity.

Indeed, the very brand of products chosen for an infrastructure can have an important impact on site activity. For example, if the hardware used to host a site is very powerful, it can cope with large volumes of traffic. Similarly, (as many Technical Teams know) some brands of software are inherently more stable that others, which means any site using them can be expected to be more reliable.

As such, it is important that information on infrastructure be reflected in a Website Standard, so staff understand the technical limits on development.

Writing a Website Standard

Having identified all the constraints on website management, the only remaining task is to express them as guidelines within a documented standard. One suggested approach is to group everything into categories based on the four elements of the Website Management Model, i.e. Maintenance, Development, Governance and Infrastructure. A document of this type allows staff to locate the guidelines they need merely by reference to the activity being undertaken. For example, a Developer who wants to identify rules for coding need only turn to the section entitled *'Website Construction'* within *'Development'* to locate the relevant entry.

However, a drawback of this approach is that some guidelines may need to be repeated in more than one place. For example, rules about *'Writing website content'* could sensibly be located within Website Development (under *'Content'*) or Website Maintenance (under *'Publishing'*). As a result, some form of compromise arrangement is probably required.

The best solution may simply be to place guidelines within the particular category that suits the business. For example, a company that publishes content very regularly could choose to place rules about *'Web Writing'* within *'Maintenance'*. In addition, a cross-reference could be placed in other relevant sections to advise readers about additional entries. For instance, a reference to *'Web Writing'* could be placed within *'Development'*. In this way, a cohesive document structure can begin to emerge, possibly reflecting the following:

Introduction

The purpose of the introduction is to explain the overall objective of the Website Standard. It could also include suggestions with regard to sections of the document that are appropriate for different audiences. For example, it might indicate that senior managers should be familiar with rules on Governance, while guidelines on Construction are most useful to Developers.

Section 1. Website Governance

This section outlines rules for the operation of the site at the highest of levels, as well as providing an outline of team structures and functions. It could also include an overview of the factors that influence and make such structures necessary, e.g. the law, company policies, technology, society, etc.

Section 2. Website Maintenance

The purpose of this section is to explain the rules to be followed for each of the six activities of maintenance:

- Publishing

- Quality Assurance

- Feedback Monitoring

- Performance Monitoring

- Infrastructure Monitoring

- Change Control

Section 3. Website Development

In many Standards, the Development section contains the bulk of all guidelines. The purpose here is to establish clear principles for ensuring production can occur in a predictable and high quality manner.

- Planning and Review

- Content

- Design

- Construction

- Testing

- Hosting

- Publicity

Section 4. Website Infrastructure

The final section of the Website Standard provides an overview of the main elements of hardware and software used within site hosting. From this, the Technical and Development Teams and can establish the scope they have for developing content.

Wording the Standard

As well as document structure, the type of language used within a Website Standard is also important. Although experienced Developers can usually be trusted to bend rules to good effect, there may be guidelines from which no deviation is tolerable, e.g. security or branding. Similarly, there may be aspects for which considerable latitude is permitted, e.g. imagery. A wording that encapsulates such a diversity of meaning is therefore necessary.

Definitions of the Internet Engineering Task Force

A useful way to achieve this is to use the set of definitions that have been developed by the Internet Engineering Task Force (IEFT)[134]. The IEFT is

---

[134] Internet Engineering Task Force. ' Key words for use in RFCs to Indicate Requirement Levels'. March 1997. http://www.ietf.org/rfc/rfc2119.txt. Accessed March 8th 2003. (Originally authored by Scott Bradner of Harvard University.)

"a large open international community of network designers, operators, vendors and researchers concerned with the evolution of the Internet architecture and the smooth operation of the Internet". In pursuit of its work, the IEFT has produced a number of precisely defined terms that indicate the stringency by which particular rules must be respected. Using these within a Website Standard ensures a high degree of confidence about how guidelines are interpreted. This helps to create the certainty that is necessary within any good system of governance.

These terms are:

- **Must.** This word indicates an absolute requirement that cannot be ignored.

- **Must Not.** This phrase indicates an absolute prohibition that cannot be ignored.

- **Should.** This word means that valid reasons may exist to ignore an item, but the full implications must be understood and carefully weighed before choosing a different course.

- **Should Not.** This phrase means that there may exist valid reasons when a particular behaviour is acceptable or even useful, but the full implications should be understood and the case carefully weighed before implementation.

- **May.** This word means that an item is truly optional.

The following examples demonstrate how such terms (classed as 'auxiliary verbs') could be used within a Website Standard:

Introduction

- "This Website Standard **must** be referred to by Developers before initiating a project or making a change of any kind to the intranet."

Section 1. Website Governance

- "The following legislation **must** be respected when making a change of any kind to the website: Data Protection Act, Criminal Damage Act, Electronic Commerce Act".

Section 2. Website Maintenance

- "The intranet **must** be checked for issues of Quality Assurance to ensure it is available and functioning correctly. This task **should** be applied weekly, but **must** be applied at least monthly".

- "Content **should** be limited to a maximum of 500–700 words per page."

- "All content **must** be free of spelling and grammar mistakes."

- "Financial information **must** be approved by appropriate parties before publishing."

- "Obscure references or quotations from literature **should not** be used in content."

Section 3. Website Development

- "The search text entry field **must** be placed in the top-right corner of the every page."

- "The names of labels **should be** as short as possible, while remaining self-explanatory."

- "Advanced search **may be** created if necessary."

Section 4. Website Infrastructure

- "The website hosting infrastructure **must** use Open Source software only."

Design Templates/Design Patterns

A final feature often included in a Website Standard is a set of graphic templates that reflect the Visual Design of a site. Templates like this allow Designers to see at a glance how new features must be created. For example, templates for the following pages may be included:

- The homepage

- A standard content page

- A featured content page

- A competition page

- A search results page

A variation on this approach called 'Design Patterns' has been advocated by the respected consulting firm User Interface Engineering[135]. In contrast to 'templates' (that describe specific pages), design patterns describe 'types of pages' or 'types of interaction'. These are useful because there might not be enough templates to cover all the design permutations that can arise on a site. For example, patterns may be created for such scenarios as:

- An online quiz

- Unsubscribing from a newsletter

- Logging into an application

Such patterns are a lot less prescriptive than templates and merely aim to highlight good design practice.

---

[135] UIE "Design Patterns – an evolutionary step to managing complex sites". August 2003.
http://www.uie.com/events/roadshow/articles/design_patterns/ Accessed Dec 2005.

Templates within Website Content Management

Both 'design templates' and 'design patterns' can be created as images in an editing tool like Adobe Photoshop, or alternatively as simple HTML. For organisations that use systems of Website Content Management (WCM), it is worth noting that such features are included by default. This is because WCM operates in a fundamental way on the basis of reproducible templates. (For more about WCM, go to page 34).

Such templates also allow Developers to experiment with new ideas in a risk free way. This is because WCM permits multiple copies of a site to be created on a hosting infrastructure. Copies of this type are called 'Preproduction' or 'Test' sites and are normally not visible to anyone except authorised personnel. The reasons why, are explained in the next and final chapter of this book, **Website Infrastructure.**

Chapter 5
Website Infrastructure

Vorsprung durch Technik[136].

The famous motto of the German automobile company, Audi, has succeeded in creating a strong expectation about the quality of vehicles they produce. As a result, customers trust them to use nothing but the very best of materials and equipment during assembly. Of course, this goes without saying—for as the old joke about German engineering asks, "Why make it from plastic, when cast iron will do?"

Yet, on another level this motto also acknowledges that success in an industry as technology dependent as manufacturing, relies fundamentally on having the right tools for the job. In a significant way, the same holds true for the systems that underlie the technical operations of a website.

For example, an organisation that promises 24-hour customer service via the internet must have a high performance infrastructure in place to

---

[136] Advantage through technology.

support it (i.e. powerful computers). If not, visitors could be denied access simply because the site cannot cope with large volumes of traffic. Over time, this would result in increasing frustration and eventually to a loss of business.

The purpose of Website Infrastructure is to ensure all the hardware, software and other systems needed for hosting are in place. 'Hosting' refers to the service that allows a website to be stored on and accessed from the internet using established protocols. As we learned in Chapter Three, there are just two options in this regard—invest in a self-made infrastructure or find an external host.

External versus Internal Hosting

External hosting is used by many organisations simply because they do not have the time, skills or money to build an infrastructure by themselves. Anyway, hosting is such a common business service that it can easily be bought on the open market. (Go to Chapter Three, page 256, to learn more about external hosting.)

However, this type of solution is not suitable for everybody.

For example, a busy Transactional site requires such careful attention that it is often easier to provide support in-house. Similarly, many organisations already maintain substantial IT infrastructures. The addition of another element to these (i.e. website hosting) is negligible in terms of overall impact.

Security is a final reason why some businesses choose to undertake hosting internally. For example, government agencies need to have an absolute assurance about the confidentiality, integrity and availability of their data. The only way to guarantee this is to retain maximum control over all aspects of site management, including infrastructure. For that reason, the safest (and possibly most economic) solution is to administer hosting internally.

In this chapter we will explore the elements from which Website Infrastructure is made. This includes a review of popular technology, as well as a rundown of the resources needed for support. Yet, it should be noted that this constitutes a very basic overview only. Any organisation that wishes to pursue this area in earnest is advised to seek additional professional advice.

As with so many other aspects of site management, the primary requirement for a successful web infrastructure is skilled staff. Therefore, to begin our exploration we will examine the duties of the people responsible for internal hosting — the Website Technical Support Team.

Website Technical Support Team

A Website Technical Support Team is the group of people responsible for creating and managing an organisation's web infrastructure. As we saw at the beginning of Chapter Two, the size of this team and the range of competencies on it depends on the scale of the site to be supported.

Basic Website	**Content**: Plain content (HTML/XHTML). **Staffing**: 1 person.
Dynamic Website	**Content**: Dynamically generated from a database. **Staffing**: 1 or 2 people (or more on a very large or busy site).
Transactional Website	**Content**: Fully transactional content. **Staffing**: From 1 or 2 people upwards (many more on a large or busy site).

Figure 84. The Three Levels of Website Complexity.

For example, the technical maintenance of a Basic website is so straightforward that it can frequently be handled by a single person. In contrast, Transactional sites require many more people, simply because of their complexity.

Notwithstanding these differences, the skills represented on such teams are generally the same, including:

Server Software Management

This encompasses everything needed to configure and maintain the software of site hosting. As we will see below, this consists of Webservers, Application Servers and Databases.

Server Hardware Management

Hardware management covers the diagnostic and repair work required to keep a site's computers and other equipment operating to a high standard. Tasks like this are sometimes carried out by engineers from the Original Equipment Manufacturer that supplied the kit (e.g. Dell, IBM, HP, etc.), on the basis of product warranty. Alternatively, they may be subcontracted to a specialist company as part of a general service agreement.

Information Systems Security

This concerns the maintenance of web security. An overview of these issues was provided in Chapter Three–Website Development, page 231.

At the head of the Technical Support Team is the individual with responsibility for the overall integrity of site infrastructure. The duties of this **Team Leader** include monitoring operational activity and representing the hosting function at meetings for site Maintenance and Development. In addition, one of her main obligations is to advise

Website Management about the effects of infrastructure on business goals.

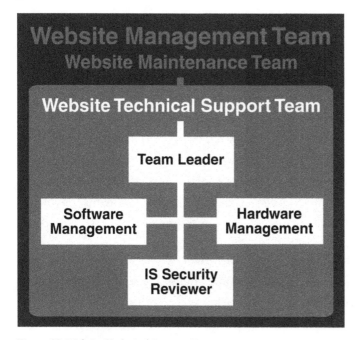

Figure 85. Website Technical Support Team.

Indeed, guidance like this is critical because of the high cost of such technology and its significance for ensuring targets can be met. In this sense, the most important advice a Team Leader can provide is a recommendation for Website Architecture.

Website Architecture

Website Architecture is the term used to describe the design of a hosting infrastructure. That is, it is a representation of how all the elements used within hosting can be structured and linked together. In fact, we have already become familiar with some of the main options in this regard.

In Chapter Two–Website Maintenance, we learned that there are three levels of site complexity, i.e. Basic, Dynamic and Transactional websites.

Each of these corresponds more-or-less to a distinct type of architecture. These are:

- Two Tier Architecture

- Three Tier Architecture

- N-Tier/Multi-Tier Architecture

Although these do not represent a complete view of how an infrastructure may be designed, they are popular as a starting point. This is because the sites they represent can support a wide variety of information and applications—from plain text though to complex transactions. Essentially, each 'Tier' reflects an extra layer of sophistication that allows more content and functionality to be delivered.

The task for the Website Technical Team is to compare their own requirements against each template and choose the solution they believe is most appropriate.

Two Tier Architecture

A Two Tier Architecture is the most basic type of site infrastructure[137]. It simply consists of a Webserver connected (via a Firewall[138]) to an internet user agent, e.g. smartphone, desktop browser, etc.

'Webserver' (sometimes called a HTTP server) is the generic name given to the main software of site hosting. A Webserver allows a computer to host a site and make it available on the internet. Confusingly, the word 'server' can also be used to refer to the hardware upon which site content is placed. In many cases, determining the distinction between the two simply depends on the context within which the word is used. For the

---

[137] It should be clear from this description that a 'one tier architecture' for Website Infrastructure is not possible. A One-Tier Architecture only consists of an internet user agent which, on its own, is not good for much!

[138] A firewall is a software package that controls traffic accessing a site.

purposes of clarity therefore, we shall use 'server' to refer to hardware only.

In a Two-Tier architecture, the first tier comprises all the user agents that access a site. The Webserver constitutes the second tier. These may also be referred to as the Presentation (first tier) and Application Layers (second tier).

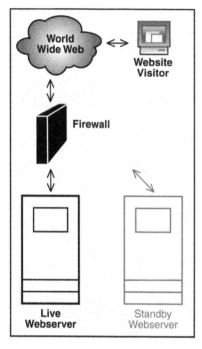

Two Tier Architectures are used to host Basic websites. As we know, sites like this are composed of plain HTML/XHTML, images, simple Client-Side Scripting and other static information. Video and audio may be included (though they occasionally require additional components).

Figure 86. (Left) Two Tier Architecture.

Although a Two-Tier architecture is simple in the sense that it can only host very basic information, this does not mean such websites are trivial. Indeed, many sites of this nature are large and busy, and provide significant value to the people who use them.

Think of the website of a transportation company that publishes online timetables for its services. Although this site may be written in plain HTML/XHTML, it could be visited by thousands of people each week. In this sense, it constitutes an important business resource and, as such, requires a high performance infrastructure to support it.

Website Performance

As we learned in Chapter Three, website performance can be measured in three ways:

- **Availability**: This is the percentage of time that a website is up and running.

- **Responsiveness**: This is the speed with which a website responds to traffic.

- **Reliability**: This equates to the number of unplanned outages, i.e. many outages = poor reliability.

The best way to ensure high performance is to invest in good technology. This means that a high spec server and other components must be purchased. We will learn more about these in the next section, entitled 'Selecting a Website Architecture'.

Server	A 'server' is the physical computer upon which a website is hosted.
Webserver	A 'Webserver' is the software program used to operate website hosting.
Application Server	An 'Application Server' is a software program used to run applications on busy transactional websites.

Figure 87. Some basic definitions for website infrastructure.

The Need for a Website Standby

But what happens if something goes wrong on a site that can only be fixed by going offline? For example, a Webserver might become infected with a virus or a server could develop a hardware flaw. If the only solution is to power-down the site, this could result in serious inconvenience for customers.

As a precaution, many organisations insist that their architecture contains at least two versions of the same infrastructure. For instance, the architecture of a Basic website (such as the transportation company above) would install two servers, two Webservers and two copies of all content. The logic is that if one infrastructure develops a problem, the other can take its place. This type of duplication is referred to as 'standby', 'contingency' or 'redundancy'.

While creating a standby may seem like a lot of expense to defend against the (hopefully) small possibility of acquiring a flaw, it remains an absolute necessity for many organisations. This is because the information on some sites is so critical that it must never be unavailable, e.g. a government website.

Some organisations go so far as to physically separate their standby and live sites. This ensures that if one infrastructure is destroyed (e.g. by flooding), the other can remain unaffected.

Three Tier Architecture

A Three Tier Architecture is an infrastructure design used for Dynamic and Transactional websites. We learned in Chapter Three that sites of this type are built to handle vast quantities of information and complex applications. For example, a site like this might be used for logging expense claims on an intranet.

The content on such a site is created by combining ordinary web pages with Server-Side Scripting and a database. It is these elements that result in the additional tiers of architecture seen in this model.

The first tier comprises the internet user agents (the Presentation Layer) that access the site, e.g. browser, PDA.

The second tier (or Application Layer) consists of a Webserver that has been configured to hold ordinary MarkUp and Server-Side Scripting, e.g. JSP, PHP, etc.

A Database forms the third tier of the architecture (also called the Data Layer). This is used to store the content that is manipulated by Server-Side Scripting.

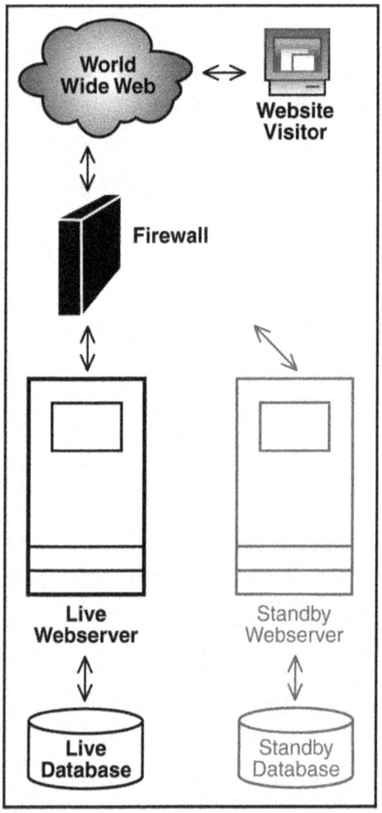

It is frequently the case that sites built on a Three-Tier Architecture are of great importance to the organisations concerned. For example, they might be used to support critical business functions or be a means of generating revenue. By necessity, this means high performance technology is needed to sustain them.

Figure 88. (Left) Three Tier Architecture.

A complicating factor when building a Three Tier Architecture is that of security. Unfortunately Server-Side Scripting has a number of inherent weaknesses that are often exploited by Crackers. As a result, sophisticated preventative security measures are usually needed, including a Firewall, strong anti-virus software and Intrusion Detection System.

(Learn more about these in Chapter Three–Website Development, page 231.)

N-Tier Architecture

Although conceptually similar to a Three-Tier Architecture, the N-Tier (or Multi-Tier) design is used by sites that contain very large numbers of applications, or that require many servers to power their operations. For example, websites like Yahoo! or Google operate on the basis of an N-Tier architecture because of the huge range of services they provide. The key difference between a Three-Tier and an N-Tier architecture is that the latter relies heavily on what are called 'Application Servers'.

An **Application Server** is a program used to execute complex interactions on a Dynamic or Transactional website. In many ways an Application Server is similar to a Webserver, in that it can host content. However, Application Servers are intended to handle dynamic features which is why they are used within an N-Tier Architecture.

It is worth noting that Application Servers almost always operate in conjunction with a Webserver. This is because the Webserver is the fundamental gateway through which requests for site content are received.

For example, when a visitor clicks a link on a site, it doesn't matter if it points to static text or to a complex application—in the first instance it is always processed by a Webserver. Only then is it redirected to an Application Server. These redirects are handled by a filter (sometimes called a Common Gateway Interface or CGI) that recognises requests for interactive content. After this has occurred the Application Server processes any necessary Server-Side Scripting with the help of an 'engine' for the language being used. Fully formed content is then returned to the visitor's user agent.

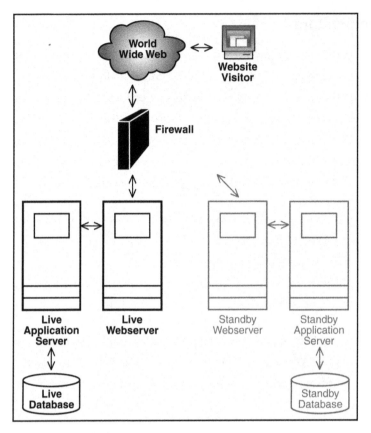

Figure 89. N-tier Architecture.

Selecting a Website Architecture

As we have seen, the main duty of a Technical Team Leader is to identify the architecture that is suitable for the site to be supported. However, very few Technical Teams have a completely free hand when it comes to selecting their preferred solution. This is because decisions of this nature must be framed within the constraints of the organisation for which they work. For example, staff skills may place limits on the type of architecture that can be deployed, while finance may restrict the components that can be purchased.

The challenge for the Team Leader is to balance all of these and still recommend a solution that allows Goals to be achieved. Thankfully, the factors that have most influence on the form of Website Architecture are few in number. By examining these, it is possible to arrive at an answer that is suitable for the organisation in question.

These factors are:

- The nature of website content

- The required levels of website performance

- Volumes of data transferred across the internet

- Volumes of website content

- Security

- IS Policies

- The skills of technical staff

- Financial constraints

The Nature of Website Content

The most important constraint on the selection of website architecture is that of the content to be hosted. We already know that most content can be accommodated by one of three types of architecture. These are:

- Two-tier = Basic HTML content and images.

- Three-tier = Dynamic content with some minor interactivity (or a low traffic eCommerce site).

- N-tier = Transactional content o a busy eCommerce website.

Once a decision on the most appropriate architecture has been made, the next challenge is to identify the hardware and software products to be used within it. The problem is that there is such a huge range of packages to choose from, e.g. OpenSource Webservers, Licensed Application

Servers, etc. As such, before signing-off on a preferred architecture, the Technical Support Team must identify the precise products they wish to deploy within it.

Webserver

Since the advent of the web in the late 1980s, the Webserver has been the principle workhorse of site hosting. This is because a Webserver is the fundamental tool that allows content to be hosted on the internet. Thankfully, the long history of this technology means it is amongst the most established of all infrastructure components. For example, the Apache Open Source Webserver alone accounts for over 70% of all installations across the entire internet[139]. The advantage of Open Source is that acquisition costs are very small (though implementation and maintenance support must be contracted from a third party).

Some other models of Webserver include:

- Microsoft Windows Server® (IIS) (Licensed Product)

- Zeus® Webserver (Open Source)

- IBM Lotus® Domino (Licensed Product)

How to Choose a Product

Although the market for Webservers is relatively small, it would be wrong to think that selecting such a product is as simple as opting for the industry leader. For example, an organisation may have an IT strategy that expressly prohibits the use of Open Source. A company like this may prefer to pay for a licensed product (e.g. Microsoft IIS) because they know backup and warranty is available.

---

[139] May 2005 Webserver Survey.
http://news.netcraft.com/archives/web_server_survey.HTML Accessed May 2005.

Consequently, there are several factors that must be reviewed before a final selection can be made. The aim is to ensure a good fit between the chosen product and the needs of the organisation. Among the most important aspects to consider are:

- **Organisational Policies.** Will policies such as security affect the choice of Webserver?

- **The Skills of Staff.** What range of technologies is staff familiar with, e.g. Open Source versus Licensed?

- **Extensibility.** Are there additional components that can be added-on to the Webserver to create extra functionality?

- **Scalability.** Can extra capacity be added to cope with any increase in traffic?

- **Performance.** How good is each Webserver in comparison with its rival for availability, reliability and responsiveness?

- **Price.** Which products are most cost effective?

The outcome of this review will allow the Team Leader to identify the products that are most appropriate to her circumstances.

Application Server

As we have learned, an Application Server is a software program used to run applications within an N-Tier architecture. Application Servers are used on busy eCommerce sites because of their suitability for dealing with large and complex processes.

Being somewhat more youthful than Webservers, there are noticeably more options when choosing this component, including:

- IBM Websphere® (Licensed Product)

- Apache Tomcat™ (Open Source)

- BEA Weblogic® (Licensed Product)

- Sun Java System Application Server (Licensed Product)

Choosing a Product

Because of its similarly to a Webserver, the process for selecting an Application Server is the same:

- **Organisational Policies**. Will policies such as Security affect the choice of Application Server?

- **The Skills of Staff**. What range of technologies are staff familiar with, e.g. what Server-Side Scripting is known?

- **Extensibility**. Are there additional components that can be added-on to the Application Server to create extra functionality?

- **Scalability**. Can extra capacity be added to cope with any increase in traffic?

- **Performance**. How good is each Application Server in comparison with its rival for availability, reliability and responsiveness?

- **Price**. Which products are most cost effective?

Databases

From discussions in Chapter Three, we know that Databases are used by Dynamic and Transactional websites to hold large quantities of information. For example, a website like Amazon.com contains such vast volumes of content that it could not be managed in any other way. The great advantage of databases is – not only can they store huge volumes of information – they can also be manipulated by Server-Side Scripting. That is why the selection of this component is such a key investment decision.

Some of the main vendors of database technology include:

- MySQL (Open Source)

- Microsoft SQL Server (Licensed Product)

- Oracle (Licensed Product)

The selection of products for this area follows the same mechanism of evaluation as that of a Webserver or Application Server. That is:

- Organisational Policies

- The Skills of Staff

- Extensibility

- Scalability

- Performance

- Price

Required Level of Website Performance

The next most important factor for designing website architecture is that of performance. As we know, Website Performance is a measure of the ability of a site to operate within expected limits. The core metrics here include:

- Availability

- Responsiveness

- Reliability

Fundamentally, the management of site performance is a balancing act. On one side is hardware and software. On the other is website traffic. The challenge for the Technical Team is to maintain a high level of performance, even as a site gets busier.

For example, a Transactional site might be able to operate very well with 1,000 visitors an hour. But what if 5,000 or 10,000 turn up? Can the servers continue to provide good Availability, Reliability and Responsiveness?

In the real world, the website of a busy eCommerce site (e.g. the low fares airline Ryanair.com) needs an infrastructure that can deliver 100% Availability. This is so customers can purchase a seat at any time. The site must also be very Responsive and Reliable, so that bookings can be expedited quickly and continuously.

As can be imagined, such a demanding level of operation depends heavily on the quality of hardware installed. In this case, Ryanair would need many high-spec servers with ultra-fast processors in order to meet its requirement of satisfying 500,000 visitors per day[140]. Most such hardware components are now manufactured in units referred to as 'rack-mounts'.

Rack-Mount Hardware

A 'rack-mount' is a large metal cabinet into which separate computers can be inserted. The advantage of this design is that servers can be added quite easily by sliding them in and out of a cabinet. In this way, it is easy to 'scale up' a site in the event of increased demand (by adding extra servers). The entire cabinet is then stored in an environmentally controlled computer room to ensure optimal performance conditions, e.g. temperature and humidity. The construction of these racks also allows for easier maintenance because each server can be accessed without difficulty.

However, the hardware of Website Infrastructure need not always be so elaborate. For example, it is perfectly feasible to host a site using an ordinary desktop computer (with a Webserver installed). Most modern

---

[140] ComputerScope. "IT for Competitive Advantage". June 2006.

computers are more than powerful enough to cope with the demands of a Basic or a low-traffic Dynamic site.

'Hot Standby' versus 'Cold Standby'

Yet, no matter what the strength of the infrastructure installed, Murphy's Law determines that at some point something will go wrong. As we know, a website that aims for high performance must also have some form of standby in place.

For organisations whose revenue depends on web traffic (like Ryanair), this is critically important. Indeed, it is very likely that Ryanair keep a duplicate (or several duplicates) of their site running alongside the live infrastructure at all times, to be turned-on at a moment's notice if need be. A back-up of this type is referred to as a 'hot standby' – meaning it is already up and running and merely requires a change in network configuration to point traffic in its direction.

On the other hand, a 'cold-standby' is one that takes some time to get going. Such a server may need to be powered up and loaded with an archived copy of website content before it can accept traffic. A scenario like this is only appropriate for organisations for whom lengthy downtime is not a problem.

Load Balancing

An interesting development as regards standby, is the adoption by many organisations of software for 'load balancing'. The advantage of load balancing is that it allows a busy site to operate on both a live and standby infrastructure at the same time. Because each site can accept traffic, this has the advantage of utilising what would otherwise be a dormant resource. However, in the event that either infrastructure was to fail, the remaining machine is powerful enough to cope with all activity (albeit with a small hit on overall performance).

Mirror Site

Finally, another useful way for dealing with high levels of traffic is to create what is termed a website 'mirror'. A mirror is basically an exact replica of a given website, hosted at an alternative web address. Mirrors are sometimes used by high traffic sites in order to respond to visitor activity more effectively. For example, users who wish to download software from a site might be told they could get a better response on its mirror. This system is used as a matter of course on such websites as Tucows.com and Sourceforge.net.

Mirrors also have other uses, including the circumvention of censorship. For example, an article that may not be legally published in one jurisdiction, can be made available on a 'mirror' without any problem.

Volumes of Data Transferred across the Internet

By dictating the speed of its connection to the web, the volumes of data transferred by a site (uploading and downloading) has a strong influence on architecture.

Broadly speaking, the required speed of a site's link to the internet is a function of the content it holds and the volume of traffic generated. For example, a website that is home to lots of video (with large filesizes) and which receives high volumes of traffic (many uploads or downloads) will have a high rate of data transfer. This necessitates a fast connection to the internet 'backbone'.

The 'backbone' is the term used to describe the central spine that connects all the main parts of the internet together. While a quiet site could happily operate at a slow connection speed, a busy site needs something better. For example, many specialist Web Hosts maintain links of 10 Gigabits per second (gigabit/s)[141] or more (though they may host dozens of sites).

A busy Transactional site should consider a link of at least 100 Megabits per second (megabit/s) to facilitate comfortable browsing. Connections like this can be purchased from specialist telecoms providers who offer services within various bandwidth ranges. These allow transfers to occur within set limits, e.g. 100 Gigabytes of data per month to be transferred over a connection of 100 megabit/s. When these limits are broken, a higher price is charged.

As with hardware and software, a standby link to the backbone should be maintained in case something happens to the main connection, e.g. a cable being severed by roadworks.

Volumes of Website Content

Content volumes influence the form of site infrastructure simply because a website with lots of information requires lots of storage space. Fortunately, the cost of data storage is very low, e.g. a 200 Gigabyte hard drive can be bought for as little as $200. In this sense, content volumes do not represent a serious problem when creating an infrastructure.

Security

The security arrangements that are appropriate for a website can be established from a review of its requirements for confidentiality, integrity and availability (as explored in Chapter Three, page 231). This includes the sensitivity of data, the nature of online transactions and the need for access control.

---

[141] One Gigabit per second (1x 10^9bits) is about 18,500 times faster than a standard dialup modem, which has a speed of 56 Kilobits per second (56 x 10^3bits). This is not to be confused with a 'Gigabyte' which is a measure of information storage.

For example, a website that collects credit card details must be able to guarantee the integrity of all its transactions. It must also make certain of data confidentiality, perhaps by using a password-based system of access control.

In contrast, the only protection a Basic website may need is a Firewall to block Hackers or Crackers. As we saw in Chapter Three, a Firewall is a software package that controls traffic accessing a site. The purpose of a Firewall is to limit the flow of traffic between different 'zones of trust'.

'Zone of Trust'

The internet is considered a zone of 'zero trust' because of the range of threats that originate from it. As a result, access by internet visitors to an organisation's public website needs strict control. However, access from within an organisation to the same site can be much less stringent. This is because an internal network constitutes a zone of 'high trust'.

In many cases, the infrastructure of a website is located somewhere in the middle between a 'safe' internal network and the 'risky' internet. This happens in organisations where a site is connected both to a private internal network, as well as to the World Wide Web. In this case, access requires particular attention because—if internet traffic can connect to the website—in theory it could also connect to other servers on the company's network. The most effective safeguard against such a dramatic breach of security is a properly configured firewall.

Indeed, for sites like this, two Firewalls may be needed[142]—one on each side of the site. If this is done, a secure zone is created into which external traffic can gain access but is prevented from connecting to any other network devices. This is referred to as a DMZ or 'Demilitarised Zone'.

---

[142] In fact, a single properly configured Firewall can adopt this role. This is because multiple instances can be created for different purposes.

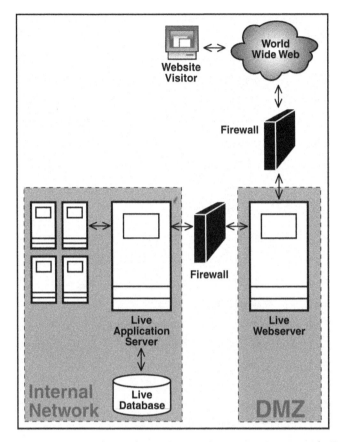

Figure 90. A Demilitarised Zone (DMZ). showing two instances of a Firewall.

Intrusion Detection

For websites that are particularly sensitive about security, an Intrusion Detection System (IDS) may be necessary. As explained in Chapter Three, IDS is software that detects unusual web activity, e.g. a change to content coming from an irregular source. Such an event could indicate that the site has been compromised by a Hacker. The IDS could then warn the Technical Support Team of this by way of an email, text or desktop alert.

Of course, other standard features of computer security such as anti-virus and anti-spyware programs must also be maintained.

Hardware Security

Finally, the security of website hardware also deserves attention. As mentioned previously, some organisations construct special computer rooms in which to locate their hosting technology. While such facilities are primarily built for reasons of performance (i.e. to ensure optimum temperature and humidity), they are also useful for restricting physical access. This helps prevent the theft or vandalism of valuable equipment.

Information Systems (IS) Policies

Many organisations enforce policies on the types of technology that may be deployed on their networks. This can have a strong influence on the form of site architecture. For example, an IS policy could stipulate that only Open Source software may be used. A clear cut strategy like this is helpful because it prevents an infrastructure becoming a jumble of different products and standards. This consistency also results in cheaper maintenance, because the variety of skills required by staff is less.

The Skills of Technical Staff

The skills of staff themselves can also influence the type of products ordered for an architecture. For example, a Technical Support Team may only have expertise in a limited range of technologies, e.g. Open Source. If other components are needed, additional personnel may have to be hired to fill the gap. If not, existing employees would need extra training to enhance their knowledge. However, both these options could quickly erode limited budget allocations.

As such, when creating a Website Architecture it makes sense to plan all aspects of technology first and then begin recruiting staff. This means the correct mix of skills can be chosen to match the preferred set-up.

Financial Constraints

Finally, a fundamental constraint on the design of Website Architecture is that of finance. Unfortunately, the cost of setting up a site infrastructure can be quite intimidating. For example, list prices for some commonly used components include[143]:

Software

- Webserver: Microsoft IIS version 6 standard edition = From $999.

- Application Server: IBM WebSphere Version 6 = From $4,000.

- Database: Microsoft SQL Server 2005 = From $5,999.

Hardware

- Rack mounted server: Dell PowerEdge Base = From $2,000.

These prices can easily be doubled if a standby infrastructure is needed. In addition, licensing costs on software may grow significantly depending on how it is deployed or how many people use it (if Open Source is not used).

Budget Submission

As we learned in the previous chapter, a Website Management Team (WMT) is responsible for acquiring the budget needed to support site operations. In this case their duty is to obtain enough money to ensure a functionally sound and secure infrastructure can be built and maintained. To do so, an estimate for all necessary components and services must be included in an annual budget submission. Some common items to be taken account of are:

---

[143] As of January 2006.

- Software licensing (if Open Source is not chosen), e.g. Webserver, Application Server, Database, Firewall, Intrusion Detection, etc.

- Hardware procurement, e.g. rack mounted servers.

- Staff costs, e.g. Data Management, Server Management, etc.

- Ancillary services, e.g. data link to the internet, consulting.

When developing a submission of this type, the Technical Team should have a firm vision of the infrastructure they wish to build. However, given the type of horse-trading involved in budget planning, it is prudent for several configurations to be proposed. The WMT can then choose the one that matches their preferences most closely.

Additional Elements of Architecture

It must be noted that the elements of infrastructure we have examined so far cover only the most basic types of architecture. Real-life websites are usually far more complex. For example, features like Search, eCommerce and Content Management require more functionality than can be provided by an out-of-the-box Webserver, Application Server or Database. As such, we will now explore some additional components that are regularly included in the design of site architecture.

Search

The continued success of Google demonstrates how important search has become as a driver of online experience. Indeed, there is evidence to suggest that up to half of all visitors to any website first attempt to find their desired content through an inbuilt Search Engine[144]. Only if this is unsuccessful do they revert to ordinary navigation in order to find what

---

[144] For example at http://www.useit.com/alertbox/9707b.html , though there are conflicting views at http://www.uie.com/articles/always_search/

they want. The clear lesson is that good quality search is essential to the prosperity of any site.

While basic search programs are often bundled free with Webservers or Application Servers, most are of fairly low quality. Consequently, many organisations find it necessary to invest in a more effective resource. This is particularly notable in large organisations that manage vast quantities of information.

In response, a number of powerful products have been developed over recent years by the following firms:

- Verity®
- FAST®
- Google
- Mondosoft
- Convera™
- Thunderstone™

In terms of how these solutions work, most offer two means of operation. These are referred to as the Standalone and Application Service Provider (ASP) models.

Standalone Model of Search

The Standalone Model requires the installation of a Search Engine directly onto the infrastructure of a site. From there, it is configured to catalogue all information and create an index of content. This index comprises a list of everything on the site, cross-referenced according to location. When a query is initiated, it is actually the index that is searched—not the website. This allows for a much faster response than would be possible if the entire site had to be searched each time.

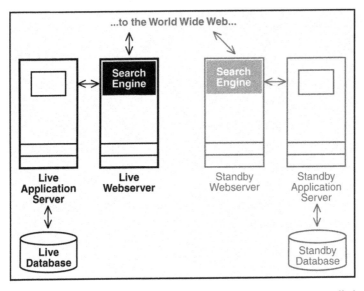

Figure 91. A Website Architecture with a standalone search engine installed.

Furthermore, to ensure the index is always up-to-date, it can be refreshed at daily intervals and configured to include or exclude certain formats, e.g. PDF, DOC, etc.

Application Service Provider (ASP) Model of Search

An Application Service Provider (ASP) is a firm that provides information or communication services over the internet. For example, the email website Hotmail can be considered an Application Service Provider, because it provides a common computer function via the web. Search can be provided in this way.

The key difference to the Standalone system is that the ASP model does not require the installation of any software. The service provider simply configures their Search Engine to crawl the contracted website from over the internet. Whenever a query is submitted, it is redirected to the ASP which returns results within a design that makes it look like it is from the original site.

Experience shows that this approach is completely seamless to visitors. It also allows powerful search to be deployed without the need for technology integration. Of course, there are some drawbacks. For example, if the ASP's servers were to fail, search would be unavailable to the contracted site (enough back-up is usually provided for this risk to be negligible).

Cost of Website Search

The actual cost of search — whether Standalone or ASP — can vary widely. For example, the list price of a good quality Search Engine is about $5,000 for 25,000 pages. This is the same for both ASP and Standalone. Costs then rise steeply as scope and functionality increase.

Indeed, some Enterprise Search Tools cost hundreds of thousands of dollars. **Enterprise Search** is software that can query a wide range of corporate systems including email, file servers, instant-messaging, chat, etc. — of which the web forms only a tiny part. At the other end of the scale, some ASPs offer free search to various online communities, e.g. clubs, societies, etc[145].

How to Select a Search Engine

Aside from the elements of technology evaluation we are already familiar with (organisational policies, staff skills, extensibility, scalability and price), three factors are commonly used to determine the suitability of a Search Engine to business needs. Referred to as Recall, Precision and Ranking, these can be used to establish the effectiveness of the mathematical algorithms that underlie a search program.

Recall is a measure of the number of relevant documents that are returned by a search query. A program with poor Recall will fail to spot

---

[145] For example, www.picosearch.com

the relevance of many documents and return only a small subset of the full possible range of results.

Precision reflects the accuracy of search results as regards the submitted query. For example, a Search Engine with good precision may return a lot of documents from NASA when the words "Mars", "Life" and "Rover" are searched for, but ignore content from the international confectionery company.

Ranking allows search results to be displayed in a manner that proposes documents with the highest precision. Ranking can be based on many factors, for example, the number of times the queried word appears in a document or the relevance of the query to other concepts in the searched content.

A demonstration of the effectiveness of a Search Engine with regard to each of these criteria can be used as a means of evaluation. These results can then be used to guide the decision making process.

'Best Bet'

A final determinant when deciding on a Search Engine is to check whether its internal algorithms can be superseded when desired. This functionality is sometimes needed so a Website Editor can deliver a set of pre-selected search results to visitors. This allows an Editor to bypass automatic results whenever he believes it is misinterpreting users' queries. This feature is called 'Best Bet'.

For example, on the banking website www.peoples.com, if a search query consisting of a string of numbers is entered, the assumption is made that the visitor is attempting to login to their account[146]. As such,

---

[146] Proceedings of "Optimising Search and Retrieval" (Ark Group), London, 12th- 13th July 2004. Ross Jenkins, eBusiness Development and Information Architect, Peoples Bank of

rather than return a list of automatic search results, a page is presented that directs customers to information about how to login. Of course, this process implies that search records are reviewed at regular intervals to extract information about visitors' search patterns. A review like this may be included as part of the activities of Website Maintenance (see Chapter Two).

Figure 92. Best Bet search results on www.peoples.com

ecommerce

For the purposes of Website Management, eCommerce is defined as the purchase of goods and services over the World Wide Web by means of a secure connection. In practice, eCommerce is often divided into different segments, based on the type of consumers being targeted. The most prominent of these are:

- **B2C** (Business to Consumer). For example, Amazon.com sells consumer goods direct to individuals.

- **B2B** (Business to Business). For example, Forrester.com sells intelligence reports to businesses over the internet.

America. "Demonstrating the value of search engine optimisation to sell the business case" (unfortunately, this feature has now been removed from the site).

- **B2G** (Business to Government). Many of the same firms that engage in B2B also engage in B2G. For example, all three categories are reflected on the Dell website, www.dell.com.

While the customer groups within each of these segments may vary, the standard tasks of eCommerce remain the same. These are:

- Collecting orders

- Processing orders

- Fulfilling orders

Any organisation wishing to get involved in this area, must have appropriate software in place to support these activities.

Shopping Carts

While a bespoke eCommerce application could be created by an experienced web Developer (using Server-Side Scripting), many solutions are already available off the shelf. Referred to as 'Shopping Carts', products of this type are designed to handle all the standard transactions of eCommerce. Some well known products include:

- osCommerce™ (Open Source)

- Comersus™ (Open Source)

- StoreFront® (from $595)

- Mercantec® (from $1,500)

(Other specialised software is also available for businesses with particular needs, e.g. airline reservation systems.)

Of course, when selecting such a technology a review of its fit to business requirements is needed. As we know, the principle factors in this regard are:

- Organisational Policies

- The Skills of Staff

- Extensibility

- Scalability

- Performance

- Price

Several other parameters also require consideration. These include:

- Security

- Functionality

- Design and Usability

Security of a Shopping Cart

The financial basis of eCommerce means that security is **the** top concern for selecting a Shopping Cart. Indeed, as most online transactions have to pass through at least three electronic transfers before completion, integrity must be absolute. These transactions are:

- Collection of payment details, e.g. a customer's credit card number.

- Processing of payment, e.g. live contact with a bank to establish credit rating of the customers.

- Expediting of orders, e.g. an order may have to be passed to a third party for manufacture or delivery.

Because each of these connections poses the risk of interception, they must be protected using encryption. In this regard, SSL has emerged as the standard means for protecting online transactions (see Chapter Three, page 237, for more).

Additionally, whenever a customer's information reaches its intended destination (e.g. a bank) it must also be safeguarded. For example, the magnetic tapes or optical disks (DVDs/CD-ROMs) upon which credit card numbers are recorded for long-term storage must be appropriately secured against theft.

Shopping Cart Functionality

While a robust system for processing orders is essential for selecting a Shopping Cart, so too is the inclusion of features that allow for the promotion of online sales. For example, many ordinary 'bricks and mortar' stores offer seasonal discounts to shoppers, e.g. January sales. The ability to replicate such campaigns in the online environment is key. At the very least the following features must be available:

- Reward Points

- Hot Deals Listing

- Wish Lists

- Popularity chart

- Out of stock Supplier alerts

- Basic and advanced Search Engine

- Currency Conversion

Additionally, a good Shopping Cart should provide some form of integration with online payment processors. A payment processor is an organisation that offers a secure means for sending and receiving payments over the internet. The best known vendors in this area include PayPal and WorldPay. Similarly, integration with the package tracking facilities of delivery companies such as FedEx and DHL, is also welcome.

Design and Usability

Finally, because design is such an important driver of website success, a Shopping Cart must be flexible with regard to aspects of usability and visual design. This ensures that the results of customer assessments and feedback can be easily incorporated into a site.

The most advanced Shopping Carts can now produce fully Web Standards compliant code (see page 171 for more about Web Standards). This is particularly important given the emerging requirement for eCommerce from mobile devices, e.g. smartphones.

Website Content Management

In Chapter Two–Website Maintenance, we learned that Website Content Management (WCM) is increasingly being used for the purposes of online publishing. Indeed, systems like this are fast becoming indispensable for the maintenance of large Dynamic and Transactional sites.

Although functionality must be at the forefront when evaluating such products, the fit to the desired web infrastructure must also be ascertained. As before, the parameters for assessing this are:

- Organisational Policies

- The Skills of Staff

- Extensibility

- Scalability

- Performance

- Price

Following the selection of an appropriate system, WCM may then be added as an 'engine' onto a site's Webserver (though individual packages may vary). Requests for pages are then directed by the Webserver to the WCM engine, which pulls information from a database and generates content on the fly.

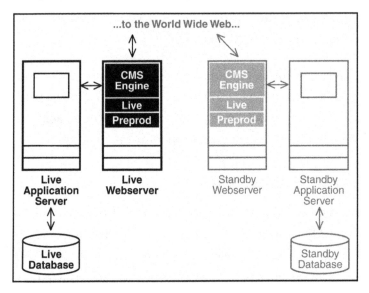

Figure 93. Website Architecture with WCM.

An interesting feature of the way WCM works is that it is often capable of hosting multiple versions of a site on just one Webserver. In this way, useful 'Preproduction' sites can be easily created.

Preproduction is a term used to describe an infrastructure where content and design changes can be prepared and evaluated, before being put live. For sites that do not use WCM, Preproduction usually comprises a completely separate infrastructure that is an exact replica of a live site. The main difference is that Preproduction is not located in a DMZ but on the internal network. This means it is inaccessible from the internet and cannot be viewed by anyone except organisational staff. This permits content to be developed in circumstances that mimic the live environment, but do not pose the risk of public access.

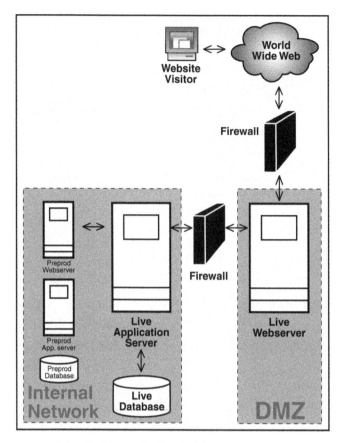

Figure 94. Standard Preproduction Architecture.

WCM offers an improved means for managing Preproduction. This is because it can host multiple versions of a site on a single server and so eliminate the cost of building a second infrastructure. Furthermore, access controls can be introduced that prevent visitors from seeing unapproved content. Only when everything has been reviewed and signed off, can it be released to the live site.

Website Infrastructure Maintenance

As anyone with experience of Website Management knows, special care must be paid to the activities of technical maintenance. Inevitably, the more complex an infrastructure is, the more time consuming and costly these tasks become.

For example, the architecture of a Transactional website may require an environmentally controlled computer room containing several cabinets of rack-mounted servers. The cost of maintaining this environment is, of course, substantially more than that of a Basic Site residing on a single desktop computer.

However, no matter what the scale of a site, the activities of Infrastructure Maintenance remain the same. These are:

Hardware Maintenance

Hardware Maintenance encompasses the upkeep of all servers, cabling and other hardware required to support site operations. As already mentioned, this activity may sometimes be handled by external suppliers.

For example, an outside firm may be hired to fix servers and swap out faulty components. They may also be required to provide additional hardware at short notice to allow the site's owners to react to surges in online activity. For example, extra memory or faster processors may be needed if traffic increases suddenly.

Software Maintenance

This area covers the upkeep of Webservers, Application Servers, Databases, internet connections, Domain Names and any other hosting software. The principal activity is to ensure each product is properly configured and kept up-to-date with new releases and security alerts.

Alerts like this may be issued to fix bugs or close security loopholes as they arise. For licensed software, e.g. Microsoft IIS Webserver, updates are provided as part of a post-sales service agreement. In contrast, updates for Open Source are issued over the internet by the bodies appointed to co-ordinate each application, e.g. Apache, Tomcat, PHP, MySQL, etc.

Security Maintenance

The activity of Security Maintenance seeks to ensure that the protections applied to website infrastructure are commensurate to the perceived threat. For example, the website of a high profile political party is at greater risk of hacking than that of an ordinary business. As such, a careful watch over site activity, new viruses and other online threats is required[147].

Data Maintenance

Data maintenance seeks to ensure site information is recorded in a secure manner. This may be required by law for some types of online transactions, e.g. changes to bank account details. The most common means for maintaining such data is to make a copy of website content every night onto magnetic tape. These tapes can then be held for use in the event of a website crash or other requirement, e.g. a court case.

Of course, the sensitive nature of some details, e.g. credit card numbers, means that the tapes themselves must be adequately secured. In this regard, many companies employ the services of specialist firms for the provision of fireproof cabinets and off-site storage depots.

Operational Level Agreement

In Chapter Three–Website Development, we saw how a Service Level Agreement (SLA) could be concluded with an external Host in order to establish a minimum acceptable level of service. While the formality of

---

[147] The advice of the Computer Emergency Response Team (CERT) provides a useful service for monitoring emerging developments in this area (www.cert.org)

an SLA may not be appropriate where hosting is provided internally, a variation on this concept—called an Operational Level Agreement (OLA)—can be beneficial for establishing basic terms of support.

For example, an OLA could specify the scope of service to be provided by a Technical Team. It could also stipulate targets for Availability, Reliability and Responsiveness—as well as commitments for data backups and other activities. In addition, one of the most important sections of an OLA (or SLA) is that which determines the procedures to be followed in the event that things go wrong.

When Bad Things Happen

Errors on a website can occur in an almost endless variety of ways. For example:

- An Application Server could become infected with a virus

- The fan on a server could jam and cause it to overheat

- A Shopping Cart could crash as a result of a sharp increase in traffic

- A Webserver could be defaced by a Hacker

There are several means by which a Technical Team can be made aware of such issues. These include:

Feedback

Website visitors are a reliable source of information about site performance. You may recall from Chapter Two, that the business intelligence firm Forrester found that 74% of alerts regarding website performance come directly from users[148].

---

[148] Copyright © 2004, Forrester Research Inc. "Managing Performance from the End User Perspective". November 2004. www.forrester.com

Website Monitoring Service

A service like this aims to detect when a site becomes unavailable to the public. For example, an external monitoring service may be contracted to automatically visit a site every 10 minutes. In the event that a visit returns an error message, this would generate an alert to be sent to the Technical Team. This type of service is available from many companies, for example SiteImprove and InterSeer.

Website Quality Assurance Review

The standard activities of Website Maintenance may uncover issues that require a response from Technical Support. This generally happens when a Maintenance Team Leader notices something wrong during a scheduled Quality Assurance review (see page 47 for more).

How to Respond

In the event that a problem is discovered, the Technical Support Team must be able to respond in an appropriate fashion. Rather than attempting to improvise, it is preferable that a set of scenarios be stipulated in the OLA as a means of assigning priority to errors as they occur. These can then be used to indicate the action to be taken. Such priorities are often separated into four levels.

Priority Three

A Priority Three issue indicates there is a bug on the site that requires fixing, but is currently having little or no impact on overall performance. The timeframe for the resolution of such issues can be set with the agreement of affected parties.

Priority Two

A Priority Two issue indicates that certain applications (e.g. on an Application Server) have stopped working, but that the website itself is still functioning. Because problems like this affect the ability of the organisation to conduct business, they require a fast response—usually within an hour or two.

Priority One

A Priority One issue indicates that a website is totally unavailable, perhaps as a result of a malfunction on the Webserver or some other element of infrastructure, e.g. Firewall. This type of error can be particularly damaging for eCommerce sites or intranets that run critical business applications. As such, an immediate response is required. In the event that an outage cannot be fixed straight away, a switch to a standby infrastructure is probably required.

Priority Zero

Aside from problems that arise as the result of statistically predictable component failure, some may also be caused by deliberate acts of sabotage. For example, a Cracker could vandalise a homepage with political messages or gain access to confidential customer data. In recognition of their seriousness, security related issues are assigned a Priority Zero rating. This demands that they be treated as extremely urgent because of the impact they could have on public perceptions, legal liability or the reputation of a firm.

Although during such an incident it is tempting to simply switch to a standby site (if one is available), that infrastructure itself may also have been compromised. As a result, the only safe course may be to completely disconnect all servers from the internet until every security breach has been fixed. During an event like this, the management of public and media relations may play an important part in protecting the image of an organisation.

Hours of Service

The final section of an OLA is that which indicates the hours of service during which support is available. For example, a small Basic site might only require assistance during standard business hours, i.e. 9am to 5pm. In contrast, a global Transactional site almost certainly needs comprehensive 24 hour service. Of course, the greater the requirement — the greater the cost, as extra staff must be employed to provide coverage. Yet, this expenditure is simply the price to be paid for ensuring business objectives and user needs can be successfully fulfilled.

Further Reading

As mentioned in the Foreword, few publications are available on the subject of Website Management. Most literature in this area comes in the form of commentaries from business intelligence firms like Gartner and Forrester, or from industry journals such as EI Magazine (Ark Group) or Communications (ACM).

However, a wealth of material is available on the disciplines from which Website Management is comprised. Some of the most widely consulted of these are listed below.

Content Critical. Gerry McGovern. Rob Norton. ISBN 0-273-65604-X.

Elements of User Experience. J.J.Garrett. ISBN 0-7357-1202-6.

Designing Web Usability. Jakob Neilsen. ISBN 1-56205-810-X.

Prioritizing Web Usability. Jakob Neilsen. Hoa Lorenger. ISBN 0-321-35031-6.

Designing with Web Standards. Jeffrey Zeldman. ISBN 0-7357-1201-8.

Homepage Usability. Jakob Neilsen. Marie Tahir. ISBN 0-7357-1102-X.

Don't Make Me Think. Steve Krug. ISBN 0-7897-2310-7

Information Architecture for the World Wide Web. Louis Rosenfeld. Peter Morville. ISBN 1-56592-282-4.

Defensive Design for the Web. 37 Signals. ISBN 0-7357-1410-X.

Useful Websites

A List Apart. www.alistapart.com

Adaptive Path. www.adaptivepath.com

Boxes and Arrows. www.boxesandarrows.com

EI Magazine. www.eimagazine.com

Forrester Research. www.forrester.com

Gartner Research. www.gartner.com

Gerry McGovern. www.gerrymcgovern.com

Jeffrey Zeldman. www.zeldman.com

Jupiter Research. www.jupiterresearch.com

Intranet Journal. www.intranetjournal.com

Pew Internet. www.pewinternet.org

Portals Advisor. www.portalsadvisor.com

The Information Architecture Institute. www.iainstitute.org

The Web Standards Project. www.webstandards.org

Usability News. www.surl.org

Useit.com. www.useit.com

User Interface Engineering. www.uie.com

W3Schools Online Web Tutorials. www.w3schools.com

Web Accessibility Initiative (WAI). www.w3c.org/WAI

World Wide Web Consortium (W3C). www.w3c.org

About the Author

Shane Diffily has many years experience in website management. He is currently employed as webmaster with one of Ireland's largest companies.

As an experienced writer, Shane has written numerous case studies on technology and business for The Irish Times "Business2000" (Ireland's leading broadsheet newspaper). He has also been published on www.alistpart.com, a leading online journal. In a previous life, he worked as a consultant with KPMG in Ireland, the United Kingdom and Belgium.

Shane lives in Dublin, Ireland. Visit his website at www.diffily.com.

Index

388

Acknowledgements

Many thanks to those who assisted the production of this book. Particular thanks are due to Ronan Diffily, Gerry McGovern, Ann Fitzpatrick, John Carton, Conor Clarke and Orla Diffily. Thanks also to Nina for tolerating my never-ending cycle of "one more draft".

Proofreading services were provided by Angela Hooper at Angel Editing.

This book was produced by the Lulu online publishing system. For more, visit www.lulu.com.

Other Acknowledgements

Screenshot of Archiseek.com reproduced with permission.
Screenshot of Wired.com reproduced with reference to guidelines at info.lycos.com/legal/tr_usage.asp.
Screenshot of Lulu.com reproduced with permission.
Screenshot of Microsoft.com reproduced with reference to guidelines at www.microsoft.com/mscorp/permission/default.mspx#ELC.
Screenshots of Gartner.com reproduced with permission.
Screenshots of Wikipedia reproduced with reference to guidelines at en.wikipedia.org/wiki/Wikipedia:Copyrights.
Screenshot of Business2000.ie reproduced with permission.
Extract from "Making the best with Flash" reproduced with permission from User Interface Engineering. Purchase this report at www.uie.com.
Extract from "Key words for use in RFCs to Indicate Requirement Levels" reproduced with permission from Scott Bradner.
Gartner Hyper Cycle reproduced with permission from Gartner.
Adobe product screen shot(s) reprinted with permission from Adobe Systems Incorporated. Adobe, Acrobat, Director, Dreamweaver, GoLive, Fireworks, Flash, Illustrator and Photoshop are either registered trademarks or trademarks of Adobe Systems Incorporated in the United States and/or other countries.
Apache is a trademark of The Apache Software Foundation, and is used with permission.

Every effort has been made to seek permission from the owners of images or information reproduced in this book. However, in some cases it has not been possible to establish contact. If you become aware of content that has not been approved for republishing please contact the author.